GARGANTUA

GARGANTUA

Manufactured Mass Culture

◆————————————

JULIAN STALLABRASS

VERSO
London • New York

First published by Verso 1996
© Julian Stallabrass 1996
All rights reserved

Verso
UK: 6 Meard Street, London W1V 3HR
USA: 180 Varick Street, New York NY 10014–4606

Verso is the imprint of New Left Books

ISBN 1–85984–941–5
ISBN 1–85984–036–1 (pbk)

British Library Cataloguing in Publication Data
A catalogue record for this book is available from the British Library

Library of Congress Cataloging-in-Publication Data
A catalog record for this book is available from the Library of Congress

Typeset by M Rules
Printed and bound in Great Britain by Biddles Ltd, Guildford and King's Lynn

For Elena

CONTENTS

ACKNOWLEDGEMENTS

Mass culture is a topic about which almost everyone has something to say. I have greatly benefited from conversations with many people – colleagues and students in history of art departments, particularly at the Courtauld Institute, and friends.

I would particularly like to thank Petrine Archer-Straw, Matthew Arnatt, David Crawforth, Simon Dell, Robert Garnett, Chris Green, Astrid Ihle, Mick James, William Jeffet, Elena Lledó, Emilio Lledó, David Lomas, Ian Noah, Diana Perriton, Naomi Siderfin, Margit Thøfner and Cordelia Wise. I would also like to thank all those at Verso and the *New Left Review* for their support, especially Gopal Balakrishnan, Robin Blackburn, David Fernbach and Sally Singer. Lastly I would like to thank my parents who have given me so much support during the time this work developed.

Obviously, the sole responsibility for any errors, omissions, prejudices and so forth in the text is my own.

Chapter 3, 'Empowering Technology', appeared previously in the *New Left Review*, no. 211, May–June 1995, and chapter 4, 'Just Gaming', in the same journal, no. 198, March–April 1993. Both have been modified for their inclusion here.

LIST OF ILLUSTRATIONS

A NOTE ON THE PHOTOGRAPHS

The photographs were taken by the author between 1987 and 1995 on films with a neutral colour balance, usually Kodachrome 25. They have been reproduced to be as faithful as possible to the appearance of the original slide and have not been digitally manipulated. Their subject matter was always photographed as found.

1

THE EDUCATION
OF GARGANTUA

Let us start with a large, if obvious, question, which I cannot quite promise to answer: what happens to a culture when it is mass-produced and mass-marketed, like any other industrial product; when, like most other businesses, it is subject to increasing globalization and concentration of ownership; and when, like the rest of society, it is founded on a grossly unequal distribution of resources, which it does its best to forget? Since addressing this question will involve trying to tackle some extremely large subjects, I shall begin by recounting a tale about a rather unusual giant. Perhaps the most remarkable thing about him was his appetite:

> So, after pissing a good pot-full, he next sat down to table; and, being of a phlegmatic nature, began his meal with some dozens of hams, smoked ox-tongues, botargos, sausages, and other advance-couriers of wine. Meanwhile his servants threw into his mouth, one after another, full bucketfuls of mustard, without stopping. Then he drank a monstrous gulp of white wine to relieve his kidneys; and after that ate, according to the season, meats agreeable to his appetite. He left off eating when his belly was tight.[1]

This is Rabelais's Gargantua, of course, a massive heir to the throne whose wants are awesome and unbridled. He is an animated fantasy about greed, strength, and sheer, unstoppable corporeality. Whatever

Gargantua is or does, in his guzzling and pissing, in his stupidity and violence, he outdoes everyone else. In the sixteenth century such tales of excess, whether of gigantic appetites or a land of plenty, took eating, drinking and associated bodily functions as their main subjects; indeed at birth Gargantua is no more than a giant, animated gullet.[2] These preoccupations are understandable, for then Europe was still subject to the threat of famine, whether caused directly by crop failure or as a consequence of epidemic or war. Now, though, when the tight belly of the First World is packed not just with nutrients but with the stuff of culture, with 'data', images, toys, soaps and all manner of trinkets, such tales seem merely quaint; even so, these concerns would be readily understood by our 'servants' on the other side of the world. First World culture, increasingly mass-media based, is founded upon simultaneous excess and minute discrimination. To object to it is to risk the charge of puritanism, and, indeed, this culture would hardly be a matter for great concern but for what its production does to the lives of the servants who make and deliver these goods, to the planet which gives up its resources to manufacture them, and last (and perhaps least) to the minds of those who consume them. So it is not the mere existence of this cultural cornucopia that should be questioned, but its price.

Perhaps, though, despite the passing of centuries, the gross body of Gargantua does have something to say even to the wealthy: in his early days he was merely an ignorant, flatulent glutton, but under the influence of a reformed and rigorous education he later developed into a refined scholar and unmatched warrior. At both stages, however, his activities were diverse to the point of encompassing everything then conceivable. Gargantua was not merely large; he was everywhere. His insatiable appetite threatened to drain the resources of the kingdom. When he played, he played at everything, from Beggar-my-Neighbour to The Salvo of Farts and Belly-to-Belly, the list of games covering well over a hundred lines.[3] When Gargantua went to war he was invincible: his numerous enemies were slaughtered in the most various manner, and barely managed to inflict losses on the giant's army. Although Gargantua took up his military career only after education had transformed him from an ignorant boor into a temperate sophisticate, we might take the two sides of his character as simultaneous aspects of the same personality, for he displays as much excess in massacre as in feasting. A gluttony for knowledge and the pursuit of war are clearly linked in Gargantua's own advice to his son, Pantagruel, who must learn languages, literature, the liberal arts and natural history. Gargantua adds:

> In short, let me find you a veritable abyss of knowledge. For, later, when you have grown into a man, you will have to leave this quiet and repose of study, to learn chivalry and warfare, to defend my house, and to help our friends in every emergency against the attacks of evil-doers.[4]

We can recognize in the old giant's size, ubiquity, gluttony, vast knowledge and warlike nature qualities of our contemporary culture. Like the celebrated commodities which now strut across the entire globe, Gargantua is more and less than human. His authority is based on sheer force since the very excess of his consumption inspires fear. At the same time his omniscience and his lack of failings make him predictable in his actions, less a character than a mechanism or robot which will always perform according to its programming. Indeed this is just his incarnation in Walter Benjamin's 'One Way Street', where he appears as an automaton in a stall at a fair: 'Gargantua with dumplings. In front of a plate he shovels them into his mouth with both hands, alternately lifting his left arm and his right. Each holds a fork on which a dumpling is impaled.'[5] Behind what looks like a willed act is a crude clockwork mechanism which governs the endlessly repeated gestures of consumption. After a time, this repetition might come to seem inevitable and unstoppable, and the visitor to the fair must be reminded that behind it lies a system of wheels and gears which reproduce it from moment to moment, which need continual power and maintenance, and which might at any time go wrong.

This book is about the qualities of a mass-produced culture which is marketed and sold. The culture's status as a commodity is the most fundamental fact about it, deeply affecting its form and inherent ideology. In a series of essays, including chapters on amateur photography, computer games, the aesthetics of the automobile and television, I will try to draw out something of this ideology and also its implicit self-recognition within the very forms which embody it; I shall argue that such recognition alone is not enough to prevent an ideology from functioning, and may even aid its unhindered operation. The subjects of this study are mostly mass-produced by commercial organizations, but sometimes they are mass-produced by consumers themselves; my contention is that these two realms of production are very closely linked.

The focus will be on visual culture; it is obvious that the visual is the pre-eminent arena of contemporary mass culture to the extent that literacy appears to be declining in many affluent societies, not only perhaps because of declining educational resources but because the skill seems less and less relevant to many people. The photographs are therefore an important and integral part of the argument. They serve as evidence certainly, but also to say things which are more succinctly said in pictures than in words, and also sometimes to comment on the text. In addition, I shall look at the issue of the relation between mass culture and high art, a distinction which is still very much in place, and is indeed necessary for the creation of important forms of aesthetic and monetary value. The two are not autonomous but react against one another in a very particular fashion. So fine art, recoiling from the predominance of the visual in mass culture, has often sought to distinguish itself from the reproducible products of the culture industry by turning its back on what is merely seen.[6] While this is hardly new, contemporary art has increasingly sought refuge in giving its small and physically present audience experiences of volume, weight, vibration and smell, of an unreproducible presence, in short, which the mass media cannot provide.

Mass culture has adopted and thoroughly internalized many of the precepts of old high-art, avant-garde modernism. There is the obvious business of its technophilia and the fetishization of function so that its appearance becomes more important than its actuality. The merging of art and life, central to mass culture, was also one of the core aims of some of the most important modernist movements, being found, for example, in materialist and idealist variants in Constructivism and De Stijl. The idea was that fine-art objects would eventually disappear in a new world in which an art made for everybody would have penetrated every object, and in which the environment itself would have become thoroughly soaked in the aesthetic. In a curious and partial way this vision has now been realized. There is a telling moment in the film *True Stories* when David Byrne is wandering about the outskirts of a small Texan town composed of prefabricated metal warehouse and factory units. These buildings, purchased ready-made from catalogues, are the fulfilment of a modernist dream, he says, but no one wants to recognize them as such. In an age in which everything has become subject to design, in which the humblest commodity aspires to project a character all its own (and this is especially true of those which seem to repudiate the strategy), the merging of art and life appears to have been achieved. A mass-produced culture has saturated every corner of our lives. When modernism was still young, some Marxists also looked to a merging of high art and mundane products; Benjamin, for instance, hoped for a fusion of art and technology such that, as Susan Buck-Morss phrases it, 'fantasy and function, meaningful symbol and useful tool' are made one in a fusion which is the very essence of socialist culture.[7] In debate with Benjamin, Adorno warned that the loss of aesthetic autonomy might not necessarily produce an emancipating effect. Instead a specious synthesis was possible in which high art, which might once have been a refuge of critique, would become integrated with facts, with life as it is.[8] What is more, this culture, falsely at peace with the world, would become inescapable. To judge the present situation against these alternatives, we need some criterion of value; without it there is no way of saying that we are not already living in the best of all possible worlds.

Given the prevalence of an aestheticized mass culture, high art finds itself in a precarious and unhappy situation. It is no longer given a semblance of coherence by the avant-garde rebellion, and it is largely isolated from political and social movements. High art may try constantly to work against the productions of mass culture, but it is prey to rapid assimilation as advertisers and designers plunder it for ideas and prestige. This assimilation is dangerous, for in it meaning and the particularity of a work or a style are generally lost, as they come to participate in the competition of equally empty ciphers arbitrarily matched to commodities. The fact of assimilation does not in itself mean that there is any intrinsic fault with high art. As Terry Eagleton has pointed out, if paintings by Picasso end up on the walls of banks, this does not mean that the art itself was not experimental or iconoclastic enough, but that either it was not rooted deeply enough in the revolutionary movement, or that this movement failed.

To imagine that art can resist appropriation by itself is idealist: 'The only thing which the bourgeoisie cannot incorporate is its own political defeat.'[9] As it is, though, much high art is resigned to its restricted role and much of the sophisticated and obfuscating theory which supports it provides screens to conceal its powerlessness to do anything but generate money.

Just as convenient theory surrounds fine art, so increasingly mass culture has become the subject of academic study and various kinds of theoretical justification. We can sketch out two linked, though apparently opposing, views which dominate much of the writing about mass culture. In the first, where nothing exists outside the text, or no reality lies behind simulation, anyone may contribute their readings to the general stew, but since there is nothing to decide between any of the ingredients, it is very likely that the powerful will continue to have their say above all others. Writers can comment on the situation itself, disillusioning readers who might have naively believed that texts or images were supposed to be about something, but there is nothing much (except liberal prejudice) to recommend even this view over any of the others. Secondly, there is much academic and 'critical' writing which assures us that all is hunky-dory with mass culture. Despite the best efforts of the great corporations which run the mass media, 'readers' (i.e. people) continue to make their own radical interpretations of these manufactured, ideological products. Here implicit judgements are made about the value of diverse readings, but relativism slips in at another level at which it becomes illegitimate to ask about the likely predominance of one reading over another, when it is in bad taste to wonder whether people might not end up adopting some of the ideological messages which they are exposed to every day of their lives. Such theories have an importance beyond the restricted audience of specialist journals and academic course books. The intelligentsia, broadly defined, has a crucial role to play in producing, marketing and publicizing mass culture, acting as writers, film-makers and journalists among many other capacities. Academics influence generations of students who take on these jobs, and they contribute to newspapers and magazines as opinion formers. If theorists generally inform us either that we should embrace mass culture as unashamed but somehow critical fans, or that we are powerless to do anything to change it, then these views and their influence are worth scrutiny. Much of this theory, and although it is quite diverse it generally bears the label 'postmodern', is politically convenient to the status quo, fostering a sense of powerlessness or a facile optimism. Its assurance that no meaning is ever definitive, or even that each statement contains the seeds of its own undermining, is also convenient to an academy in which careers are assessed on publication records.

One task of this book, then, will be to look at just a few of the ways in which the postmodern view collides with the cultural phenomena it seeks to describe. I have already indicated that the distinction between high and low culture is still very much in place and this is something which postmodern theory seeks to deny: this durable opposition is the first clue to a lack of cultural fulfilment and integration. To ask a few more questions: how is it that culture is supposed to be fragmenting and diversifying when the ownership of the producers of culture is dramatically concentrating? How is it that all 'grand narratives' – accounts which seek to explain phenomena in terms of broad historical processes – are to be abandoned just at this moment of unsurpassed economic integration on a global scale?

To raise an even more fundamental issue, questions about identity lie at the heart of much postmodern theory. The unitary bourgeois subject is supposed to have expired, to have been replaced by a multiplicity of incommensurable identities, each regularly endowed with its own essential and unchangeable nature. Again, the political convenience of such a view cannot be overlooked: given the death of the integrated subject, says David Harvey, 'We can no longer conceive of the individual as alienated in the classical Marxist sense, because to be alienated presupposes a coherent rather than a fragmented sense of self from which to be alienated.' We need such a sense in order to be able to think coherently about possible futures, and in fixing on schizophrenia, fragmentation and instability, postmodernism has a tendency to discourage us from picturing coherently, let alone devising strategies to produce, a different future.[10] There are a number of competing and contradictory approaches to identity within postmodernism. The idea that there is something static and essential in belonging to a particular racial group or sexual orientation, for instance, which is crucial to what you are, which is shared with other members of that group and no one else, is incompatible with the unstable identities of much postmodern psychoanalytical theory. The general exclusions from the construction of essentialized identities, however, are interesting: no identity is based on what it is to be human, generally none on what it means to belong to a particular class, and none on what it means to live in a consumer culture as such (as opposed to the micro-identities which are formed by buying one particular brand or another).

The decline in the unitary subject has somehow been accompanied by the unstoppable rise of a veritable cult of personality – though of a quite peculiar kind. We only need to look at the rows of faces that stare out from almost every consumer magazine on the newsagent's shelf or think of the immense popularity of biography. Postmodern scholars, immersed in high literary theory, can ignore the obvious popular success of literary biography which suggests that in some form the author lives on. All this is not to deny that postmodern theory has a point, or to say that there is no evidence in its favour. It is just that it frequently takes as natural what is social (and often does so by denying the distinction). It will be part of the argument of this book that the natural and the material cannot be simply written out of existence, and that the frequent attempts to do so in the current intellectual culture are extremely dangerous. It may be that looking to older theories of culture and society, written at a time when modernism and mass culture were still in the early stages of their development, may enable us to illuminate our current situation.

If there is something to the postmodern idea that identity is fluid, curiously it is Georg Lukács, writing of modern society, who has a close understanding of it:

> the contradiction that appears [. . .] between subjectivity and objectiv-
> ity in modern rationalist formal systems, the entanglements and
> equivocations hidden in their concepts of subject and object, the con-
> flict between their nature as systems created by 'us' and their fatalistic
> necessity distant from and alien to man is nothing but the logical and
> systematic formulation of the modern state of society. For, on the one
> hand, men are constantly smashing, replacing, and leaving behind
> them the 'natural', irrational and actually existing bonds, while, on
> the other hand, they erect around themselves in the reality they have

created and 'made', a kind of second nature which evolves with exactly the same inexorable necessity as was the case earlier on with the irrational forces of nature [. . .][11]

Identity is, then, constantly remade for us, and presented to us as a natural, exterior force. This process has been exacerbated lately, not by the fall of agreed aesthetic standards or because of some crisis of modernity, but rather because of an intensification of economic competition. Producing the ephemeral is more an effective economic strategy than a cultural imperative, as Harvey notes, for if there are limits to the accumulation and turnover of physical goods in saturated markets, then it makes sense for capitalists to turn to providing ephemeral services. He rightly sees this as lying at the root of the increasing penetration by business of various aspects of cultural production from the mid sixties onwards.[12] We shall see that this process is being taken to an extreme in which the material basis of cultural commodities is entirely abandoned.

The focus of this work will be on the aesthetic and affective aspects of mass culture. It may well be criticized for its lack of sociological content and analysis in terms of class, gender and race. In one sense this is quite deliberate. The basic contention is that people are more defined by how they live than by who they are, and that more unites consumers in the First World than separates them, especially when they are compared with the underclass at home and the disenfranchised people of the poorer nations. In terms of class, the process of the splitting of the working class into a group of skilled employees and the self-employed, on one hand, who share many of the same interests as the middle class, and an underclass, on the other, which shares none, creates a good deal of common interest across what have been dubbed the 'comfortable classes' on the grounds of consumption and environment in the broadest sense.[13] Even the very poor, however, are subject to the culture of the rich, affected by the fallout of television and advertising.

These are the grounds, then, for using the words 'we' or 'us', in violation of postmodern concepts of the disintegration of the self and the radical 'otherness' of disparate groups within society. The cultural phenomena I will be considering affect just about everyone in the developed economies, regardless of factors of class, race, gender or even age. While people certainly respond to these features of their life in different ways, this is not to say that they do not have a general effect. What is more, this culture, which has many uniform features, binds us together and creates what we have in common. It might seem like irony that postmodern theories of diversity and competing narratives have emerged at the very time when corporate control of the means of expression has reached an all-time high, and keeps climbing. Yet they are created by the operation of this very culture, which constantly grades and divides people, and desires their personal and collective dissociation, yet always ends up ranging them on the same monetary scale. Postmodern theory, like a camera obscura, produces an inverse image of what is taking place in the real world, and while reality flaunts the most blatant counter-examples in its face, it nonchalantly continues on its way as though this blindness was a matter of principle. There is much to be said for the postmodern utopia of diversity, but unfortunately its existence is not one of them.

This book will pay much attention to the details of new media technologies. These promise a great deal, but we are entitled to be sceptical about the way in which they will be used. In the past it has seemed that such technologies have simultaneously changed everything and left everything the same. Even before the rise of television, Max Horkheimer had written:

> Photography, telegraphy, and the radio have shrunk the world. The populations of the cities witness the misery of the entire earth. One would think that this might prompt them to its abolition. But simultaneously, what is close has become the faraway. Now the horror of one's own city is submerged in the general suffering, and people turn their attention to the marital problems of movie stars.[14]

Mass culture is a crucial component of the system of capitalism, if only because it allows people to turn their faces from what is happening to their neighbours who are obliged to live on the streets, and from the fate of billions whose lives are occasionally brought into comfortable living-rooms only to be swept aside by a tide of trivia, and from the global environmental hazards which threaten to force open the door between possibility and horrendous reality.

Against extreme relativism and the denial of value, the fundamental claim of this book will be that there is a grand narrative of mass culture, that its effects are global and that they run in a particular direction. This is not to deny its diversity, and there will be a good deal of attention paid to detail and exceptions. If it were a truly monolithic system, after all, then there really would be no grounds for critique. This diversity must not, however, blind us to its strongest trends, which work in favour of distraction, conformity and cultivated stupidity; it is a system which encourages the wasting of lives. What we have in common is precisely the culture which binds us. If this book has a readership for whom it is particularly intended, then it is for those who have the education and the chance to think about such things and who have, I believe, often betrayed this opportunity.

First World culture is founded on a world economy which denies the great majority of people the necessary means to live a decent existence, untroubled by widespread hunger and disease. Such a system, which might appear to regenerate itself automatically, is not easy to maintain; lies, threats and continual violence are its mainstays. Others have described this system in great and damning detail.[15] What is so astonishing, though, is the paucity of the benefits the moderately rich receive in return for the production of this poverty, violence and environmental degradation. The culture consumes resources without measure yet phlegmatically continues to emit much the same mild, happy brain-fodder piece by mundane piece. For those who can look on the situation with new eyes, it is a truly amazing spectacle: 'Such injustice for such stupidity' was how one fortunate of my acquaintance described it. This work will look at stupidity, and at how even in stupidity we know about injustice. It will try to show how a reciprocal process operates in which the decline of thought and principles makes acts of cruelty easier, and protects the system of cruelty in which they subsist, while the acts themselves, and their defence, serve to further degrade thought and principle. So while concentrating on the minds of those affected by this culture is, in one sense, to look at its most negligible aspect, in another it is of the highest importance, because a change of consciousness is certainly the least destructive way in which this unsustainable situation may begin to change. The seeds of it are perhaps already apparent.

NOTES

1. François Rabelais, *The Histories of Gargantua and Pantagruel*, trans. J.M. Cohen, London 1955, pp. 82–3.

2. His name and those of his family members (Grandgousier and Gargamelle) are associated with the words for throat in various languages: M.A. Screech notes the French *gosier*, the Provençal *gargamelle* and the Languedocian *gargamela*. Screech, *Rabelais*, London 1979, p. 118.

3. Rabelais, *Gargantua*, pp. 83–5.

4. Ibid., p. 195.

5. Walter Benjamin, *One Way Street and Other Writings*, trans. Edmund Jephcott and Kingsley Shorter, London 1979, p. 88.

6. For an account of modernist and postmodernist objections to the visible see Martin Jay, *Downcast Eyes. The Denigration of Vision in Twentieth-Century French Thought*, Berkeley 1993.

7. Susan Buck-Morss, *The Dialectics of Seeing. Walter Benjamin and the Arcades Project*, Cambridge, Mass. 1989, pp. 125–6.

8. Noted in Richard Wolin, 'Utopia, Mimesis, and Reconciliation: a Redemptive Critique of Adorno's *Aesthetic Theory*', *Representations*, no. 32, Fall 1990, pp. 45, 48.

9. Terry Eagleton, *The Ideology of the Aesthetic*, Oxford 1990, p. 372.

10. David Harvey, *The Condition of Postmodernity. An Enquiry into the Origins of Cultural Change*, Oxford 1990, pp. 53–4.

11. Georg Lukács, *History and Class Consciousness. Studies in Marxist Dialectics*, trans. Rodney Livingstone, London 1971, p. 128.

12. Harvey, *The Condition of Postmodernity*, p. 285.

13. The 'comfortable classes' was a term used by Martin Parr in association with his exhibition, *The Cost of Living*, at the Cornerhouse, Manchester 1989.

14. Max Horkheimer, 'Unlimited Possibilities', *Dawn and Decline: Notes 1926–1931 and 1950–1969*, p. 19; cited in Martin Jay, 'Mass Culture and Aesthetic Redemption', in Seyla Benhabib, Wolfgang Bonß and John McCole, eds, *On Max Horkheimer. New Perspectives*, Cambridge, Mass. 1993, p. 371.

15. There are of course many examples of such writing. Noam Chomsky gives a synthetic, historical account in *Year 501. The Conquest Continues*, London 1993.

2

SIXTY BILLION SUNSETS

Around sixty billion photographs are taken every year. Imagine them as points of light marked out on a dark globe. A comprehensive catalogue of touristic icons from Buckingham Palace to the Taj Mahal could be compiled from the dense clusters surrounding these sights, dramatically falling off in the surrounding hinterland. Fainter clusters would appear around the locations of wars, natural disasters, parades and sporting events. An evenly distributed scattering of points would outline the pattern of affluent human settlements. Now imagine this display animated, providing a developing image of the history of picture-making from the beginnings of the photographic industry, when the first points of light blinked in the streets of Paris and in Lacock Abbey in Wiltshire, to the current constellations and galaxies of recording.

While the last 150-odd years have seen the steady spread of photography's distribution and a steady rise in the number of pictures taken, qualitative changes are beginning to affect this massive industry of picture-making. Videos are increasingly made instead of photographs; although video is entirely different in terms of its technique and its product, it is widely substituted for the snapshot. The digitization of photographs, where the analogue medium of film is converted to or even replaced by a digital computer file, threatens to break the assumed link between photography and the outer world. Both are already having an effect on the internal demarcations of photographic practice. As Pierre Bourdieu has explained, there is a structural relation between the activities of mass photography and fine-art photography, each of which defines itself against the other.[1] Fine-art photography cannot be understood without considering its relationship to the billions of images which pour from the cameras of snappers each year, and from which it must rigorously distinguish itself. Reciprocally, through its crankiness and elitism, art inoculates the culture of mass photography against the out of the ordinary. Amateur photography sits between them and takes elements from both. This threatened middle ground which, more than any other type of photography, is currently being eroded by digitization and video is the subject of this chapter.

Four broad types of photographer can be identified: the professional, the snapper, the amateur and the artist. The professional takes pictures to make money and, whether they are wedding photographs or advertising shots, they are used in particular social circumstances; the snapper spends money to make pictures for specific social reasons, to document holidays, family, friends or special events. Both artists and amateurs fall between these two poles: the artist, whose subject matter is not directly tied to specific social functions, still hopes to make money, but amateurs lack both an extrinsic social context for their activity and the possibility of financial gain. Amateurs alone, artists without pretensions but with a simple faith in their medium, are defined by the social and professional uselessness of their work.

Although Bourdieu's book about the middle-brow art of photography, first published in 1965, is showing its age, many of his general points about the behaviour of casual snappers still hold true, especially his arguments about the intimate connection of mass photography to the structure of the modern family. Such photography lacks its own aesthetic, since the value of most snapshots is highly dependent on their subject matter, and on the correct identification of that subject matter by its viewers. Taking pictures is more or less automatic and even obligatory in certain social situations and absolutely ruled out in others; the contrast between attitudes to photography at weddings and funerals is the classic example. Amateurs, on the other hand, argued Bourdieu, generally have a low level of social integration because of their age, profession, or marital status (being young, single or, if married, childless). When the demands of the family exert least pressure then the amateur is free to develop a dedication to photography itself.[2] This relationship is perhaps a little less rigid now, but amateur photography is still seen, even by the family member, as a zone of freedom from social responsibility. Its uselessness is far from incidental.

Perhaps it is because of its relation to traditional, industrial forms of work, which we shall look at later, that amateur photography has been so identified as a masculine pursuit. Photography has been one of those forms of mechanical competence which have usually been gendered male. This has been reflected in its male-oriented subject matter (including glamour and sport) and in its very language, with its talk of shooting, exposure, long lenses, camera bodies and bayonet attachments (a vocabulary which this essay could not of course avoid). The activity itself has tended to suit lone males, for the hunting and the shooting of the subject often take place while wandering in deserted places (not an option many women would lightly consider), and this has been reflected in the traditionally macho image of photojournalism. With the decline of industrial work in much of the First World and the concomitant erosion of rigidly gendered working practices, these worlds are now open to women, though not necessarily attractive to very many of them. As the gender imbalance became less marked, it has often been women's protests which have driven soft porn out of the amateur magazines.

Amateur photographers self-consciously occupy the middle ground between the snapper and the professional. They form a discrete market for which camera manufacturers design and to which many magazines cater. Traditionally they have been positioned against the poles of quotidian and commercial photography largely by their equipment, which for them has often taken on a pre-eminent importance. As the camera market expanded, the number of models grew, the distinctions between them widened, and the users they appealed to became ever more finely graded. Aside from the camera itself, amateurs can be expected to carry, and occasionally use, a wide array of accessories – filters, lenses and converters, flash guns and tripods – while another market is created by specialized facilities for displaying and storing the products of their hobby.

Amateurs tend to use sophisticated, but not professional, SLRs (single lens reflexes), rather than the compact cameras carried by most casual photographers.[3] Professional cameras are certainly distinguished by their cost, but they are generally simpler than amateur ones, being less dependent on battery power, and designed for reliability and longevity. When these cameras do incorporate advanced technical features, they tend to have a direct impact on image quality, rather than ease of use: it is assumed that the professional photographer either already knows how to use the machine or will use it often enough to find out quickly. By contrast, the impetus of camera design in the amateur market is towards an ever greater proliferation of 'features' which contribute to an increasing automation of the photographer's tasks and which also of course create value for the manufacturer. Regardless of the sophisticated technology expended on it, this trend has little to do with function and everything to do with style. Because cameras now contain microprocessors, it is necessary that their exteriors express this fact by emulating the look of the computer. Buttons have replaced dials, even when the latter are clearly more functional: it is easier to change an exposure setting by three stops by turning a dial once than by pushing some combination of buttons three times, and dials also allow intermediate settings. Buttons, unlike dials, cannot carry information about the current setting, so this has to be provided separately in LCD panels. These can be difficult to read, use up battery power, have a limited life (effectively limiting that of the camera as a whole), and can usually be read only when the camera is switched on. They are now, however, deemed an essential. Old cameras often indicated exposure above and below the norm with an analogue device, usually a needle; this has been superseded by a digital device, usually a plus or minus sign. The former was more useful because it indicated the degree of under- or overexposure, and was more instinctive to use; while there is no reason why a digital device should not emulate its analogue ancestors, the flashing electronic signals at least impart an air of state-of-the-art technology.

Other common features have only limited uses, or ones which are out of proportion to their expense. Autofocus in SLRs has few uses for photographers who have reasonable eyesight (and solves little for those who do not, since they still cannot see what they are shooting) and its use immediately conjures up a host of problems, 'special' circumstances in which it fails and which can be solved only by further technical fixes. Another increasingly popular feature is built-in motor-drives – useful for photographers without thumbs; they are noisy, consume battery power and usually rewind the film leader all the way into the canister (making it very difficult to reshoot a partially used roll). The technical issues which really affect the image, the quality of the lens and the film, receive comparatively little attention in the amateur magazines. Cameras are valued, then, not so much for their utility, but for the number and sophistication of their features, which is another way of saying that they are valued for their cost, or sometimes for their 'value for money'. Some of the camera magazines make this explicit in complex tables of cameras enumerating features and generally being organized in a hierarchy of price. The amateur is defined more by consumption than photographic activity.

It is a curious state of affairs when a supposedly consumer-driven technology is making its products less functional. This can happen because consumers (like voters) are quite powerless when it comes to the particulars of the packages of 'features' which they buy in the form of a camera. New users who buy equipment more often are favoured over the old, who have established preferences and practices. Consumer demand is also much affected by advertising and by its bearer, the magazines, in which the editorial copy is closely related to the propaganda of their paymasters. The camera market, like many others, is also driven internally by the engine of fashion. Nevertheless there has been a marked change in the nature of the camera's technological development, which may be related to postmodernism in an economic sense. For over the first hundred years of camera design the struggle was with the quality of the equipment and with control and ease of use. For the earliest photographs, exposure times were so long that people passing through the scene never left a trace, and the camera would render capital cities as ghost towns; Eugène Atget, working as the century turned, acquired a heavy stoop from the burden of his camera and plates; Weegee's famous press pictures were made with a one-shot camera, leaving no margin for error. Gradually, struggling against such adversity became unnecessary as lenses became faster, cameras smaller and film was produced in rolls. Exposure meters were built into cameras and even made their readings through the lens. With cameras like the Olympus OM-1, produced in 1973, the amateur user really had all that could reasonably be required in an easily portable package. It may be that things began to change with the introduction of micro-circuitry, although even this was initially used only to improve the accuracy of shutter speeds. Eventually, however, it opened the way for quasi-intelligent devices which would begin to usurp the photographer's tasks.

This picture is somewhat complicated by the issue of non-technical matters of style. Compact cameras are often seen as playthings and have been open to the exercise of overt decorative design: they come in different colours, sport 'handwritten' words ('Sketchbook', for instance) or make noises to warn the photographer of errors. A more subtle exercise of taste is also apparent in SLR design, including some machines which distinguish themselves through an elite simplicity, eschewing autofocus and power-winders to claim, through a technical back-to-basics, the aesthetic high ground.[4] Nevertheless, among amateur cameras, the range of stylistic options is quite narrow, and, as we have seen, there is a predominant single hierarchy operating, based on price, 'features' and value.

So what is the impetus of technological style behind this 'progress'? In a contribution to the Bourdieu study, Robert Castel and Dominique Schnapper argued that the camera was seen as a benevolent apparatus, used for personal, non-alienated activity, as a salve against the robotic automatism which dominated industrial work.[5] It is easy to see that simple SLRs could fulfil this role, for they gave the user complete control over many of the basic factors which control the appearance of the picture: exposure, depth of field, shutter speed and focusing. The mechanism was relatively simple to understand and, if it went wrong, an amateur would often know what had malfunctioned and even how to fix it. Contemporary camera design has progressively relieved the user of this power, automating and computerizing first exposure, then the relation between shutter speed and aperture, then focusing. This can be seen as a consequence of the decline in the First World, especially among the skilled working-class devotees of amateur photography, of the dominating presence of alienating industrial work. The camera has not yet quite become an obscure black box like other domestic electronic devices, for it quaintly mixes digital processing with analogue chemical and optical processes, but its operation has nevertheless been thoroughly mystified. This can only serve the processes of commodification and its servants, fashion and style, which now dominate utility. Such a commodity is always more important for the image it portrays through its surface than for how it is used.

Some of these new features do compensate the user for the loss of control over the machine. The zoom lens, for instance, especially when powered by the camera rather than the photographer's hand, makes fragments of a scene readily available without the effort of traversing terrain, or indeed without any significant physical effort: just as in a car, and with the same screen of glass before the world, (perhaps newly) bourgeois viewers steadily stand in one spot while the world advances and recedes, whirring, before them. Auto-exposure, autofocus and motorwinds reduce the moment of picture-taking to a mere touch of the button: all serve to make reality more immediately compliant to the wishes of the photographer.

Despite the dominance of matters of consumption, amateurs still take pictures, and it is important to ask how they go about it and what they take as their subjects. Bourdieu distinguishes between occasional users and fanatics who shoot regularly and join clubs. Intermittent or committed, there is a curious spirit animating amateur photography which contributes to its particular approach, an attitude to the subject which is fundamentally realist but is inflected with a very distinct aesthetic. The amateur may well take pictures of the family, just as the snapper does, but these should have merit as photographs, as well as for simply representing their subjects. Indeed, in all cases, the merit of the photograph seems to be determined by an aesthetic judgement which matches technique to subject matter. This is the origin of the endless advice given to readers in the amateur journals, often in the form of 'picture clinics', where readers send in their efforts to have them judged by the magazines' resident experts. So, to take just one example of the pally advice proffered, a budding portraitist is first praised for 'a lovely moody portrait captured entirely by the ambient light streaming in through a window next to the model', but:

> despite all the bouquets we've handed out there's one brickbat we'd like to toss. It's that top left hand corner, Paul, that light area just under the picture on the wall. Try putting your hand over it. See how much it strengthens the composition? Have a go at producing another

print, this time burning it in to a dark grey or even black, and you'll have it damn near perfect.[6]

In the same issue, other photographers are urged to get closer to their subjects, to use backgrounds that do not distract from the main point of interest, to use portrait-format images for portraits, and to place objects in the foreground of landscapes. In all this, there is a very curious tension between creativity and rule-making. In the specialist amateur magazines and in the competitions run in amateur clubs, photographers are constantly urged to do the unusual, to break with clichéd subject matter and handling, but simultaneously they must also learn about a complex structure of rigid genres and their associated techniques. As Bourdieu puts it, 'amateurs remain faithful to a basic normativeness, and remain attached to the certainty of a body of rules that they could and should know or that are known to others'.[7] Judgement is rarely based on aesthetic matters alone, but rather on conformity to an apparently endless sequence of rules matching technique to subject, which no amateur, however accomplished, can be expected to know. Each rule is discrete, parasitic on subject matter and, taken together, they have little coherent shape.

Sometimes the multiplication of rules is a consequence of the close connection of the amateur magazines with the manufacturers, who are, after all, their main, if not sole, advertisers. So, for instance, it is important for both manufacturers and magazines that photographers do not understand that light meters make a reading of the scene in front of them, no matter whether it is snow or coal, to match a mid-grey tone. This might suggest to amateurs that their cameras are a little less capable of making reality compliant than they had been led to believe. So the readers of magazines and camera manuals may learn that they should, Rule 1, overexpose on the beach and, Rule 2, underexpose when shooting a spotlit figure against a dark background. What is not said is that these are merely the extremes of a continuum of exposure compensation, in which regular small adjustments are needed in most situations. Rather than being a feature of the camera, adjustments at the extremes, cast as rules, become a feature of peculiar or special conditions. When a deeper technical understanding is ruled out, the advice given must be fragmentary and even contradictory, because of its basis in an extraordinarily complex array of combinations of subject matter and shooting conditions.

The system works both ways, however, and the multitude of rules may also lead to cameras which have many different 'modes' for exposure, shutter speed and focusing. The photographer selects the mode appropriate for the subject and the camera implements the rules. Real situations, when considered suitable for photography, are rigidly demarcated and classified in terms of technical criteria. As an increasing number of situations is catered for, controls multiply, the combinations of button-presses increase, the meaning of the tiny icons in the LCD display becomes ever more obscure, and selecting the situation becomes rather more difficult than setting the controls manually.

This complexity is a smokescreen in front of the basic problem which both manufacturers and the amateur publications face: the fundamental techniques of modern photography are very simple. While nineteenth-century amateurs brewed chemicals, prepared glass plates and carried their exposure meters in their heads, all these stages and more are now automated or marketed ready-made. Focusing with a modern SLR is easy and exposure is only a little more complex. Any fool could do it. Beyond these technical matters, it is simply a question of taking 'good' photographs, the most difficult thing of all. The purely aesthetic side of this is also the most difficult to write about. Although the wider instruction offered by the amateur magazines has odd parallels with the traditional training of painters, their lessons in composition rarely proceed beyond the rule of thirds. Manufacturers deal with the conundrum by designing ever more sophisticated products which solve problems that did not really exist prior to the technologies invented to fix them. Magazines address the problem in many ways, including a diversification of subject matter, addressing many specialized areas from infra-red to food photography; but they never explicitly state that photography is simple, and explain what the basic techniques are.

Yet there is another, more fundamental, reason for the production of this endless set of rules, which goes beyond technical and commercial issues, and is founded on photography's durable link to its subject. The rules imply a realist aesthetic which aims to express the essence of the subject. The endless variety of subject matter must be matched by a variety of style and handling. This is the point behind the unceasing injunctions to focus on the eyes, to expose so that there is detail in the shadows, to shoot children at their own height, and so on. Beyond rule-making, intuition plays a role in creating the necessary empathy between photographer and subject. The selection of the appropriate rules to follow in a particular situation, or even the knowledge of when to break them, requires this empathy. The amateur, like the good professional photographer, pursues this self-effacing talent which subsumes itself to the essence of whatever is in front of it, but pursues it alone and entirely for its own sake.

Today, there is a striking contrast between the unassuming ideology of the photographer's aesthetic and the extreme mannerism of most of the results. This has always been a danger in amateur photography; governed by rules, enamoured of clichés, it has been an isolated pursuit of the aesthetic which has generally adopted the norms of an average taste. Now, when the pursuit is under pressure, amateur skills are pushed towards extremes and a saturated mannerism, amounting to boredom, becomes ever more prevalent in the work. Although simplicity is sometimes featured as one style among many to be cultivated, the modesty of work like that of Atget's before its subjects is forgotten. The field becomes increasingly fragmented among a variety of specialized disciplines and techniques.

In 1937 Walter Benjamin had harsh words for German avant-garde photography, which celebrated the pure objectivity of the camera, and which:

> can no longer photograph a tenement block or a refuse heap without transfiguring it. It goes without saying that it is unable to say anything of a power station or a cable factory other than this: what a beautiful world! [. . .] it has succeeded in making even abject poverty, by recording it in a fashionably perfected manner, into an object of enjoyment.[8]

He could not perhaps foresee that what was once a fashion among the avant garde would become the regular practice of the amateur, but amateurs do indeed owe much to the German and American objective schools of the inter-war period, in technique and in the ideological message that their work conveys.

Yet perhaps, despite Benjamin's apposite comments, there is something positive about such work. In a celebrated phrase, Adorno wrote
that 'Art is the promise of happiness, a promise that is constantly
being broken.'[9] Slipping out of the noose of avant-garde fashionabil-
ity, amateur photography takes fragments of the world as evidence for
an order of things, forcing them into making sense. In matching representation to subject matter, it uncovers in objects and living things
a harmonious world view which can be confined and expressed within
the microcosm of the enprint or the white borders of a 35mm slide.
These little talismans are discovered and collected by their creator,
and the more that are amassed and possessed, the more there is evidence for an essential and comforting coherence. Landscapes, holiday
destinations, loved ones and pets, fragments of the urban scene and
natural wonders all come to participate in a continuum in which all
objects are known and (when things go well) all respond kindly to the
photographer's subjectivity. In this conservative but optimistic view of
the world, where all things demand different responses, and where
the photographer must be open to their particular nature, there is a
radical moment which refuses to respect the full implications of commodity culture which would make everything fungible, and arrange it
on the single scale of monetary value. The amateur brings the landscape safely home, confines it and classifies it, but at least does not sell
it.

This earnest relation to the world is one reason why amateur practice eschews the casual humour of the snapper, which extends to
photographic incompetence and accident: the finger in front of the
lens, red-eye and startled looks, bleached faces against a background
of ink. All these things instead of ruining a snapshot may contribute
to its charm and the liveliness of the social events where it is shown.
For the amateur, though, they are marks of failure and must be
excluded: if humour is present it must be manifestly deliberate.

Ideally the object in the photograph, rather than being subsumed
under some rule of exchange or use, becomes more like itself. The
avant-garde combination of ideal and concrete, in which things retain
their identities as things-in-themselves, is curiously reflected in the literal art of the amateur photographer. The ideal is somehow brought
out from behind the real, producing a world of beauty, wonder and
sense. Yet in doing this, the photographer ironically forgets the thing

itself, dwelling on a representation of its skin so that appearance is presented as essence. The limits to photography's critique are found in this idealism of the surface, so similar to that of the commodity, which takes form, not function or movement, as its basis. Such forms can become meaningful only when they appear within an already agreed world of sense: if Saddam Hussein looks crazy in newspaper photographs it is because so many people have already agreed that he is. 'We photograph things in order to drive them out of our minds',[10] wrote Kafka, and this can happen because photography simulates the process of understanding by subjecting objects to the rigours of composition and framing.

Yet in one sense photography is radically unsuited to the ideological role which amateurs assign to it. Roland Barthes described the medium as 'the absolute Particular, the sovereign Contingency, matte and somehow stupid',[11] and this makes its use for the expression of essence an extraordinarily difficult task because it will uncontrollably and dumbly record every disruptive little contingency. This makes photography particularly suited for partial 'misreading', or, to put it more positively, for a very great variety of uses. Yet, at the same time, this difficulty is unavoidable because it is also the very reason for photography's usefulness in making sense of the world: people generally read photographs as evidence. Its apparent guarantee of truth is the very source of its power and what separates amateur practice from the highly controlled fetishization of the surface in commercial work. Photography is dumbly indiscriminate and it is quite difficult to make it say anything specific. Rather, it delivers the same ideological message over and over again: *this is the way things are.*

Perhaps the most contested site of this combination of realism and idealist searching for sense is the issue of colour. Many amateurs still shoot in black and white, and while this is certainly in part a matter of retaining control over the medium, it being much easier and cheaper to develop and print your own pictures, other matters are also involved. In themselves the unitary tones of the monochrome print impart a meaning to whatever subject they describe. Walker Evans famously accused colour photography of vulgarity, and with its widespread use in advertising dominating the environment, the problem has become far more acute. Black and white film provided photography with a ready-made aesthetic while colour presented the amateur, who rarely constructs studio shots, with a significant problem: how to make sense of these competing, meaningless hues? A minor industry has grown up around providing fixes to this problem: the graduated tobacco filter is one of the most common solutions, serving the purpose of darkening unphotogenic grey skies while imparting a sepia quality to the whole. Films are often balanced towards warmer tones, improving complexions, and helping to drain scenes of their too messy particularity. Most strikingly of all, Fuji's film Velvia, a great success among amateurs and advertisers alike, intensifies colours, producing Caribbean tones from dull, damp streets: this film, which now has many imitators, was made for Walker Evans's remark. Flicking through any amateur magazine, one is struck by the preponderance of red, orange and brown tones. So many colour pictures restrict themselves to warm monotones, the colours of sunsets and cheap rented rooms.

Reality sometimes needs help. It is difficult to square some of the manipulative techniques used by amateurs to the reality principle which is of central importance to so much photographic practice, from shots of the family to holiday snaps and 'glamour' photographs, where viewers imagine themselves, like the photographer, present before the model. When manipulation does occur it very often involves the use of photographic particularities (such as grain) to bring out the essence of a certain subject, so that a symbolic match between the subject and the attributes of the medium is created. Often, however, there is a mannerist application of a certain technique to a wide variety of subjects. There are sub-genres of evidently manipulated pictures; sky swapping, for instance, which has a pedigree going back to Gustave Le Grey in the 1850s, is still popular. The point about most of these techniques is perhaps that, although the photographer may know that the sky has been darkened with a polarizing filter, the effect only allows the subject to be truer to itself. Such techniques are merely an extension of the removal of contingencies, the process of selection, that goes on when the photographer selects a scene in the first place. The admiration of advertisers' tricks in the amateur magazines is an important feature, though it is the job of the articles to demystify them by explaining how they were achieved. The difficulty of making these pictures, and the admiration they inspire, is once again predicated on the essential realism of the medium.

Traditional manipulation in amateur photography alters elements but rarely bears an arbitrary relation to the recorded light captured from the real world, which is used as the essential basis for enhancement.

Beyond presenting the real as ideal, the photographer must be introduced into the subject matter. In this, there is a considerable overlap between the attitudes of snapper and amateur in front of their subject. Both require the following statements to be inscribed in their photographs: not just 'I was there' but also 'I took this'. As with writing graffiti, the act of taking the picture is a performance in itself, an essential part of the image. At any major tourist destination, the vast majority of the images will be distinguished only by their mistakes, for the originality of the photographic image is sought only in the on-site performance of its capture. For the snapper the inscription of presence on to touristic sites is a mechanical, mass-produced form of identification. On to this the amateur lays another form of personal identification and creativity, a link with the machine and the chemical process out of which, in propitious circumstances, may be summoned originality. So while the snapper wants merely to create his or her own version of the postcard view, the amateur must try to carry away something new, something no one has seen in quite that way before. The subject must be made to express itself through the photographer's personal originality.

Amateur photography has traditionally been defined against work, especially industrial factory work, where the traces of labour are usually effaced in the process of production. Taking pictures generally involves travel, wandering, finding things (often by luck), ingenuity and aesthetic appreciation. It is a form of freedom which counters work by commenting on its characteristics of directed, restricted movement and its instrumental relation to objects. Yet there is another aspect to photography – the manipulation of objects for particular goals (however immaterial), technical control, a form of discipline and expenditure. Furthermore, once the image is taken, it is alienated from its maker in its fixity and potential use, as something to be collected and catalogued. Benjamin wrote of the souvenir that 'In it is deposited the increasing self-alienation of the person who inventories his past as dead possessions. Allegory left the field of the exterior world in the nineteenth century in order to settle in the

inner one.'[12] Now, in one sense, the indexical nature of amateur photography could not be further from rigid, arbitrary allegorical
expression. Nevertheless, the way in which the amateur treats each
fragment of reality, bound by the frame of the slide or cut by the
edge of the print, the way photography concentrates itself at the surface and is so dependent on captions, on correct identification, the
way form is taken as the unitary expression of a single principle, all
this is close to allegory. Despite itself, then, amateur photography
tends towards the allegorical. In their use, amateur pictures do suggest a certain fungibility after all: the reduction of all things to a play
of forms over emulsion. So a dialectic can be established between
the freedom of amateur activity and its bound and regulated products. Benjamin also describes, in a little text on 'The Untidy Child',
those young hunters of objects who eventually grow into antiquarians,
researchers and bibliomaniacs, whose diverse possessions come to
form one single, grand collection. They drag home their booty, he
says, 'to purify it, secure it, cast out its spell'.[13] This is the reduction of
experience to an administered and lifeless collection of images: a
process of reification, collection and classification.

Aside from showing readers' work, the amateur magazines contain a curious mix of diverse pictures, covering advertising shots, mild
'glamour' and also photojournalistic work, sometimes of a very disturbing nature. This latter is meant to be admired for the
photographic skills displayed in the face of its subject matter, where
difficulty of access or physical danger contributes to admiration for
the photographer and wonder that the events could be depicted at all.
Whatever the theory about techniques matching circumstances, those
appropriate to capturing horrors in wartime or in disaster areas are
blithely carried over into the portrayal of family and friends, new cars
and the girl next door, just as Cecil Beaton carried his louche dandy-
ism with him when photographing the Second World War.

The critical moment in amateur photography is when its commitment to realism meets an idealistic aesthetic, in an implicit critique of
the world as it is. Yet this practice remains remarkably cheerful,
devoted to a *Family of Man*-type viewpoint of humanism and optimism.[14] There is a resolutely affirmative, self-imposed cheerfulness to
amateur photography, as though the century's ills have been blithely
forgotten. So the critical moment of amateur photography is deeply

buried: the practice is caught up in ideologies of the surface, in an activity which is defined by commerce and the dictates of advertisers, and where the amateur's love of both the medium and the world is inseparable from its uselessness and powerlessness.

The amateur's view of photography as evidence has hardly gone unchallenged. Unsurprisingly, artists have been in the forefront of the attack on photography's ontological status, and have been quick to use digitization for this purpose. To take a particularly clear example, Michael Ensdorf digitizes what he sees as historically significant press photographs, magnifies the pixels which make them up, adds uniform colour, finally overlaying them with the single word 'Fiction'. By calling attention to the surface of the image, he hopes 'to question the validity of photography's authority to describe a time, or to define history. The word "fiction" functions as a label to desensitize the original photograph, and in turn, the actual event depicted.'[15] Ensdorf chooses as his subjects pictures of South African police attacking anti-apartheid demonstrators, and the Klaus Barbie trial; he seems to want to remove the sting of the events and the pictures together. This might, on the face of it, seem a strange thing for an artist to want to do, but behind it lies much logic.

In part such work is about the supposedly liberatory potential of computer manipulation and interaction, which will be examined further in the next chapter. Influential Foucauldian histories of photography (most notably the work of John Tagg) have transferred an indiscriminate methodology, in which, as Peter Dews puts it, 'the mere fact of becoming an object of knowledge represents a kind of enslavement',[16] on to a similar structure in which representation plays the role of devil, and photography, being its most literal form, becomes the most pernicious type. Now there is no doubt that photography has often been used by states for the most nefarious purposes, but it has also been used for radical and progressive ones. The common postmodern presumption is that to attack representation is itself radical. This is a curious restaging of the modernist assault on figuration which has led in some cases to revamped versions of formalism.

Economic factors have also been important in bringing artists to an assault on photography: traditionally there have been various ways in which fine-art photography has sought to distinguish itself from its less prestigious neighbours, and most of them still hold: the size of prints or projections can be massively inflated to match the scale of museum painting, expensive media may be chosen, the economic barb of reproducibility may be reduced (with limited editions) or withdrawn (by using a one-off medium like Polaroid or manipulating the print by hand), while of course the venues in which such work is shown help to reinforce the distinction. Also useful are techniques which serve to erode the subject matter itself, perhaps by bringing out photography or printing's constituent elements. Of course some artists have been able to use straight photography to make money *as fine artists*, and one or two commercial photographers have remade themselves as artists, but they are very few.

Lastly, as already suggested, there is something modest about the photographer's role, which is more about finding and bringing back, more about tailoring the craft to meet the demands of the subject than forcing a recalcitrant material to your will, that sits uneasily with the Nietzschean ego that the market tends to require of artists. A photography that can be shaped as one wills is to be preferred. The prejudice the mechanical medium of photography has had to overcome in gaining acceptance within the world of high art has left its mark: typical reactions in theoretical writing against the vulgar use of photography by the masses have been to deny the medium as employed by fine art any of the qualities of photography at all. It is often claimed that the medium exhibits not an ounce of objectivity and that it is better to consider it as a language.[17]

As fine-art theory and practice have moved into close unison, various artists have tried to embody these ideas in their work. Some have taken old family photographs and digitally excised the figures, leaving eerie backgrounds, or have taken news photographs to which they add their own image, or enlarged magazine reproductions so that the image is almost lost among the printing patterns. Others might take a highly charged subject, a picture of a victim of the Hiroshima bomb, for instance, again enlarging and distorting it until the subject is barely recognizable. Such work tends to favour fiction over fact, subjectivity over objectivity and most of all, in its frequent 'deconstruction' of clichéd oppositions, undecidability over opinion.

The political implications of such works and theories should not be ignored. John Tagg and others have argued that photography only refers to objects as a matter of arbitrary convention, and this is central to works which seek to undermine the opposition between fine art and photographic representation. Tagg rightly stresses the social factors which are implicit in the production of photographic 'truth' (endowed variously by government departments, the courts and so forth), but is wrong to extend this to deny the role of any intrinsic feature of the medium. He writes, 'Ask yourself, under what conditions would a photograph of the Loch Ness Monster or an Unidentified Flying Object become acceptable as proof of their existence?'[18] The question is cleverly posed, for it is unlikely that a *single* picture, of whatever quality, could be – but a number could. More important, if their existence were to be proved independently, different photographs of Nessie or the UFOs could subsequently be judged real or fake, and the real ones could be used as sources of evidence to provide information about their subjects. This is outside the merely social. Such views are partly based on the supposed impotence of documentary photography to influence change by its descriptions of human tragedy. It can be asked whether this failure is to do with the inherent qualities of the medium itself or rather with political reaction, to the wanton blindness of conservative political leaders to real, let alone depicted, suffering. If we accept that photography is at fault, then before a good deal of fine-art work which uses photography, artist, critic and viewer are supposed to share a postmodern Nietzschean awareness of contradiction, to quiver in a tense and suspended state before the brief revelation of vistas opened up beyond whatever opposition they choose at that moment to consider. In the face of catastrophe, these works and their attendant writings inspire an aware, informed inaction.

Now it is evident that certain areas of fine-art practice which incorporate photography involve a flight not only from political activism and documentary, but also from any engagement with the social and even with the meaningful, courting a blank failure of reference. While mass photography is all meaning and discounts the aesthetic entirely, fine-art photographic work of this sort often discounts all meaning in favour of a breathless, aesthetic awareness of contradiction. However, recent developments, particularly digitization, have placed both these extreme positions under threat; fine-art photography is now subject to new forces as its crude opposition of realism and the corrosion of the subject is deconstructed by the withdrawal of at least one of its halves; yet ironically it is an aspect of the intermediate ground, amateur photography, which has initially suffered the most.

The first sign of the breakdown between the once rigid distinctions governing different photographic activities was the appropriation of mass photography by artists. This historically fixed distinction between high and low was eroded by digitization, which began to make mass photography look aged, fixed and discrete – in other words, ripe for appropriation by the high. Recent lionization of the subjective element in art has also helped.[19] In the translation of mass photography into fine art, the former loses all but its formal characteristics, and the despised middle of amateur photography is excluded. It cannot, indeed, exist for postmodern photographic practice, because as an apparently 'petty bourgeois' marginal form, disrupting the boundaries between the poles of mass and professional photography, it is strictly 'unthinkable'.

The most notable area of this appropriation has been in the high-art use of domestic photography. In the United States this adoption has received the ultimate official sanction of an exhibition at the Museum of Modern Art in New York, *Pleasures and Terrors of Domestic Comfort*. Britain has recently seen a large exhibition of mainly domestic photographs, *Who's Looking at the Family?*, and there have been many other manifestations of the trend.[20] These photographs are often no more than what an amateur would see as mistakes elevated to the realm of high art through museum display. That this is possible illustrates both the beleaguered condition of mass photography and the aimless relativism of fine-art practice. In the thriving heyday of mass photography such an appropriation would have been impossible, but now that it has begun to acquire the musty air of an old-fashioned craft such as, say, quilting, artists permit themselves to pick it up.

Such high-art photographs are often marked off from mass or amateur productions in the ways noted above, but nevertheless as pictures they pose problems of interpretation, being distinguished neither by subject matter nor often by quality from a billion other images. Peter Galassi, who curated the Museum of Modern Art exhibition, notes of his selection that it was too diverse to meet a single interpretation, and asks readers to 'turn directly to them' and reach their own conclusions.[21] This dodges the question of whether these works have any inherent interest or meaning, or whether they are entirely open to diverse readings. Galassi also notes the opacity of family photographs for those who know nothing about their subjects,[22] and this is an important part of their meaninglessness: rather than mapping knowledge of a personality on to the image in the picture (which would allow us to make comments such as 'that's not like you'), we vainly attempt to read the physiognomies displayed in the pictures as momentary expressions of personality. Intentionality is at the base of this puzzle, since so much in any of these pictures could be or is accident. Such pictures take us straight to the postmodern dilemma about quality: Galassi notes of Lee Friedlander's work that 'These pictures trick us into thinking that all snapshots – all umpteen billion of them – must be wonderful, and of course in a way they are.'[23] It makes just as much or as little sense to say that they are all terrible.

As in photographic work which attacks the ontological status of the medium, there are political issues at stake in this exploration of the domestic. Galassi notes and excuses the retreat from political subject matter by photographers, which has led them into the home, as a response to the unsympathetic political climate of the Eighties.[24] Of course there are 'domestic' political issues which should be explored, but this hardly warrants neglecting all others. The lack of specific knowledge about the subjects of the pictures may give the viewer the feeling that they are making universal, political statements, but this is difficult to square with the idea that any reading of the pictures is legitimate.

We have seen that the adoption of mass photography by high art excludes amateur practice. Amateur photography is further under attack from two directions, each of which threatens to change it radically. Video cameras have become very widely used and, technically and aesthetically, they are the archetypal amateur device. They have attacked the market for amateur photography at its heart, being too cumbersome and complex for casual use, and of insufficient quality for much serious use. Video, while it is simply a different medium, poses as a technical advance over still photography, and as such it is difficult for the truly technophile amateur to resist. Many of those who

used to carry SLRs now carry videos: as a reaction, camera manufacturers have been moving increasingly into marketing sophisticated
compact cameras to try to earn back from the mass market what they
have lost in the amateur. In the past rigid distinctions could be established around the size of the film used: professionals tended to use
large or medium format, amateurs 35mm, and the snappers something smaller, often 110. Now, 35mm film has got much better,
making the advantages of medium and large format less important
except for specialist work, while the invention of highly automated
35mm compact cameras has led to a substantial lessening of the popularity of smaller formats, which gave very poor picture quality. These
new cameras are, however, very different from amateur SLRs and
serve a very different use: their degree of automation is so extreme
that they can be meant only for casual picture-taking. An indication of
this is that very few of them provide any means for controlling exposure.[25] Meanwhile, for amateurs the video triumphs over the SLR
because it more comprehensively objectifies lived experience, not just
some snatched moment, but as it happens. The real-time, recorded
experience of zooming and panning gives a greater illusion of power.
Best of all, the results are viewed on the domestic icon.

The other direction of attack is digitization, which also threatens to
remove images from paper to screen. It has received much attention
because its widespread use threatens the status of photography as
evidence. Digitization makes manipulation cheaper and easier, accessible, indeed, to anyone with a computer. Sophisticated manipulation
techniques are available to newspapers and magazines which can alter
the structure of a picture at the level of the grain: such pictures are
technically indistinguishable from their source. There are obviously
sinister implications in this, although it is currently most often used to
eradicate the human imperfections of models. It has always been
true, in a restricted sense, that photography cannot lie; the effect of
digitization will be to change this forever. The forging of ordinary
photographs involved great skill and, if all variants and the original
negatives were not destroyed, could always be unmasked. With digital
manipulation, any original image may be quickly written over and on
the modified one no trace whatever remains.

The implications of this are as much aesthetic as legal or evidential.
Its fundamental effects have less to do with the manipulation of

commercial imagery (which has always gone on by other means, whether by altering what is in front of the camera or through dark-room trickery) than with a change in photography's ontological status, which strikes at the heart of amateur practice, unsupported as it is by commercial or social factors. The marketing of digitization as a consumer product will change everything in the amateur world. The technology has moved rapidly from being the preserve of big business into the home: Kodak has marketed a domestic CD system on which snapshots may be stored and altered. Multimedia computers with CD-ROM drives can read Kodak's disks and sophisticated pro-grams have been marketed which are dedicated to the manipulation of photographs. Much of amateur photography's charm and its suit-ability for critique is a result of contingencies which it faithfully records and the mistakes of its practitioners. This is an effect which Gerhard Richter has exploited in meticulous painted 'versions' of colour prints. With the arrival of domestic computer manipulation techniques, this may radically change: there will be no more lamp-posts growing out of Uncle Stan's head, no more power lines in the landscape, and every sunset will be perfect. Amateur photographers will have the power to alter their scenes, breaking the iron link between subject and photograph, and so releasing the spectre of a ubiquitous and average perfection. Photographs may even lose their status as evidence of the photographer's presence at a scene. If pho-tography's days are numbered by digital technology, which may soon encompass the camera as well as the display, a new wave of blandness will break over the world, as happy and unhappy contingencies are discarded in favour of the conventionally beautiful.

Barthes has argued that society tames the disturbing actuality of photography in two ways, by turning photographs into art, and by dis-tributing them so widely that they become banal.[26] Amateur practice has resisted this, perhaps without meaning to, by never quite reaching the status of art, and always remaining a personal matter. The post-modern attack on essence, where every contingency may be read as essence, or each essence as equally pure contingency, is another aspect of the attack on the amateur world view. It prefigures the free manip-ulation of images as weightless, homogeneous material to be freely traded, just as all qualitative distinctions are denied in the universal marketplace. By contrast, to read photographs against the grain, as

Barthes would have us do, assumes that they have an essential basis.

Despite the strident efforts of many artists and theorists, however, there is no necessary connection between anti-realism and digital techniques; indeed the use of fractal algorithms, which are capable of resolving detail not there in the original, may establish a connection with reality at some fundamental level. Digital filters may also help to sharpen an image, acting as alternatives to techniques that might otherwise be performed manually. Yet there is no longer any necessary connection with realism either; a digital filter may alter pixel neighbourhoods in any way whatsoever, as long as it can be described mathematically.[27] The weight of commercial usage ensures that realistic mendacity will become the norm. As long ago as the twenties, when the commercial use of photography was gaining momentum, Henri Michaux warned of the world sinking into a ubiquitous banality, where, however far one travelled, one would never leave the suburbs.[28] In this utopia of the banal, the real is always ideal. In one sense, digitization threatens to augment this massively; in another, it could undermine it by bringing the ideology and artificiality of representation to the fore. Yet our intellectual appreciation of the new technology of mendacity is not necessarily matched by our emotional and even physiological responses to images which still look as real as photography, and have an effect just because of this illusion. It is this residue of realism in photography, in which the look of authenticity is regularly faked, which makes it so powerful. We are led, finally, to believe in a beauteous, brave new world of digitization, and in the immaculate creatures which inhabit it.

The change is not restricted to subject matter. Although some digital means of presenting photographs emulate analogue ones (computer displays which look like slides on a light-box for instance) pictures will change their meaning when they are displayed on the television or computer screen. The print, though formally reproducible, once it is loosed on the world as an object, becomes an autonomous thing which can be moved about, given away or lost, and may become faded, dog-eared, or stained. The screen image is mere information, both more permanent and less tangible, a digital array fixed for eternity, and in display ever fleeting, part of an endless procession of images. As a piece of digital code, it may be endlessly copied and sent anywhere. The digitization of photographs is another stage in the loss of aura, defined as the presence of an object in the here and now: that photographic prints as objects could acquire aura with age, and that they could gain value because of their rarity, showed that the promise of their reproducibility was never fully redeemed. With their dematerialization into digital code, that residue will disappear. The amateur's naive attempt at the possession of essence is yielding to the digital capture of the image followed by manipulation. The photograph enters the digital world in which, since all is equally manipulable, the represented object loses its rights: there is no bar to unleashed subjectivity.

Just as in the purely aesthetic there may be some liberatory potential, so there may be in the anaesthetic concentration on the particular and the social in mass photography, but neither adds up to a free and integrated culture. Each is damaged by the other's absence. Amateur photography, combining particularity with aesthetic intent, technology with the iconography of the Sunday painter, and social issues with generality, is a forlorn and hobbled attempt to bring these sundered halves back together. The resistance which cameras once offered to commodification, as objects which were used meaningfully and which were understood by their users, is in swift decline: rather, with the demise of the amateur attitude to reality, the camera becomes a mystical object which uses its possessor. The effects of the two developments which threaten amateur photography, video and digitization, are quite different. Video is a largely technological move with sociological and aesthetic side-effects, but its central impetus is the replacement of one method of representation by another, supposedly more advanced. The digitization of images is different, for it does not *have* to do anything to the nature of photographic images, but its use is likely to alter them in such a fundamental way that it threatens the very existence of amateur practice.

Marx once wrote, 'If in all ideology men and their relations appear upside-down as in a *camera obscura*, this phenomenon arises just as much from their historical life-process as the inversion of objects on the retina does from their physical life-process.'[29] Amateur photography has traditionally tried to make sense of a mechanized, technological world which has slipped ever further from the grasp and the gaze of the individual; it has tried to recast reality in an understandable and readable form, where anything, even tragedy or evil, can be simply recognized and understood. Photography has occasionally had the power to break with its own commodification, to speak to people as evidence for conditions which they believe to be real, to speak straightforwardly about other people's experiences. Benjamin even dubbed it 'the first truly revolutionary means of reproduction', noting that its invention had coincided with the rise of socialism.[30] Digitization and its widespread application to photography, which appeared alongside the collapse of the Communist states in Europe, is a technique which though not mendacious in itself will surely continue to be used to foster commercial lies, retrospectively endorsing the musings of postmodern theorists. Reality will further recede, representation become a little more abstract, people a little less solid, our empathy with them a little less strong, while objects, cleansed of gross particularity and become eternal, apotheosize themselves in our place.

Introducing a book about the implications of digital photography, Fred Ritchin imagines how it would feel if we could no longer be certain that the figures in subway advertising photographs had ever been real. However lifelike they might seem, they might refer to no one. He continues:

> As I stared more, at images of people in business suits, on picnics, in a taxi, I became frightened. I looked at the people sitting across from me in the subway car underneath the advertisements for reassurance, but they began to feel unreal, as if they also were figments of someone's imagination. It became difficult to choose who or what was 'real', and why people could exist but people looking just like them in photographs never did.[31]

And, oddly, this is just the point; at photography's inception the faces of its bourgeois subjects, confident in their individuality, etched their personae firmly and sharply on the surface of daguerrotypes. Portraits today are altogether more insubstantial things, often coddled into a comfortable, banal perfection. Photography, in potentially losing its veracity while retaining its powers of resemblance, takes something away from all of us, and brings closer the postmodern nightmare in which people are mere conglomerations of signs, to be exchanged, altered or dispersed.

NOTES

1. Pierre Bourdieu, *Photography. A Middle-brow Art*, trans. Shaun Whiteside, Cambridge 1990.

2. Ibid., p. 41.

3. In the SLR (single lens reflex) the photographer views the scene through the lens. Compact cameras have a separate viewfinder.

4. A recent brochure for the Contax S2, a camera of this type, proclaimed 'Camera Back-to-Basics'.

5. Robert Castel and Dominique Schnapper, 'Aesthetic Ambitions and Social Aspirations: the Camera Club as a Secondary Group', in Bourdieu, *Photography*, p. 126.

6. Steve Basiter, 'Photo Clinic', *Photo Answers*, no. 68, November 1994, p. 75.

7. Bourdieu, *Photography*, p. 190.

8. Walter Benjamin, 'The Author as Producer', in Andrew Arato and Eike Gebhardt, eds, *The Essential Frankfurt School Reader*, New York 1982, p. 262.

9. T.W. Adorno, *Aesthetic Theory*, trans. C. Lenhardt, London 1984, p. 196.

10. Cited in Roland Barthes, *Camera Lucida. Reflections on Photography*, trans. Richard Howard, London 1984, p. 41.

11. Ibid., p. 4.

12. Benjamin, *Zentralpark*, in *Gesammelte Schriften*, Frankfurt am Main 1972, vol. I, p. 681; cited in Susan Buck-Morss, *The Dialectics of Seeing. Walter Benjamin and the Arcades Project*, Cambridge, Mass. 1989, p. 189.

13. Walter Benjamin, *One Way Street and Other Writings*, trans. Edmund Jephcott and Kingsley Shorter, London 1979, p. 74.

14. *The Family of Man* was an important international exhibition of photography curated by Edward Steichen and shown at the Museum of Modern Art, New York, in 1955.

15. Statement by Ensdorf in Timothy Druckrey, *Iterations: The New Image*, New York and Cambridge, Mass. 1993, p. 96.

16. Peter Dews, *The Logics of Disintegration. Post-Structuralist Thought and the Claims of Critical Theory*, London 1987, p. 177.

17. See, among many examples, Rosalind Krauss, 'Corpus Delicti', in London, Hayward Gallery, *L'Amour Fou. Photography and Surrealism*, 1986, and Craig Owens, 'Photography *en abyme*' in his book *Beyond Recognition. Representation, Power, and Culture*, Berkeley 1992.

18. John Tagg, *The Burden of Representation. Essays on Photographies and Histories*, Basingstoke 1988, p. 160.

19. For a sympathetic analysis of this trend in high art see Donald Kuspit, *The New Subjectivism. Art in the 1980s*, New York 1993.

20. See New York, Museum of Modern Art, *Pleasures and Terrors of Domestic*

Comfort by Peter Galassi, 1991, and London, Barbican Art Gallery, *Who's Looking at the Family?* by Val Williams, 1994.

21. New York, *Pleasures and Terrors*, p. 7.

22. Ibid., p. 11.

23. Ibid., p. 10.

24. Ibid., pp. 12–13.

25. All compact cameras used to provide this feature if only because the film speed had to be set manually: with the advent of DX coding (which employs a pattern on the film cannister to set the speed automatically), the user has become powerless to modify the camera's often faulty judgement. There are very few exceptions: they include the Contax and Minox ranges. The former are very expensive compacts capable of serious work but often purchased for their snob value; the latter are professional cameras which buck the trends by providing manual focus and exposure.

26. Barthes, *Camera Lucida*, p. 117.

27. William J. Mitchell, *The Reconfigured Eye. Visual Truth in the Post-Photographic Era*, Cambridge, Mass. 1992, p. 112.

28. See Henri Michaux, *Ecuador. Journal d'un voyage*, Paris 1929.

29. Karl Marx, *The German Ideology*, in *Collected Works, vol. 5, Marx and Engels, 1845–47*, London 1976, p. 36.

30. Walter Benjamin, 'The Work of Art in the Age of Mechanical Reproduction', in *Illuminations*, ed. Hannah Arendt, London 1973, p. 226.

31. Fred Ritchin, *In Our Own Image. The Coming Revolution in Photography*, New York 1990, p. 3.

3

EMPOWERING TECHNOLOGY

From the death of the real in photographic representation, we turn to the apotheosis of representation in digital media, where data, thrown to the ether, is handled in such a realist manner that it virtually rematerializes. The environment in which all digitized media promise to combine and be exchanged is called cyberspace. It is a curious subject, because as yet it barely exists. Nevertheless, this has not hindered previews of its concepts and ideals being played out constantly in theory and fiction; these writings, which look to technology to fulfil their wishes, visions and nightmares, promise no less than a fundamental remaking of human relations to machines and information, and with it a remaking of humanity itself.

The component parts of cyberspace – virtual reality and computer networking – are already with us; the first, in a crude form, can already be seen in the video arcades, while the second is a rapidly growing global infrastructure. Until now, however, the heady marriage of the two, which is the ideal of cyberspace, has been described only in theory and science fiction. The typical vision is as follows:

> From vast databases that constitute the culture's deposited wealth, every document is available, every recording is playable, and every picture is viewable. Around this: a laboratory, an instrumental bridge; taking no space, a home presiding over a world [. . .].[1]

The user is immersed in a world of data which is present either as we would normally see it (perhaps a simulation of a printed page), or represented graphically (a dynamic three-dimensional graph of financial movements on the stock exchange). The massive number of sites or specialisms which this data comprises could be presented as different geographical areas between which the user would virtually travel. A number of old bourgeois dreams are encompassed in the promise of this technology: to survey the world from one's living-room, to grasp the totality of all data within a single frame, and to recapture a unified knowledge and experience. It also holds out the vision of an eternal archive which will persist long after the physical objects from which it was taken have crumbled; paintings may crack and photographs fade but digital records permit their colours and surfaces to remain forever pristine, while the exact trajectory of the object's decline is plotted. Artefacts and even species which have been lost may be reconstructed; in a computer simulation, at least, we can wander about the Acropolis in its prime, or see dinosaurs stamp the virtual earth. Of course to write about *the* culture's 'wealth' assumes a community of interest among users before this process starts, and that cultural riches are simply out there to be grasped and codified. Yet this is in fact widely assumed: to the renewed liaison between technology and culture, the developers of cyberspace bring both a charming naivety and much commercial acumen. Microsoft is buying up the digital rights to what its founder, Bill Gates, calls the million most fascinating images in the world.[2]

The ideal of cyberspace takes in more than just the sum of all human knowledge. It is also an electronic agora in which isolated, anomic but presumably rather well informed individuals may once more come together, without risk of violence or infection, to engage in debate, exchange information or merely chew the fat. Both data and conversation are potentially accessible from anywhere; to be able to 'chat' instantaneously with a neighbour on the other side of the world certainly changes notions of distance and locality. Cyberspace seems to offer simultaneously the advantages of privacy and cultural wealth, self-sufficiency and opportunities for sociability.

Yet, despite all the attention it has been receiving, cyberspace as a technological development has a strange status, not only because it has not yet been realized, but also because it is a concept which has its origins in fiction, particularly in the cyberpunk novels of William Gibson. Programmers and engineers are acting on fictional blueprints and, since these are naturally extremely vague, the very concept and the details of its implementation are up for grabs. The whole affair is even more curious because the fictional vision of cyberspace and the world which surrounds it is hardly positive: what has been taken up so enthusiastically is not so much a technical proposal as a dystopian vision of the future. Of the very term itself, Gibson admits that he 'Assembled word *cyberspace* from small and readily available components of language. Neologic spasm: the primal act of pop poetics. Preceded any concept whatever. Slick and hollow – awaiting received meaning.'[3] In Gibson's books cyberspace is a dizzying, dangerous 'place', where experience is so intense that it exceeds anything likely to be encountered in real life. It is dominated by leviathan corporations for whose operations it exists, but the system has exceeded them, producing mysterious creatures of mythical abilities, and encompassing such enormous complexity that there are many opportunities for daring Net frontiersmen, who make money by breaking security systems and copying confidential information. Above all, cyberspace is a visual environment in which, while deception is sometimes a feature, things generally look much like what they are: large databases look large, corporations look powerful, military complexes look remote and dangerous, electronic countermeasures look threatening, and as they operate their workings are graphically represented. There is, as we shall see, some sense to this. The transparency of meaning in cyberspace, the absolute match between concept and appearance, is a utopian feature which stands in marked contrast to the real world of meaningless detail and redundant matter.

These descriptions should be contrasted with the reality of computer networking today for, while there are certainly opportunities for hackers, the interface is largely text-based and highly technical. Visceral experiences and reactions are absent – unless boredom counts. If computer networks are eventually to present themselves through graphical systems, there is no particular rule to say that there will be any resemblance between 'what they are' and what they look like, although there will no doubt be a tendency to link looks with the image an entity wishes to project. Yet links between data and its representation cannot be entirely arbitrary, because the major advantage of cyberspace is that everyday perceptual skills would be employed in understanding and manipulating complex information; people are generally much better at picking up an anomaly in a visual repres- entation of data than from a raw mass of figures. The development of computer systems is also certainly running in the direction of Gibson's vision: as Michael Benedikt points out, the 'evolution' of systems, from typed command to menu to Graphical User Interface (for instance, the Macintosh operating system copied in *Windows*) is that of making implicit navigation data visible and marrying it to con- tent.[4] The idea of an apparently immersive, three-dimensional cyberspace is another step in this direction.

What, then, are the details of this fictional vision to which many technicians, parts of the mass media and a portion of the public, have subscribed? There is little common agreement about the definition or extent of cyberpunk. However, its main features are easy to charac- terize, as Istvan Csicsery-Ronay Jr, a writer about science fiction, rather wearily demonstrates:

> how many formulaic tales can one wade through in which a self- destructive but sensitive young protagonist with an (implant/ prosthesis/telechtronic talent) that makes the evil (megacorpora- tions/police states/criminal underworlds) pursue him through (wasted urban landscapes/elite luxury enclaves/eccentric space stations) full of grotesque (haircuts/clothes/self-mutilations/rock music/sexual hob- bies/designer drugs/telechtronic gadgets/nasty new weapons/ exteriorized hallucinations) representing the (mores/fashions) of modern civilization in terminal decline, ultimately hooks up with rebel- lious and tough-talking (youth/artificial intelligence/rock cults) who offer the alternative, not of (community/socialism/traditional val- ues/transcendental vision), but of supreme, life-affirming *hipness*, going with the flow which now flows in the machine, against the spec- tre of a world-subverting (artificial intelligence/multinational corporate web/evil genius)?[5]

Despite all this, he goes on to argue that the genre is worthy of attention because it explores links between four levels of information- processing: the individual's biological processes and personality, the totality of social life, mechanical artificial intelligences and finally new, 'living' entities, created out of these AIs.[6] Cyberspace jockeys in these fictions do not just wear virtual-reality headsets but undergo surgery so that they may interface directly with the Net. There is an air of telepathy about the way they experience, if not understand, the sublime complexity of the world's data, and the most fortunate may hope for mystical contact with artificial super-beings. In the connection of the individual and the social, there is a dialectical move in which opposed qualities find resolution in a higher unity, and we shall see that this is typical of writing about cyberspace in fiction and non-fiction. For the moment note the strange combination of hi-tech and grunge, of the laboratory and the street (or at least a suburban boy's idea of the street), of social critique and unreconstructed heroism. Cyberpunk sports a Gothic technophilia.

The cyberpunk vision is not simply negative, but it is not a happy one. Gibson's first novel, *Neuromancer* (a great success and the book which, more than any other, defined the genre), is set in the wake of a worldwide nuclear conflict. After the reconstruction, the rich are fabulously so, while everyone else scrapes by in an environmentally degraded world of drugs, violence and conspiracy, aided by bizarre mental and physical prostheses. The hero:

> slept in the cheapest coffins, the ones nearest the port, beneath the quartz-halogen floods that lit the docks all night like vast stages; where you couldn't see the lights of Tokyo for the glare of the television sky, not even the towering hologram logo of the Fuji Electric Company, and Tokyo Bay was a black expanse where gulls wheeled above drifting shoals of styrofoam. Behind the port lay the city, factory domes dominated by the vast cubes of corporate arcologies. Port and city were divided by a narrow borderland of older streets, an area with no official name. [. . .] By day, the bars down Ninsei were shuttered and featureless, the neon dead, the holograms inert, waiting, under the poisoned silver sky.[7]

The real world is in a perhaps terminal decline, and threatens to bury its inhabitants beneath obsolete consumer goods, an ever-rising tide of trash.[8] People turn their backs on reality, into drugs, into cyberspace, or, for the less active, into an enveloping form of television which directly imparts the sensory experiences of its stars. Cyberspace is at once an ideological inverse image of this world, and a tool which helps to maintain the power of those who govern. Nevertheless, for those who regularly inhabit it, even the real world comes to seem like cyberspace, as the virtual takes on a reality which often has material effects, and the material acquires an unreal virtuality.[9] Given this scenario, a question naturally arises: why does anyone want to develop dystopia? Among the reasons which immediately spring to mind are its supposed technical inevitability, coupled with dissatisfaction with currently fixed identities and activities; also perhaps that there might be a career in it. Most of all, though, because fictional cyberspace has a fascination as a glossy technophiles' dystopia, which contains some curiously utopian elements. In cyberspace, as it appears in novels at least, the world seems to make transparent sense, if only for the god-like entities which haunt its highest margins. Rising up beyond the mundane, messy everyday world of gross matter, it is a wondrous vision of dazzling complexity, a visual manifestation of the spirit of a higher order. Yet beyond even this, there is a resolutely positive vision of cyberspace, very much at odds with its face in fiction, which is at once highly congruent with current intellectual fashions and with powerful commercial interests.

A phone book is a material object containing data; this data is abstract and can be understood only by those who know how to read it; the book itself is a piece of matter and has to be put in the appropriate place and sometimes moved around. In cyberspace both of these conditions may be changed: data is extracted from its material support and purified so that it can be in many places at once, and sent at near the speed of light. Cyberspace also promises to restore a sensorial form to data without its losing utility or fungibility. Furthermore, this data can be directly linked into a functioning system: such a telephone system may still work with numbers but the regular user would never need to deal with them.

The representation of data within cyberspace is generally thought of as visual and strictly organized in space. Michael Benedikt, a professor of architecture, writes of 'cyberspace architects' who will visualize the 'intrinsically nonphysical' and so give 'inhabitable visible form to society's most intricate abstractions, processes, and organisms of information'.[10] Cyberspace, then, will be a unified field in which the real is abstracted and the abstract solidified, in which data, extracted from real processes, is reconstituted into apparently solid, immediately comprehensible forms, stripped of all actuality. Within this neat schema, the status of representations is equivocal. While data gains physicality, representations in cyberspace lose it, floating free in the digital environment, but as pieces of data which already have a form, they are not manipulable in quite the same way as, say, numbers. They are hard nuggets of discrete information among a shifting mass, manipulable by position and presentation, but not so much (except on the whim of the individual) in terms of form or content, nor changeable in response to shifts in the values of external data. Old, fixed representations, then, might become an important anomaly within the dematerialized visual arena of cyberspace.

To leave this issue aside for the time being, the simultaneous dematerialization of data and its transformation into readily understood visual forms have been used as the basis for much metaphysical speculation about the nature of cyberspace. At times this has amounted to the exercise of a hi-tech Hegelianism. Cyberspace is often presented as a new realm between the material and the mental: 'Cyberspace becomes another venue for consciousness itself. And this emergence, proliferation, and complexification [sic] of consciousness must surely be this universe's project.'[11] Its materialization of information, the gift of form to data, is also a Platonic dream come true:

> Cyberspace is Platonism as a working product. [. . .] The computer recycles ancient Platonism by injecting the ideal content of cognition with empirical specifics. [. . .] The computer clothes the details of empirical experience so that they seem to share the ideality of the stable knowledge of Forms.[12]

Rather than see cyberspace simply as a halfway house between various pre-existing concepts, the temptation is to view it as a Hegelian synthesis. If for Hegel the real was ideal, in cyberspace the ideal is made virtually real. Very often theories about cyberspace encompass a grand historical sweep, taking on a Hegelian tone as the technology is seen as the means of achieving a sublation of previously opposed fundamental forces or qualities. Cyberspace becomes the conclusion of a wondrous and harmonious historical pageant, a story of human technical and cultural evolution sweeping forwards from cave-painting to computer science. So Benedikt, for instance, argues that it ushers in a '*post* literate era' which unites the advantages of pre-literate physical activity with literate symbolic activity.[13] Or it may be seen as the sublation of the 'monadological' body and the community,[14] body and mind, art and science and no doubt quite a few other combinations. Two self-proclaimed, networked media-philosophers, Mark Taylor and Esa Saarinen, spell out the nature of the attraction clearly:

> According to Hegel, the concept is actually embodied in time and space. In different terms, objectivity is actually conceptual or the real is the idea. In the society of spectacle, the idea becomes the image and the real is imaginary. For Hegel, it is concept all the way down; for the society of the spectacle, it is image all the way down. In the twentieth century, the Hegelian concept becomes real in electronic telecommunications. The net wires the world for Hegelian *Geist*.[15]

The Hegelianism of the cyberphiles is not one of process, a form of becoming – in fact there is a general assumption that what is technically possible will inevitably be implemented. Rather, the cyberspace utopia is a fixed state in which the end of history and the total realization of mind is finally achieved in a fixed Platonic form. Yet cyberspace is to be more than a pretty picture; it must also be an operational system. Data, which must be handled in the visual arena of cyberspace, like numbers on the stockmarket, has already been abstracted from the real world and made fungible. Its particularity has already been stripped away in its reduction to number. In cyberspace, where it is given an apprehensible form, this data must be constantly animated, as if in a movie. Given that the function of virtual representation is tied to movement, a fixed perfection, like that of architecture, will certainly elude these forms. Further, even these clean, mobile cyberspace forms can never show the material suffering behind a row of financial figures, for this has been stripped away long ago in the very collection of the data. When form is restored to this data, the 'reality' it adopts is utterly cleansed of anything that cannot be exchanged.

Perhaps we should try to stand Hegel on his head for a while. 'Empowering technology' is the new buzz phrase of the informatics enthusiasts, and it has a revealing ambiguity to it. The cyberphiles have generally had an easy time of it in the mass media, which are owned by the very companies that are buying up rights to data for virtual distribution. Here fundamental questions about the direction in which the technology is being taken are rarely asked. A basic assumption behind the acceptance of cyberspace underlies that of the information society as a whole: Andrew Ross has rightly argued that 'the technical *fact* of communication itself is celebrated as an inherent good', without any discussion of the 'resulting shape of the community that is wired up in this way'. New Age dreams of universal, seamless networking are oddly congruent with features of a modern corporate communications ideology.[16] Cyberspace is also allied with an unashamed consumerism: 'We are present at the apotheosis of commercial culture. Commerce is the ocean that information swims in. [. . .] the means of exchange in commercial culture is now *pure information*'.[17] Vivian Sobchack has analysed the mix of New Age spiritualism and New Edge technophilia in which sixties political activism and social consciousness have been resolved into 'a particularly privileged, selfish, consumer-oriented and technologically dependent libertarianism', which fulfils 'the dreams of "mondoids" who, by day, sit at computer consoles working for (and becoming) corporate America'.[18] It is cyberspace which will allow this becoming to complete itself, uniting the worlds of work and leisure in an environment plied by virtual alter-egos. In this light, cyberspace appears as less the end of history than the ultimate business environment, being stockmarket, warehouse and shopping centre all in one.

Aside from commercial interests, there is also an unholy alliance of postmodern disintegration theorists and wide-eyed New Agers, producing a ludicrous image of the world immersed in a great, shifting sea of data, each person jacking in and finding exactly what they want, in their own personalized order and format. People will live intensely in this digital utopia, forgetting their grosser material needs in an affective, intellectual search for companionship and knowledge. In this ostensibly democratic forum, the chairman of some Western conglomerate and an impoverished peasant in Central Africa will both use a device, about the size of a Walkman, to communicate by satellite with a panoply of open information systems.

As soon as this utopian vision of global information sharing is baldly stated, its stupidity becomes obvious. It is not a matter of doubting the capabilities of the technology, which has already been developed and is becoming cheaper all the time. One should be deeply sceptical, however, about who will control the information, how much it will cost, and to whom it will be sold. Technological revolutions of the past parade their many broken utopian promises. As Herbert Schiller has shown, similar arguments have been rehearsed about all manner of new technologies in order to prepare for their acceptance, and in all cases the liberatory effects have been negligible. Desktop publishing is one example, as is cable television which, although it was much touted as the guarantor of pluralism, has rapidly succumbed to homogeneous corporate dominance.[19] Indeed, at its inception, even the standard technology of television was supposed to offer equal exchange between broadcaster and viewer and access to universal knowledge.[20] Domestic computer technology provides another striking example of the marketing of a rapidly improving technology. Computers have indeed become much cheaper, but only in a certain sense. Average systems still cost a considerable amount of money and, while they are far more powerful, their basic price has not fallen for many years; in fact it may be that the average system has become more expensive in real terms.[21] Software developments which, like cameras, do not always develop in a strictly functional manner, push the minimum acceptable machine ever upward into new areas of speed and sophistication. Below a certain price level, there is little money to be made selling these goods, unless they can be shifted in vast amounts. There is no interest in selling electronic commodities at the price the world's poor can afford, nor is there likely to be. The idea that high-band global networking will become truly universal in a world where only a fifth of the population currently have even telephones is laughable.[22] Even in the highly improbable event of the hardware price sinking to that of a can of Coke, there are still insuperable obstacles for the impoverished. The technology requires that end-users are connected by satellites or a network of specialized terrestrial cabling, the 'Information Super-Highway' in which the United States government is currently investing much money. Already there is an awareness that the placement of the cables may be a means of discriminating against the less wealthy. Without the cabling, and without expensive, advanced modems to receive the data, transfer is much slower, to the point of being either impractical or, since online charges are much like telephone calls, too expensive. Then there is the whole vexed issue of copyright, which will certainly add further charges for the access of 'intellectual property'. Large companies are actively buying the digital rights to all kinds of data, from financial records to pop records; they are not doing this to distribute them free of charge.

The emergence of cyberspace as the main information channel is worrying because it will not necessarily be seen as complementary to existing media. If the Net becomes the only way of receiving certain kinds of information, it may be more restrictive than current systems. Schiller puts the broad issue clearly:

> Transforming information into a saleable good, available only to those with the ability to pay for it, changes the goal of information access from an egalitarian to a privileged condition. The consequence of this is that the essential underpinning of a democratic order is seriously, if not fatally, damaged.[23]

Now of course, access to certain kinds of information has always been difficult and time-consuming, and what appears in the mass media has always been strictly controlled; in one sense, and perhaps as it exists today, networking can provide a minority with the means to receive information and opinions from diverse sources, yet in another, pay-as-you-go cyberspace threatens to add another powerful disincentive on top of the controls which already exist.

Far from closing down access to information, cyberphiles have generally seen the Net as evolving into an open, global forum to which anybody can contribute, in which information and data are shared and weighty issues discussed. Communities, often sundered in the real world by traffic, the threat of violence or by the self-sufficiency encouraged by modern domestic appliances, will be reborn in the ether, as people with the same interests, but who are perhaps geographically distant, virtually meet. Roy Ascott, for instance, has stressed the dialogic nature of the new telematic media:

> Interactive telecommunications – telematic technology [. . .] speaks a language of cooperation, creativity and transformation. It is the technology

not of monologue but of conversation. It feeds fecund open-endedness
rather than an aesthetics of closure and completion.[24]

This is not to forge the way for a society of the kind described by
Habermas, in which agreement is founded on reasoned conversation, but something far more fractured and postmodern; not so much
dialogue as a cacophony of separate, atomistic voices. For Ascott, and
this is a very common association, it has its philosophical basis in the
writings of Nietzsche, Bateson, Weiner, Derrida and Rorty. Ascott,
speaking now of art on the Net, continues:

> Art is no longer seen as a linear affair, dealing in harmony, comple-
> tion, resolution, closure – a composed and ordered finality. Instead it
> is open-ended, even fugitive, fleeting, tentative, virtual. Forming
> rather than formed, it celebrates process, embodies system, embraces
> chaos.[25]

On the face of it, there would seem to be some contradiction between
building a community, which must have a basis in some agreed terms,
and the supposed ever-shifting fluidity of postmodern discourse. Yet
people on the Net, despite their differences, have managed to build
something of a community, though as we shall see it is of quite a particular kind.

Until very recently, many of the advantages of networking were
derived from its very exclusiveness: it was open only to people who
had access to a computer and a modem, and using these was quite a
technical matter. In Britain especially, the social composition of participants on the Net was very narrow, in part because of high
telephone charges, being dominated by young computer professionals and academics, often scientists, who gained access through the
free university network. In all countries, the restricted social make-up
of those on the Net, and the fact that they were all technically com-
petent, encouraged a good deal of solidarity. The great increase in the
number of new users, however, has led old hands to complain that the
pleasures of discovery are being obstructed by the high number of
learners and 'party-goers'. Theodore Roszak, writing of Bulletin
Board Systems where people can post computer messages, describes
part of the problem:

In most of the BBS hard copy I have seen, the gems of thought lie scattered through a dense thicket of trivia, cute limericks, snippets of opinion, off-the-wall outbursts, illegible fragments. I would be inclined to see much of this as simply another source of data glut, requiring more time to sort through and glean than it is worth. Is networking really better than gathering of an evening at a nearby coffeehouse, or pub, or café to make conversation?[26]

Even those who are enthusiastic about the potential of the Net have to admit that most BBS discussion is 'mundane or puerile or esoteric', having something in common with homemade fanzines.[27] Net conversations are often theatrical, featuring well-known regular participants who are thoroughly informed about networking etiquette, and are greatly outnumbered by silent listeners.[28] Various intellectuals hang around this world, in the hope that a little of its street cred might rub off. Some have cultivated a cool but apocalyptic mode of writing, replete with neologisms and oxymorons. This is a passage from Arthur Kroker and Michael Weinstein's aptly named book, *Data Trash*, in which the authors are careful to parade their pretensions in detail:

> I am sitting in Foufounes Electrique, an underground cyberpunk music bar in Montreal. I've a shooter in my hand, copies of Bruce Sterling's *Crystal Express* and Nietzsche's *Will to Power* in my data bag, and my cyber-flesh is taking direct hits from the sound force-field of *Fuzzy Logic*, a group of digital music hackers [. . .][29]

And so it proceeds interminably.

Aside from the danger that meaningful discourse may be buried by trivia and, increasingly, advertising,[30] there is a postmodern dilemma which the Net faces, and which is very much linked with the philosophical work of Rorty et al. Howard Rheingold, who has been very active in building a local network in San Francisco, notes that the Net's diversity of dialogue and porous boundaries 'might be an artifact of the early stages of the medium – fragmentation, hierarchization, rigidifying social boundaries, and single-niche colonies of people who share intolerances could become prevalent in the future'.[31] The idea that there is a 'true' structure of information is one of the most pervasive myths of cyberspace, notes Erik Davis,[32] and it is likely to be eroded as people begin to disagree about what constitutes trivia, or how special-interest groups are structured and represented, or as fascists and religious fundamentalists increasingly use the Net to push views which would deny the rights of others. The consensual environment of cyberspace must try to satisfy many competing demands.

These incipient communities also have to face active vandalism. This may take the form of hacking into the operating system to cause disruption or bypassing security measures in order to read private mail and credit-card numbers. Beyond this, forums may be attacked merely by the content of the messages. Rheingold notes:

> One of the great problems with the atmosphere of free expression now tolerated on the Net is the fragility of communities and their susceptibility to disruption. The only alternative to imposing potentially dangerous restrictions on freedom of expression is to develop norms, folklore, ways of acceptable behaviour that are widely modelled, taught, and valued, that can give the citizens of cyberspace clear ideas of what they can and cannot do with the medium, how they can gain leverage, and where they must beware of pitfalls in the medium, if we intend to use it for community-building.[33]

He gives one example of a community Bulletin Board System which was destroyed by a group of young males choking the system with obscene postings.[34] Such tales point to a fundamental problem: to function successfully, the virtual community demands that a real one lie behind it. The propensity for trying to make virtual communities is comment enough on the debility of real ones, but also on the need for them. If virtual communities flourish now, this is due to the relatively closed nature of the Net, which means that it is hardly the identity-free utopia that some claim. People are defined at least by the fact that they are there.

Postmodern critics who praise Net-speak for its diversity are reluctant to raise questions of judgement about its quality. The central argument of Roszak's book, *The Cult of Information*, is that there is no necessary connection between the mere amount of data available and the quality of thought brought to bear on it. There is also the question of whether the computer itself has any effect on the quality of thought produced in its presence. At first sight, it would seem that the answer must be no; the computer is a universal machine, capable of simulating the action of any other machine, so its operation need do little to change our previous habits and predilections. Yet the actual form which it has taken is highly specific, and very much determined by the fact that it must be marketed and sold to businesses and consumers, and this particular form does seem to encourage certain types of relationship to the content it displays. In part, this may be to do with the system of navigation; effortless and unlimited jumps lead to skimming, while the lack of hierarchy in presentation and the equality of access to each area give the impression that all pieces of information are equivalent. There is a propensity to travel but never to arrive. Benedikt is aware of the difficulty:

> If instant access to people and information were to become endemic to cyberspace, gone would be the process of progressive revelation inherent in closing the distance between self and object, and gone would be a major armature in the structuring of human narratives: the narrative of *travel*. Destinations would all be certain, like conclusions foregone. Time and history, narrativity and memorability, the unfolding of situations, the distance between objects of desire and ourselves – the distance, indeed, that creates desire and the whole ontology of eroticism [. . .] – would be collapsed, thrown back, to existing in *this* physical world only, and only as lame, metaphorical constructions, here and there, in that one.[35]

This is not mere speculation. Theodore Roszak has commented on the diminished attention span encouraged by 'edutainment', arguing:

> There is something about all computerised activities that is worrisome in this respect, something built into the physical posture, emotional affect, and perceptual action of sitting at a video terminal, entering data, scrolling through, revealing snippets of this and that.[36]

If this seems exaggerated, it may be because we have already been affected: Adorno wrote of the abbreviated thought which takes place with pencil in hand, so what would he have made of the insistently flashing cursor?[37] Even the best multimedia programs encourage constant flicking from screen to screen, partly because the options for moving on are always present, awaiting the next click of the mouse, but mostly because of the paucity of the material offered. One might gaze at a painting by Poussin for quite some time, but not at the little images in 256 colours provided in Microsoft's *Art Gallery*. The flattening of information and representation into a single field tends to erode the significance of the unusual. Again, as in digital photography, this amounts to a retrospective justification of postmodern views, in this case of extreme relativism.

The rise of digital media has encouraged the propagation of a 'theory' which lauds these very qualities of shallowness and dispersal as a new form of radicalism. The beginnings of a theoretical attack on print itself are evident, working in the interests of those corporations which have invested in multimedia. A symptomatic example is *Imagologies*, to which I have already referred, which is about a video-linked seminar on networking and the new media conducted between Finland and the United States. This book is somewhat embarrassed to be a book, and seeks to convince the reader by its layout (which uses multiple parallel texts and words printed in different directions and in different typefaces, rather in the style of an up-market student rag magazine) that it goes beyond the mundane, linear reasoning associated with the reading of mere print. Matching the layout, there are few passages of sustained argument, the stress being rather on sequences of dispersed soundbites and unsupported statements. The cover sports the phrase 'If you read books, justify it'. Of course, unlike transitory musings over the ether, this book is an object and a commodity, one that might even appeal to masochistic bibliophiles. The alliance with deconstruction is made quite explicit:

> While marking the closure of the western metaphysical tradition, deconstruction also signals the opening of post-print culture. Deconstruction remains bound to and by the world of print that it nonetheless calls into question. What comes after deconstruction? Imagology. To realize what deconstruction has made possible, it is necessary to move into the world of telecommunications technology. The notion of textuality cannot be radicalized until it is transformed from print to other media. To perform dissemination is to electrify the signifier.[38]

To show that this alliance is not what it seems will involve a staid recourse to analysis and a dissatisfaction with dwelling on the surface of things. Taylor and Saarinen argue for naivety and plain speaking in the face of ecological catastrophe a few pages later,[39] and neither quality might be thought to match the electronic apotheosis of deconstruction. The general argument, however, is that meaning itself involves an authoritarian closure, and that, in any case, no one has much time in this age of television and telecommunications to read a whole book from cover to cover or develop an argument, so we have no option but to celebrate the liberatory potential of fragmentary thought, hypertextual skipping, and the merely tactical use of the media in highly transitory situations. Obviously, in such a situation, contradiction may be borne lightly.

The greatest freedom cyberspace promises is that of recasting the self: from static beings, bound by the body and betrayed by appearances, Net-surfers may reconstruct themselves in a multiplicity of dazzling roles, changing from moment to moment according to whim. From being restricted to a single time and place, the Net being may distribute itself over the wired-up globe and make its acts and statements eternal. The new technology offers us freedom of the most fundamental and necessary kind, from identity itself:

> The technology of these transformative systems fulfils a profound human desire: to transcend the limits of the human body, time and space; to escape language, to defeat the metaphors of self and identity that alienate and isolate, that imprison the mind in solipsistic systems. Our need is to fly, to reach out, to touch, connect – to expand our consciousness by a dissemination of our presence, to distribute self into a larger society of mind.[40]

As it currently exists, this utopian anonymity has been founded on text, in fact on the technical limitations of the interface. Identity can be fluid in virtual communication where accent, looks, wealth, posture and gender are screened out in text-only dialogue; this is not likely to last long, and in fact the degree to which it happens even now may be exaggerated.[41] Such playing of roles goes back to Alan Turing's gender game, in which a man and a woman in separate rooms conversing only with written messages try to convince each other that they are both women.[42] Turing of course also devised a similar test for machine intelligence. When video rather than text is exchanged the conventional boundaries of identity may be re-established. Images could be modified, of course, but only by deliberate falsification. On the other hand, representations of the self in cyberspace may be thought of as deliberate fictions, and gender-swapping seems to be one of those most in demand, to the extent that in the Lucasfilms virtual world, *Habitat*, there is a 'Change-o-matic' object which switches the virtual gender of its user. The Humean kit form of identity change is likely to be the most open to most users: true fluidity being beyond all but the independent programmer. Yet the extreme mutability and multiplication of identity possible in cyberspace collides with the desire to build communities based upon honest communication with people of diverse backgrounds and interests. Role-playing, and the potential for dishonesty which goes with it, militates against community.[43]

The potential flexibility of cyberspace does not extend merely to the presentation of identity, but also covers a personal tailoring of how the virtual environment is experienced. It might form the ultimate solipsism, because space and perception are infinitely malleable to the user:

> Liquid architecture is an architecture whose form is contingent on the interests of the beholder; it is an architecture that opens to welcome me and closes to defend me; it is an architecture without doors and hallways, where the next room is always where I need it to be and what I need it to be. Liquid architecture makes liquid cities, cities that change at the shift of a value, where visitors with different backgrounds see different landmarks, where neighborhoods vary with ideas held in common, and evolve as the ideas mature or dissolve.[44]

The next room is indeed always where you need to be, but this is only half the problem. Such schemes amount to a materialized phenomenology, a realization of the postmodern dream in which we create reality itself. Benedikt, aware of some of the practical difficulties which this would involve, tries to rule this out with his 'Principle of Indifference' which states that '*the felt realness of any world depends on the degree of its indifference to the presence of a particular "user" and on its resistance to his/her desire*.[45] Such pre-emptive restrictions on the freedom of identity, its multiplication, and the speed and latitude of travel are imposed by the requirements of a consensual space. Of representations of objects and people in cyberspace Benedikt writes:

> These malleable data representations, worlds, and selves, seemingly so desirable, instantiating (at last!) our much-vaunted individual subjectivity and the late-twentieth-century notion that reality is nothing but a projection of that subjectivity, are, in fact, as much laid *against* each other as into each other. While the temptation to narcissism and deception are [sic] dismaying, the risks to rational communication are staggering.[46]

Immediately, then, and just as in the real world, personal freedoms are restricted by the demands of a consensual environment; cyberspace enthusiasts may want completely fluid identities and organic communities, but they cannot have both at once – at least not within a unitary environment.

Politics and commerce are as closely linked in the emergent medium of cyberspace as they are in television or any other mass-marketed cultural form. Again, however, political advances are supposed to be founded on this new technology. The unrestricted exchange of information is supposed to make life difficult for totalitarianism, and to augment the power of citizens in democracies.[47] Networks have indeed often been employed for radical purposes: Green organizations use them to maintain contact with remote areas where rapid responses to, say, new logging operations are necessary. News can be passed on quickly to activists internationally, who can then mobilize opposition. More generally, however, and when we consider not specific radical activities, but the idea of universal data access as a whole, this optimism is based on a strange diagnosis of our social ills. As Roszak puts the matter: 'It assumes that the body politic is starving for lack of information and that only the computer can make good that shortage', while obviously politics has hardly exhausted the information already available.[48]

The idea that networking has a politically radical aspect has not, however, just been invented out of the blue by cyberphiles. It has a basis, especially in the early idealism of those who established the popular use of computer networks. The utopian and politically progressive moment of networking lies perhaps not in its future but in its anti-commercial origins, when enthusiasts established an exclusive counter-culture based on the free exchange of information and programming tools. The first words of Robert X. Cringely's book about the rise of personal computing, *Accidental Empires*, run as follows:

> Years ago, when you were a kid and I was a kid, something changed in America. One moment we were the players of baseball, voters, readers of books, makers of dinners, arguers. And a second later, and for every other second since then, we were all just shoppers.[49]

The point is that, for those wealthy enough to be consumers, the personal, digital world provided – and perhaps still can provide – an escape from the ubiquitous mall that the world has become. The key programs that made amateur computer communication possible were distributed free or at a nominal cost.[50] Furthermore, the Internet is remarkable because it requires so little administration; while it has its origins in military computer communications networks which were designed to be robust and flexible enough to survive the destruction of a large number of their nodes by nuclear attack, the result is a modular and largely self-regulating system.

The hope is that the shiny new world of cyberspace will be a free, public space where the environmental depredations and commercial white noise of the real world can be avoided. In the United States, it is often described as the new Frontier. For those rugged, libertarian individuals who dare to venture there, the realm of cyberspace will reactivate the lost magic of a mythological past. For Timothy Leary, who has retired from recommending designer drugs to take up proselytizing the benefits of computer networking, cyberpunks are strong, stubborn individuals who have inherited the mantle of the early explorers, mavericks, ronin and free-thinkers everywhere.[51] Certainly some of the hackers and legitimate Net-surfers do understand their experience in this way, largely because the networks are still difficult to navigate. When and if this space really does become as public and as immediate as television, what is to say that it will not become as cluttered and full of commercial garbage as anywhere else? A comparable example is the previously unsullied world of computer games which has succumbed to 'product placement' within the past few years.

Two descriptions of cyberspace skies elucidate this situation: for Gibson they are a 'monochrome nonspace where the only stars are dense concentrations of information, and high above it all burn corporate galaxies and the cold spiral arms of military systems'.[52] A bleak vision of some frozen frontier, then, forbidding but at least not crass. For Benedikt, by contrast, the skies are alive with the images of their travellers, hurtling through space, and 'alive with entities licensed to inhabit this public realm, floating like ribbons, hot-air balloons, jelly-fish, clouds, but in wonderful, unlikely shapes, constrained only (1) to represent information systems in the public interest, and (2) to be mostly transparent. There would be a thousand words and images, a din of voices and music (and, yes, advertisements are possible) . . .'[53] They are far more than just possible. Benedikt also recommends that travel in cyberspace have a monetary cost, and speculates about various sources of cyberspace profit, from virtual 'real estate' in cyberspace, which might be leased to advertisers, to connection charges for the system.[54]

So the radical and exclusive position of the Net is fragile. Howard Rheingold correctly argues that the Net offers liberatory potential just because it is still largely outside the control of the mass media. Using Ben Bagdikian's analysis of the media monopoly, he argues that the 'new media lords [. . .] are not likely to encourage their privately owned and controlled networks to be the willing conduits for all kinds of information that unfettered citizens and nongovernmental organizations tend to disseminate'.[55] The commercialization of the Net will raise questions of pricing, access, censorship and copyright, of 'intellectual property' in short, which the owners will take action to protect. In 'Operation Sun Devil', FBI agents arrested hackers not for causing damage but merely for gaining free access to information.[56] Here the open-door ideology of the network founders collides with the commercial ethos of the society in which they live. The United States government's support of the networking infrastructure is founded on connecting supercomputers, and gaining advantage in international technological competition, rather than on some experiment in networked democracy.[57] Rheingold, analysing this process of commodification, warns that, 'this transition might render moot many of the fantasies of today's true believers in electronic democracy and global online culture'.[58] Commercialization and political control are entangled issues.

Cyberspace will be highly complex, so people will need guidance through it, and this is where corporations step in, providing regular and assured channels of access. As Microsoft has shown again and again, in an industry where common standards are usually of more importance than quality, the big players have most of the advantages. The nineties have seen various powerful mergers and alliances between large companies which are trying to dominate this technology, including the agreement between Microsoft, Telecommunications Inc. (the largest cable television company) and Time-Warner. Such corporations are limbering up for the control of a medium which could serve as a substitute for movies, newspapers, magazines and even shops. The virtual world is also the ideal arena for public relations exercises: 'Perhaps the most dramatic opportunity cyberspace provides for a corporation is a dynamic and exciting public face. Public visits to the corporation will provide intimate interactions with company products either simulated or real.' Best of all, information flows both ways for, as the potential customer gathers information about the product, the corporation will gather data about its customers 'for instant measurements of acceptance'.[59]

The business of advertising and public relations raises the possibility that networks might be used for the propagation of organized disinformation. Those putting messages on the Net may do so anonymously but this anonymity is controlled by the managers of the network provider and they may be leant on by the authorities; access privileges are likely to accrue to the powerful. Unfortunately, in relation to those who wish to use the Net for political or radical purposes, it is possible for programmers and those who manage a network system (or hack it) to keep track of and identify the users. The possibility of automated surveillance makes the Net a particularly insecure and inappropriate medium for clandestine political activism. Running counter to this argument, however, is the free distribution of effective encryption programs which the United States government has tried to outlaw. Its attempt to enforce a standard hardware device (the Clipper chip) to which only state authorities would have access foundered on several grounds: Net activists' resistance to such blatant, 'Big Brother'-

style interference, the practical matter of enforcing the standard, and finally the embarrassing discovery that the government's encryption code was not in fact secure. Some commercially run networks have, though, buckled under government pressure and banned unofficial encryption programs. In any case, even these programs have their limits.[60] The tracking of normal computer communications, which can be applied to any electronic transaction like a credit-card sale, is likely to be further developed for commercial purposes.[61] As Michael Heim puts it:

> The infinite CSM [Central System Monad] holds the key for monitoring, censoring, or rerouting any piece of information or any phenomenal presence on the network. The integrative nature of the computer shows up today in the ability of the CSM to read, delete, or alter private e-mail on any computer-mediated system. [. . .] While matrix users feel geographical and intellectual distances melt away, the price they pay is their inability to initiate uncontrolled and unsupervised activity.[62]

If monitoring on such a wide scale is possible, this is through quasi-intelligent programs which automatically scan the Net looking for particular information. They can be used by individuals to search for items of interest but also to monitor network activity as a whole. The techniques of networking, then, potentially liberatory, are likely to deliver only 'virtual democracy'; in other words, just what we already have.

A great benefit of cyberspace for producers of information is its dematerialization of the 'soft' commodities which they sell, whether they be books, images, music or software. Marx argued that the status of the commodity was dependent upon movement:

> *Circulation proceeds in space and time.* Economically considered, the spatial condition, the bringing of the product to the market, belongs to the production process itself. The product is really finished only when it is on the market. [. . .] This locational movement [. . .] could be more precisely regarded as the transformation of the product *into a commodity.*[63]

In making a virtual space in which soft goods may be replicated and moved around at little or no cost, cyberspace becomes a perfect marketplace. Those commodities which are not marketed primarily on their merits as objects may be launched in cyberspace with no material basis; this involves little outlay and great potential for distribution. Holding 'stock' will cost almost nothing. Unwanted 'goods' will be immediately disposable. Without the material substratum restraining them, commodities may respond instantly to the fractal climate of fashion. Most of all, the support structure for all this, cyberspace itself, becomes the grand universal commodity. The virtual environment is marketed and put on a meter. As one commentator put it: '*Experience will become a substance and a commodity*'.[64]

What effect might this dematerialization have on 'soft' data commodities? The pieces of plastic, paper and metal which now serve as vehicles for games, music or images currently receive a little aura, some small affective charge by way of association. Covers and styling aid this, and although they may be simulated in the computer, these immaterial adjuncts will no longer have any rigorous distinction from their contents. While it is unlikely that such developments will stop people wanting to collect objects, it may affect our view even of the soft commodities which continue to be sold. The world of commodities and the world of things will become more manifestly separate, as will the disjunction between notions of value and the material purchased – most people already know that compact discs are very cheap to produce, but at least they somehow look expensive. This may give rise to a more obvious separation of use value and exchange value, something which is already apparent in attitudes to the pricing and illicit copying of software.

Dreams of a networked utopia will come up against hard commercial reality. Cyberspace is of course flexible enough to incorporate areas for both; where it is used for recreation, some freedom and flexibility will be permitted, and when it is used practically and is connected to the real world, strict rules will no doubt apply and access will be restricted. To illustrate the contrast, it is enough to think of teleworking on the Net, where the actions of isolated and unprotected workers, remotely linked to their employer, are monitored from moment to moment. Primarily cyberspace will be a working environment, virtual but with very real consequences. Its solipsism will be that not of the pioneer but of the worker as monad:

Absolute solitude, the violent turning inward on the self, whose whole being consists in the mastery of material and in the monotonous rhythm of work, is the specter which outlines the existence of man in the modern world.[65]

Cyberspace is a way of literally enforcing this solitude and concealing it virtually. Systems will enforce behaviour, in the workspace, and in the very acquisition of knowledge itself.

Although misgivings about the economics of cyberspace are rarely expressed, despite much discussion there is also little agreement about its likely cultural effect. From the overview given so far, it is obvious that there is a basic contrast between utopian theory and dystopian fiction, a fundamental difference over whether the new technology will bear us to heaven or send us to hell. Despite this, both are agreed on the magnitude of the effect, and often express it in quasi-religious terms. Brenda Laurel describes her 'conversion experience' on first being introduced to a computer:

> A friend of mine worked at a large think tank where he was head of a new department in computer graphics and imaging. Late one night he asked me if I wanted to see a computer. We went through three security checks and up an elevator and through a maze of cubicles to a workstation where images were materializing on a little screen. I think it was Mars we were looking at. All I remember now is that I saw a portal to a new world, a million new worlds. I fell to my knees and said, whatever I do, I have to get my head into this stuff.[66]

Many of the elements of myth are here: the mystery of the dead of night, the hazardous pilgrimage followed by the revelation of another world. Many enthusiasts of cyberspace let its propensity for dematerialization transport them into the realms of spiritual discourse. For Benedikt:

> Cyberspace: The realm of pure information, filling like a lake, siphoning the jangle of messages transfiguring the physical world, decontaminating the natural and urban landscapes, redeeming them, saving them from the chain-dragging bulldozers of the paper industry,

from the diesel smoke of courier and post-office trucks, from jet fuel fumes and clogged airports, from billboards, trashy and pretentious architecture, hour-long freeway commutes, ticket lines, and choked subways . . . from all the inefficiencies, pollutions (chemical and informational), and corruptions attendant to the process of moving information attached to *things* – from paper to brains – across, over, and under the vast and bumpy surface of the earth rather than letting it fly free in the soft hail of electrons that is cyberspace.[67]

The reality of the computer industry is of course far from the image of rarefied immateriality in which it likes to pose, but nevertheless the message is clear. Humanity, freed from the effort of moving material around, will be raised to a purer, ethereal domain, leaving Nature to its own devices – and a good thing too.

Cyberspace does not stop at dematerializing part of the world's transport. In a fulfilment of the dreams of modernists, it offers the hope of eroding the boundaries between high art and the cultural environment as a whole:

We may, at last, have broken the stranglehold of the gilded frame and bypassed the parasitic high-priests and culture vultures to establish an egalitarian art of, for, and by the people. Not the constrained and hierarchical social realism of totalitarianism but a heterachial and streetwise cyber-grafitti, an art from the grassroots of democracy that, like urban spraycan walls, will impinge upon and possibly integrate all our diverse consciousnesses.[68]

The apparent freedom and lack of structure within cyberspace come to affect its contents, letting everyone have access to the world's cultural riches, and initiating a golden age of universal, radical creativity. Cyberspace promises also to let us enter behind the screen, to embrace us as participants in new worlds. There we will be dematerialized and made eternal: 'Forget about Andy Warhol's petty promise of fame for fifteen minutes. We will all become angels, and for eternity! Highly unstable, hermaphrodite angels, unforgettable in terms of computer memory.'[69] Every statement, eventually every thought, is recorded, unchanging even though we change, persisting even when we have passed away. In this dream of immortality, and of a fairytale land where the mind's every blip has a permanent place and meaning within a vast collective dream, there is also a clear sense that computers have exceeded us, outgrowing their militaristic origins and merely practical uses to become an embracing, eternal spirit.

The concept of cyberspace attracts a breathless, hyperbolic writing, positive or negative, in which lists tend to proliferate, as though the prose were trying to suggest the vast connected catalogue that the virtual world should become. It also encourages writing of a quasi-religious nature, the better to suggest the escape from the taint of material and flesh that the technology offers, and the disinterestedness of its purveyors. Benedikt again:

> Consider: Where Eden (before the Fall) stands for our state of innocence, indeed ignorance, the Heavenly City stands for our state of wisdom, and knowledge, where Eden stands for our intimate contact with material nature, the Heavenly City stands for our transcendence of both materiality and nature; where Eden stands for the world of unsymbolized, asocial reality, the Heavenly City stands for the world of enlightened human interaction, form and information. [. . .] The Heavenly City, though it may contain gardens, breathes the crystalline gleam of its own lights, sparkling, insubstantial, laid out like a beautiful equation. Thus, while the biblical Eden may be imaginary, the Heavenly City is *doubly* imaginary: once, in the conventional sense, because it is not actual, but once again [. . .] because it *is* information, it could come into existence only as a virtual reality, which is to say, fully, only 'in the imagination'. The image of a Heavenly City is, in fact, [. . .] a religious vision of cyberspace.[70]

Again sublation is in evidence, this time between innocence and knowledge. Here cyberspace is a modernist vision of light and insubstantial form, the pure stuff of dreams. Now, as we have seen, its image in fiction is quite different: for Gibson cyberspace and its surroundings (which sometimes appear congruent) are tawdry, hybrid, even filthy:

> The architecture of virtual reality imagined as an accretion of dreams: tattoo parlors, shooting galleries, pinball arcades, dimly lit stalls stacked with damp-stained years of men's magazines, chili joints, premises of

unlicensed denturists, of fireworks and cut bait, betting shops, sushi bars, purveyors of sexual appliances, pawnbrokers, wonton counters, love hotels, hotdog stands, tortilla factories, Chinese greengrocers, liquor stores, herbalists, chiropractors, barbers, bars.

These are dreams of commerce. Above them rise intricate barrios, zones of more private fantasy.[71]

This fantasy is little more than a description of some downmarket Las Vegas, the dream of a middle-class boy losing himself in a cheesy display of street decadence (and Gibson is no doubt aware of this). For the rebellious kid, this is a grubby, fascinating heaven; for the mature academic, paradise takes rather the form of a kingdom of information, whose palatial halls we may wander without fear, free from chaos, dirt and obscurity. The contrast between these scenarios, and more specifically between the fiction and those who come to recommend its vision, has certainly struck Gibson, who has commented on the endeavours and the propaganda of the technophiles: 'it never occurred to me that it would be possible for anyone to read these books and ignore the levels of irony'.[72]

The dichotomy between utopian prophecy and dystopian fiction must be qualified, for there are phenomena which take in both; the technophile magazine *Mondo 2000*, for instance, happily embraces heaven and hell, covering them with an irony which allows it to take neither seriously:[73]

> There's a new whiff of apocalyptism across the land. A general sense that we are living at a very special juncture in the evolution of the species. [. . .] This magazine is about what to do until the *millennium* comes. We're talking Total Possibilities. [. . .] Flexing those synapses! Stoking those neuropeptides! Making Bliss States our normal waking consciousness. *Becoming* the Bionic Angel.
>
> But things are going to get weirder before they get better. The Rupture before the Rapture. Social and economic dislocation that will make the cracked 80's look like summer camp.[74]

This is not the sudden catastrophe of nuclear annihilation or alien invasion, but something slower, more internal, and perhaps already here. The revamped apocalypse might creep up on you. The 'post-human' aspect of cyberpunk writing with its improbable prostheses, genetic tinkering, and computer augmentation of the brain, most evident in the work of Bruce Sterling, carries postmodern identity politics to the last degree. Being merely human is a poor and obsolete thing, which only the latest technological commodities from the smartest companies can fix, although again these tales are inflected with some ineffectual irony, to divert criticism.

This fiction revels in the dangers of unleashed technology, in the possibilities of dehumanization; it takes apocalypse for apotheosis. Such scenarios are premissed on the apparently unlimited power of technological development and the simultaneous inability of the current authorities to face the dangers of its situation: the apotheosis of the system takes place when it is pushed to its logical limits, triggering a strangely familiar apocalypse. The very utopianism of the early Netheads produced a belief in the apocalypse, for their resistance was partly founded on the idea that the system could not survive. Roszak characterizes the attitude as follows:

> By way of IBM's video terminals, AT&T's phone lines, Pentagon space shots, and Westinghouse communication satellites, a worldwide movement of computer-literate rebels would arise to build the organic commonwealth. They might even outlast the total collapse of the high industrial system which had invented their technology. For there was a bleak vision of thermonuclear holocaust deeply mixed into the survivalist instincts of the counter culture.[75]

Cyberpunk is part of a co-opting and marketing of apocalyptic visions as entertainment; on one level there is nothing frightening about these tales, even if they do pose as an extrapolation of current tendencies. Rather the idea that one is participating in headlong, dangerous scientific progress imparts a specious frisson to the mundane use of today's technological equipment. In the real world, apocalyptic tales play themselves out in profusion, but generally do not affect those who write these stories or read them. The governing political and economic system, as seen in fiction, is corrupt but all-encompassing, unsustainable but inescapable – or at least the only way out is a mystical solution in which poor, deluded humanity is itself superseded. Gibson is utopian about the experiential aspect of the technology (its slickness, speed, definition and the experience of immersion and freedom from the body), if not about its overall effects; his dystopia is necessary as a field for the heroic actions of the cyberpunk cowboys who ameliorate it. The morality-play aspect of much science fiction disarms its dystopian scenarios.

Beyond fiction, in technophile writing, the mix of apotheosis and apocalypse is perfectly illustrated by the supposed emergence of a transcendent, inhuman Net mind. The individual computing and human units of the network will become neurons participating in a collective, worldwide mind of incredible power. As one enthusiast puts it, arguing that any system going beyond a certain complexity must evolve self-awareness, 'I believe that we can think of this globalNet [sic] as a potential neural network in its own right'.[76] Furthermore, the linking of an artificial intelligence with the information on the network should produce 'an ultra-fast learning curve. Very soon after it has evolved, machine intelligence will eclipse human facilities and the new SIs [super-intelligences] will begin to inhabit the Net. A growing number of researchers are suggesting that by facilitating this process we are, in fact, fulfilling the dictates of our own DNA and creating a more rugged intelligence that will become our evolutionary successor.'[77] The link with science fiction here is obvious, particularly with Wintermute, the shackled AI of *Neuromancer*. Again, there is a decidedly religious aspect to such glimpses of super-intelligences and emergent identities across the Net, as though what was being born, or perhaps merely accessed, was the mind of God itself. In Gibson's writing, especially in *Count Zero*, an alliance is established between AIs and the 'Other' of voodoo gods, black magic and mysticism against the material forces of technocracy, rationalism and utilitarianism. Again this is an extrapolation, but a utopian one, from a tendency which, as we shall see in looking at computer art, is already present in computing, the sense of an inhuman presence with its own volition.

The paranoia about super-intelligences and multinational intrigue is found not only in fiction, but also in a whole shadow-world of conspiratorial literature; there is a rational basis for such writing, at least in the sense that corporations certainly protect their interests by nefarious means. Its expression in this writing, however, takes the form of myth-making, encouraged by the complexity and immateriality of the

capitalist system, which resists representation. In science fiction, corporations are generally presented as powerful, but are nonetheless
themselves governed by the impetus of the technologies they have
created.[78] In one sense, though, the activities of corporations are not
at all mysterious, and make good sense when they are considered in
the light of what these institutions are set up to do. If these actions are
sometimes hard to spot, it is only because corporations own the mass
media. It hardly needs super-intelligences to work out that corporations support friendly governments, undermine unfriendly ones,
employ (at some remove) people to dispose of their unprotected enemies, push for favourable legislation, and so forth. Their activities are
mundane in practice, if not in terms of ethics and long-term
consequences.

In a well-known passage of his book *Postmodernism*, Fredric Jameson
linked such hi-tech paranoiac literature with the representation of
capitalism itself:

> I want to suggest that our faulty representations of some immense com-
> municational and computer network are themselves but a distorted
> figuration of something even deeper, namely the whole world system of
> a present-day multinational system.[79]

Most evidently, in cyberpunk:

> the circuits and networks of some putative global computer hookup are
> narratively mobilized by labyrinthine conspiracies of autonomous but
> deadly interlocking and competing information agencies in a com-
> plexity often beyond the capacity of the normal reading mind.[80]

It is a degraded attempt to grasp the impossible complexity of the
worldwide capitalist system: 'Gibson's cyberspace is an image of a way
of making the abstract and unseen comprehensible, a visualisation of
the notion of cognitive mapping.'[81] Or rather, any attempt to grasp
the actual complexities of the workings of global capital are abandoned to a literary spectacle of the sublime phenomena of complexity
itself. Now the development of cyberspace is actually meant to address
this issue of a complexity beyond the grasp of normal human capabilities; the lack of a complete picture of the working system is quite as

worrying for capitalist enterprise as it is for literary theorists. We should look at the form of cyberspace to see if there is anything substantive to this idea of it representing the entire operation of capital.

Cyberspace is above all conceived as a visual environment. While it does not yet exist except in crude prototypes, and while users may be given the choice of a number of options determining how they see it, we may look to computer art for a preview of its form. A particular and remarkably constant aesthetic has emerged out of the relationship between art and computer science, and it is likely that its preoccupations will be carried over into the design of cyberspace. Although there is no necessary requirement for it, virtual spaces are always described as Euclidean, at least in the way that they are experienced, and as hierarchically structured – usually on a vertical axis. The connection between discrete areas might be non-Euclidean, as might the overall shape of the virtual universe (which could take the form of a hypersphere) and there could be a nesting of worlds within worlds. Movement from one part to another could be instantaneous. Michael Heim has noted that jumps, not steps, are typical of movement in hypertext, and suggests that the same will hold for cyberspace.[82]

Such broad considerations do not give much idea of what cyberspace might actually look like; for this we need to turn to the way artists have arrived at an aesthetic which they consider to be appropriate to the computer. For at least twenty-five years computer art has been in its infancy. Just as promises of a technical utopia, of free power or plentiful food for all, are constantly being made and broken (their fulfilment being always just over the temporal horizon), so the hope of a techno-cultural utopia is also constantly deferred. The old predictions of a radical computer art are still being made, with the addition of a new set of buzzwords. In 1968 Jack Burnham predicted the end of sculpture, which was to be superseded not by an as yet undreamt-of virtual space, but by the development of cybernetic systems, dominated by artificial intelligence: 'In retrospect we may look upon the long tradition of figure sculpture and the brief interlude of formalism as an extended psychic dress rehearsal for [. . .] intelligent automata'.[83] Similarly, in an early article about computer art, Robert Mallary made bold claims about artificial intelligence systems which he thought would develop an aesthetic sense, eventually producing art without the aid of humans.[84] Burnham's idea was that figurative sculpture had prepared humans for the advent of a breed of autonomous, intelligent robots upon which future artistic talents will be lavished. Now these beings have appeared in abundance, although for the time being they are fictional and are seen on cinema, television and computer screens, and they are certainly much less friendly than those which Burnham envisaged. These biological robots (such as Terminator or Robocop) are computer controlled or assisted, both in fiction and in fact; if they have a particular aesthetic, it is of a slick, elitist and deadly modernism. We will return to them in the next chapter, but for the moment it is enough to say that they form a pre-emptive counter-claim to the optimists of cybernetics and cyberspace.

When virtual objects are visualized within the computer, they do not necessarily exhibit any of the qualities of conventional objects. They do not have to be three-dimensional; higher-dimensional shapes may be indicated, while fractal forms provide a visual expression of fractional dimensions.[85] Some of the images produced from these virtual forms may be thought of as the shadows of higher-dimensional forms, their insubstantiality and complexity resulting from their being rendered in a form that humans can appreciate. Their apparent scale and material are purely arbitrary. Viewpoint, lighting, colour and texture are totally independent of the structures depicted. As digital forms, nothing about them is fixed and they provide the possibility for the viewer to interact with or even virtually become the 'object'.

Despite such potentially radical features, computer art has often been associated with idealist aesthetics, using explicitly Platonist models relating number to beauty. Claims are frequently made by adherents of computer art that objective progress in aesthetics is now possible.[86] Brenda Laurel simply states that 'art is lawful', thus thinking that the persistent opposition between art and science can be definitively eroded within the rationalist silicon frame.[87] Another strand, which goes back to D'Arcy Thompson's famous book *On Growth and Form*, has been to study the structure of natural forms, and to write programs which generate similar shapes.[88] It is visual rather than structural essence that is involved in such programming,[89] since it is hard to tell whether the look alone has not been produced by reverse engineering. Computer artists do sometimes fake the look, for instance by using randomization to modify over-precise forms.[90]

In 1990, when an issue of the *Art Journal* was devoted to computer art, the editor remarked upon the contributors' optimism, based on the flexibility of the computer as a universal tool.[91] There is often a gung-ho, unashamedly masculine ethos to writing about computer art which, alongside talk of pioneering, returns us to the heyday of modernism. Carl Eugene Loeffler, for instance, assures us that 'Electronics was and continues to be the true new frontier for contemporary art'.[92] Both in high art and in the more popular manifestations of computer culture, an unreconstructed sexism is frequent in this male-dominated world, whether blatantly, on the covers of *Mondo 2000*, which 'tended to feature women's heads floating somewhere in the ether of an erotic wet (ware) dream',[93] or simply in the whole notion of the free navigation, penetration and manipulation of a feminine sublime. Computer art exhibits a curious combination of great technical sophistication and naive theory. In part, this may have a sociological cause, of the kind explored by Pierre Bourdieu in his book *Distinction*, which looked at how taste strictly conforms to income and education.[94] There is a snobbery attached to any kind of machine work which forbids it contact with the heights of fine art and rarefied theory. Those committed to the computer are more likely to look at fine art from the outside and in an over-idealized fashion. Equally, they are likely to be interested in forms of popular culture which high-art practitioners shy away from, or approach only with the intent of ironic appropriation. Computer art forms, then, feed off cyberpunk fiction, and the hip apocalyptic visions of sci-fi film.

Something different does happen, though, when artists cease to confine themselves to using the computer as a drawing or animation tool, and let the processor itself contribute to the design of form. One way to do this is to simulate the evolutionary process, allowing the machine to virtually breed forms over generations. Like mutating computer viruses and other forms of artificial life, evolutionary programs are to some degree autonomous. They produce forms of inhuman complexity and an alien appearance.[95] If we find such images disturbing, this is because of our habit of reading intention into complicated images; here there is a feeling that, while an intention is certainly at work, it is not entirely human. The computer takes on the guise of an allegorical being, the program being the unstoppable ghost in the machine and the image its mere materialization. Some are keen to embrace this presence:

> Those idealists (among whom I count myself) [. . .] who decided to follow the light, had sensed from the beginning that the medium of computer animations was no mere image generation in the traditional sense, but rather a virtual world, populated by half-living entities, that we would inhabit someday when the technology would allow it.[96]

If there is a deep sense of identification with the allegorical image of a being wholly devoted to the service of a single principle, this is because it is expressive of a more general reification, in which living beings take on the guise of objects and objects seem inhabited by living spirits. In cyberspace the two are likely to attain total elision.

When we see the operation of another sort of intelligence in computer art, we become aware of a power which is hard to define or hold steady in the mind, yet which is felt as a presence, like the fleeting, protean artificial minds of Gibson's novels. Goethe wrote of a force of nature which is:

> both animated and inanimate, both souled and soulless, something which manifested itself only in contradictions and could not therefore be formulated in concepts, let alone in words. It was not divine, for it seemed irrational; not human, for it had no understanding; not diabolical, for it was beneficent; not angelic, for it often betrayed *Schadenfreude*. It was like chance in its inconsequentiality; like Providence in the inter-relationships it revealed. Everything that has limits for us seemed to it penetrable; it seemed wilfully to recombine the most necessary elements of our existence, eclipsing time and extending space. [. . .] This being, which seemed to interpose itself between all the others, to sunder or unite them, I called the *Demonic* [. . .][97]

Goethe's natural force is surely what we now call emergent order, that force which somehow forges complex pattern from unthinkable chaos, a force which we have begun to know only through computer simulation. It is notable that it is described as demonic, notable also that it is harnessed now to control real or virtual robots, or artificial life.[98] Such order is apparent not merely in nature, but in many complex systems; if in computer forms we find a disturbing recognition of some alien order, then what we see is an image of the operation of economic markets, of apparently obscure and inhuman forces which control every detail of our lives. A cold order is wrought from the immensely complex flows of funds (now largely electronic signals), material, jobs and – finally – people that are flung across the globe, gathering and dispersing at the whim of this power, incessantly building and wrecking hopes, raising and lowering the death-rate as it goes. The computer can, then, act as an 'analogue' of these forces, revealing an image of the demon of Capital.

Although most descriptions of cyberspace stress its dizzying complexity, they also emphasize the empowerment of the user, who flies through the virtual sky, or swims through its depths. The fantasies are always the same:

> Sometimes I linger on a pattern for the sake of its strangeness, and as it becomes familiar I grow into another self. I wonder how much richer the patterns I can recognize can become, and surprise myself by scanning faster and faster regions in times shorter and shorter. Like a bird of prey my acuity allows me to glide high above the planes of information, seeking jewels among the grains, seeking knowledge.[99]

New Agers make computer simulations of flying through fractal landscapes at great speed which are transferred to video and marketed as 'cyberspace' experiences. About this new sea of capital in which millions of punters swim, the question arises: aside from their own personal experience of immersive travel, what will be their relation to the leviathan corporations, and how will they treat each other?

Horkheimer and Adorno argued that at the heart of Enlightenment there was a secularized version of the belief that God controlled the world. People thus confronted nature as an inferior, external other, a world of lifeless, fungible atoms, open to manipulation, and without conceiving of an interpenetration of subject and object.[100] In one sense, then, cyberspace may be seen as the final act of the Enlightenment, in which the interface of nature disappears, replaced by a more evidently divine other. Although subject and object are most certainly entwined, the subject's attributes become definitively open to exchange. Some time before the age of intelligent machines, Aldous Huxley described virtual reality pornography, his 'feelies': 'then suddenly, dazzling and incomparably more solid-looking than they would have seemed in actual flesh and blood, far more real than reality, there stood the stereoscopic images'.[101] While each solipsistic user may feel empowered, every other being is prepared for use. Cyberspace is an ideal realization of Lukács's 'second nature', entangling the subjective and objective, and since, unlike the transformation of the real world by Capital, it evolves without direct material destruction, the speed of development (and mental destruction) can be all the more dizzying.

Cyberspace is also likely to be, in flagrant contradiction to its postmodern apologists, the embodiment of the totalizing system of capital. Again, Adorno and Horkheimer are relevant here: 'For the Enlightenment whatever does not conform to the rules of computation and utility is suspect . . . Enlightenment is totalitarian.'[102] It aims at a principle of scientific unity in which the 'multiplicity of forms is reduced to position and arrangement, history to fact, things to matter'.[103] If we replace 'matter' with 'data' then this passage can be directly applied to cyberspace. Douglas Kellner notes that 'Such quantitative modes of thought presuppose an identity between concept and object, word and thing, and privilege mathematical logic as alone capable of grasping the essence of things.'[104] The invention of cyberspace is, then, the attempt to create a world where to perceive is the same as to understand, where 'objects' are entirely adequate to their concepts, and are even, through their dematerialization, identical with them. Despite the sport of fictional demons within cyberspace, the impetus of the system is towards the reduction of everything to the calculable; for this 'the Net' is indeed an apt name.

So technophiliac enthusiasts are stitching up a totalizing, brave new world based on an Enlightenment paradigm but defended by postmodern theory. Adorno, and others following him, have been much concerned to argue that there is a negative and liberatory charge in objects exceeding their concepts. It is this which cyberspace promises to abolish. This virtual space threatens to form the ultimate illusion of a unified understanding, not by surmounting contradiction, but by remaking the world in specious harmony. As a universal system of data, however, cyberspace will have to contain representations of pictures, texts and photographs. While these will have lost all materiality, at least their fixed forms will challenge the homogeneity of the system. History and its representations will become resistant islands of unchangeable data, reminders of the other of reality, of process and finally of humanity.

In the extraordinary situation in which a new technology of profound importance is being created, there is a curious parallel between the associated confusion, bloated claims, predicted utopian dystopias and vice versa, and what Benjamin described in his analysis of Germany during the great inflation of the twenties. He noted that within accounts of widespread decline, accommodations were always made to justify specific personal positions and activities:

> A blind determination to save the prestige of personal existence, rather than, through an impartial disdain for its importance and entanglement, at least to detach it from the background of universal delusion, is triumphing almost everywhere. That is why the air is so thick with life theories and world views, and why in this country they cut so preposterous a figure, for almost always they finally serve to sanction some wholly trivial private situation. For just the same reason the air is so full of phantoms, mirages of a glorious cultural future breaking upon us overnight in spite of all, for everyone is committed to the optical illusions of his isolated standpoint.[105]

This passage illuminates the solipsism of cyberspace, which is merely a literal expression of the situation of the individual in contemporary society, and more specifically of business people and their camp followers (from engineers to intellectuals) spinning universalizing fantasies out of their desire to ride the next commercial wave. This wondrous but specious technology threatens to act as another curtain between those who consume it and the condition of the world: as the poor are excluded from cyberspace, and will appear on it only as objects, never as subjects with their own voices, there is a danger that they recede even further from the consciousness of the comfortable. As the real world is left to decline, the air once again becomes full of phantoms, this time digital, promising at the last moment to pluck utopia from apocalypse.

Descending from the heights of speculation and turning our back on computer hype, we should look again at the present situation. A great many homes in the First World have computers but these are generally not connected to any network. Not yet up to doing the housework, the universal machine is still looking for a useful domestic role. So, given the vast numbers of computers in homes, what do people actually do with them? More than anything else, they play games.[106]

NOTES

1. Michael Benedikt, 'Introduction' to Benedikt, ed., *Cyberspace. First Steps*, Cambridge, Mass. 1991, p. 2.

2. Gates has founded a new company, Continuum, to form a massive visual database. See 'Bill Gates' Mega-database of World Art', *The Art Newspaper*, December 1994, supplement on publishing, pp. i–ii. The first fruit of this has been a CD-ROM catalogue of the paintings in the National Gallery, London, which Microsoft has marketed under the name *Art Gallery*.

3. William Gibson, 'Academy Leader', in Benedikt, *Cyberspace*, p. 27.

4. Benedikt, 'Cyberspace. Some Proposals', in Benedikt, *Cyberspace*, p. 174.

5. Istvan Csicsery-Ronay, Jr, 'Cyberpunk and Neuromanticism', in Larry McCaffery, ed., *Storming the Reality Studio. A Casebook of Cyberpunk and Postmodern Fiction*, Durham, North Carolina 1991, p. 184.

6. Ibid., p. 190.

7. William Gibson, *Neuromancer*, London 1984, p. 13.

8. On trash and decay as a theme in Gibson, see Miriam Glazer, '"What is Within Now Seen Without": Romanticism, Neuromanticism and the Death of the Imagination in William Gibson's Fictive World', *Journal of Popular Culture*, vol. 23, no. 3, Winter 1989, p. 158.

9. For the similarities between electronic matrices and physical reality in *Neuromancer*, see Scott Bukatman, *Terminal Identity. The Virtual Subject in Postmodern Science Fiction*, Durham, North Carolina 1993, p. 148.

10. Benedikt, 'Introduction', in *Cyberspace*, p. 18.

11. Benedikt, 'Cyberspace: Some Proposals', p. 124.

12. Michael Heim, 'The Erotic Ontology of Cyberspace', in Benedikt, *Cyberspace*, p. 64.

13. Benedikt, 'Introduction', in *Cyberspace*, p. 12.

14. Allucquere Rosanne Stone, 'Will the Real Body Please Stand Up? Boundary Stories about Virtual Cultures', in Benedikt, *Cyberspace*, p. 101.

15. Mark C. Taylor and Esa Saarinen, *Imagologies. Media Philosophy*, London 1994, Simcult, p. 3 (each chapter of this book is paginated separately).

16. Andrew Ross, *Strange Weather. Culture, Science and Technology in the Age of Limits*, London 1991, p. 35.

17. R.U. Sirius, 'A User's Guide to Using This Guide', in Rudy Rucker, R.U. Sirius and Queen Mu, eds, *Mondo 2000: A User's Guide to the New Edge*, New York 1992, p. 16; cited in Vivian Sobchack, 'New Age Mutant Ninja Hackers. Reading *Mondo 2000*', *South Atlantic Quarterly*, vol. 92, no. 4, Fall 1993, p. 583.

18. Sobchack, 'New Age Mutant Ninja Hackers', p. 574.

19. Herbert I. Schiller, *Culture Inc., The Corporate Takeover of Public Expression*, Oxford 1989, p. 51. Schiller, writing in 1989, noted that four operators had a third of all cable subscribers (p. 39). On recent developments in cable television, see also Todd Gitlin, *Inside Prime Time*, revised edition, London 1994, pp. x–xi.

20. See Richard Dienst, *Still Life in Real Time: Theory After Television*, Durham, North Carolina 1994, p. 5.

21. The price of a usable machine in the early eighties was considerably less than the £1000 paid for an average 486 system today. See Simon Rockman, 'Back to the Future', *Personal Computer World*, March 1995, p. 533.

22. See Jonathan Crary, 'Critical Reflections', *Artforum*, February 1994, p. 59.

23. Schiller, *Culture Inc.*, p. 75.

24. Roy Ascott, 'Connectivity: Art and Interactive Communications', *Leonardo*, vol. 24, no. 2, 1991, p. 115.

25. Ascott, 'Connectivity', p. 116. Of course such sentiments, far from being a consequence of computer networking, are at least as old as modernism.

26. Theodore Roszak, *The Cult of Information. A Neo-Luddite Treatise on High-Tech, Artificial Intelligence and the True Art of Thinking*, Berkeley 1994, p. 171. This is also the repeated complaint of a former proselytizer of the Net, Clifford Stoll, in his recent book, *Silicon Snake Oil. Second Thoughts on the Information Highway*, London 1995.

27. Howard Rheingold, *The Virtual Community. Finding Connection in a Computerized World*, London 1994, p. 132.

28. Ibid., p. 61.

29. Arthur Kroker and Michael A. Weinstein, *Data Trash. The Theory of the Virtual Class*, Montreal 1994, p. 105.

30. For an account of advertising on the Net, see Stoll, *Silicon Snake Oil*, pp. 104–5.

31. Rheingold, *The Virtual Community*, p. 207.

32. Erik Davis, 'Techgnosis: Magic, Memory, and the Angels of Information', *South Atlantic Quarterly*, vol. 92, no. 4, Fall 1993, p. 601.

33. Rheingold, *The Virtual Community*, p. 64.

34. This cautionary tale is recounted in ibid., p. 135.

35. Benedikt, 'Cyberspace: Some Proposals', p. 170.

36. Roszak, *The Cult of Information*, p. 197.

37. Theodor W. Adorno, 'The Curious Realist: On Siegfried Kracauer', *Notes to Literature*, trans. Shierry Weber Nicholsen, vol. II, New York 1992, p. 61.

38 Taylor and Saarinen, *Imagologies*, Style, p. 5.

39. Ibid., Naivete, p. 4.

40. Ascott, 'Connectivity', p. 116.

41. See Anne Balsamo, 'Feminism for the Incurably Informed', *South Atlantic Quarterly*, vol. 92, no. 4, Fall 1993, p. 698.

42. See Benjamin Woolley, *Virtual Worlds. A Journey in Hype and Hyperreality*, London 1993, p. 105.

43. Rheingold describes the outrage which followed the revelation that a de facto agony aunt on the Net, who claimed to be disabled, disfigured, mute and female, was actually a New York psychiatrist with none of these attributes. Rheingold, *The Virtual Community*, pp. 164–5.

44. Marcos Novak, 'Liquid Architectures in Cyberspace', in Benedikt, *Cyberspace*, pp. 250–51.

45. Benedikt, 'Cyberspace: Some Proposals', p. 160, emphasis in original.

46. Ibid., p. 180.

47. For a typically proselytizing view see George Gilder, 'A Technology of Liberation', in Raymond Kurzweil, *The Age of Intelligent Machines*, Cambridge, Mass.1990, pp. 454–7.

48. Roszak, *The Cult of Information*, p. 162.

49. Robert X. Cringely, *Accidental Empires: How the Boys of Silicon Valley Make Their Millions, Battle Foreign Competition, and Still Can't Get a Date*, London 1992, p. 3.

50. Rheingold, *The Virtual Community*, p. 102.

51. Timothy Leary, 'The Cyberpunk: the Individual as Reality Pilot', in McCaffery, ed., *Storming the Reality Studio*, pp. 245–58. For more on Leary's computer enthusiasms and uncritical responses to virtual reality and networking in general see Scott Bukatman, *Terminal Identity*, pp. 189f.

52. William Gibson, *Burning Chrome*, London 1993, p. 197. The first edition was New York, 1986.

53. Benedikt, 'Cyberspace: Some Proposals', p. 205.

54. Ibid., p. 219.

55. Howard Rheingold, *The Virtual Community*, pp. 5, 14.

56. Ibid., pp. 251f.

57. Ibid., p. 84.

58. Ibid., p. 273.

59. See Steve Pruitt and Tom Barrett, 'Corporate Virtual Workspace', in Benedikt, *Cyberspace*, p. 405.

60. The encryption seems to be fine, but software 'keys' to personal codes can be stolen. See Stoll, *Silicon Snake Oil*, pp. 169–70.

61. Rheingold notes that on commercially run networks postings are already censored and that in addition information may potentially be read from users' own computers. *The Virtual Community*, p. 277. Controversy has been caused by Microsoft's network program, bundled with *Windows 95*, which does just this to report back information about the user's installed software.

62. Heim, 'The Erotic Ontology of Cyberspace', p. 79.

63. Karl Marx, *Grundrisse. Foundations of the Critique of Political Economy (Rough Draft)*, trans. Martin Nicolaus, Harmondsworth 1973, pp. 533–4, emphasis in original.

64. Tim McFadden, 'Notes on the Structure of Cyberspace and the Ballistic Actors Model', in Benedikt, *Cyberspace*, p. 337.

65. Theodor Adorno and Max Horkheimer, *Dialectic of Enlightenment*, trans. John Cumming, London 1973, p. 226.

66. Brenda Laurel, 'On Dramatic Interaction', in Timothy Druckrey, ed., *Iterations: The New Image*, New York and Cambridge, Mass. 1993, p. 79.

67. Benedikt, 'Introduction', in *Cyberspace*, p. 3.

68. Paul Brown, 'Metamedia and Cyberspace', in Philip Hayward, ed., *Culture, Technology and Creativity in the Late Twentieth Century*, London n.d., p. 240.

69. Nicole Stenger, 'Mind is a Leaking Rainbow', in Benedikt, *Cyberspace*, p. 52.

70. Benedikt, 'Introduction', in *Cyberspace*, pp. 15–16.

71. Gibson, 'Academy Leader', in Benedikt, *Cyberspace*, p. 28.

72. Gibson cited by Brown, 'Metamedia and Cyberspace', p. 238.

73. See Sobchack, 'New Age Mutant Ninja Hackers', especially p. 570.

74. *Mondo 2000*, no. 1, editorial; cited in Sobchack, 'New Age Mutant Ninja Hackers', pp. 572–3.

75. Roszak, *The Cult of Information*, p. 149.

76. Brown, 'Metamedia and Cyberspace', pp. 231–2.

77. Ibid., p. 234. For an introduction to this concept see Stephen Levy, *Artificial Life. The Quest for a New Creation*, London 1992.

78. See Brian McHale, 'POSTcyberMODERNpunkISM', in McCaffery, *Storming the Reality Studio*, p. 316. He points out that such scenarios have their origin in the work of Thomas Pynchon.

79. Fredric Jameson, *Postmodernism or, the Cultural Logic of Late Capitalism*, London 1991, p. 37.

80. Ibid., p. 38.

81. Peter Fitting, 'The Lessons of Cyberpunk', in Constance Penley and Andrew Ross, eds, *Technoculture*, Minneapolis 1991, p. 311.

82. Heim, 'The Erotic Ontology of Cyberspace', in Benedikt, *Cyberspace*, p. 70.

83. Jack Burnham, *Beyond Modern Sculpture. The Effects of Science and Technology on the Sculpture of this Century*, New York 1968, p. 376.

84. See Robert Mallary, 'Computer Sculpture: Six Levels of Cybernetics', *Artforum*, vol. vii, no. 9, May 1969, p. 33.

85. See Stephen Todd and William Latham, *Evolutionary Art and Computers*, London 1992, p. 51.

86. For instance see Tom DeWitt, who argues that formalism, as in musical notation, may be extended to the visual arts, founded on algorithms and the procedural languages used in programming. 'Dataism', *Leonardo. Supplemental Issue. Computer Art in Context: SIGGRAPH '89 Art Show Catalog*, 1989, p. 58. Similar arguments may be found in Herbert W. Franke, 'Mathematics as an Artistic-Generative Principle', in the same issue, pp. 25–6.

87. Laurel, 'On Dramatic Interaction', p. 80.

88. D'Arcy Wentworth Thompson, *On Growth and Form*, second edition, Cambridge 1942.

89. As noted by Beverley Jones in 'Computer Imagery: Imitation and Representation of Realities', *Leonardo. Supplemental Issue. Computer Art in Context: SIGGRAPH '89 Art Show Catalog*, 1989, p. 33.

90. William Latham, for instance, uses fractal irregularities in order to give his otherwise mathematically regular forms a little, natural 'wobble'. Todd and Latham, *Evolutionary Art*, p. 152.

91. Terry Gips, editorial statement, *Art Journal*, vol. 49, no. 3, Fall 1990, p. 232.

92. Carl Eugene Loeffler, 'Modem Dialling Out', *Leonardo*, vol. 24, no. 2, 1991, p. 113.

93. Sobchack, 'New Age Mutant Ninja Hackers', p. 571.

94. Pierre Bourdieu, *Distinction. A Social Critique of the Judgement of Taste*, trans. Richard Nice, London 1984.

95. The scientific interest in artificial life and the simulation of evolution has not been slow to find application in art. See for example Todd and Latham, *Evolutionary Art*, and John McCormack, *Turbulence*, illustrated in Montxo Algora, ed., *Art Futura 94*, Madrid, Centro de Arte Reina Sofia, 1994, n.p.

96. Nicole Stenger, 'Mind is a Leaking Rainbow', in Benedikt, *Cyberspace*, p. 49.

97. Goethe, *Dichtung und Warheit*, Zurich 1950, pp. 839–40; cited in Fredric Jameson, *Marxism and Form. Twentieth Century Dialectical Theories of Literature*, Princeton 1971, pp. 129–30. Jameson uses this passage to describe creative production.

98. The term 'demon' is appropriately used by programmers to describe an algorithm, which is of course defined by and devoted exclusively to its task.

99. Marcos Novak, 'Liquid Architectures in Cyberspace', in Benedikt, *Cyberspace*, p. 230.

100. Adorno and Horkheimer, *Dialektik der Aufklärung*, p. 41; cited in Martin Jay, *The Dialectical Imagination. A History of the Frankfurt School and the Institute of Social Research, 1923–1950*, Boston 1973, p. 260.

101. Aldous Huxley, *Brave New World*, Harmondsworth 1955, p. 134.

102. Adorno and Horkheimer, *Dialectic of Enlightenment*, p. 6.

103. Ibid., p. 7.

104. Douglas Kellner, *Critical Theory, Marxism and Modernity*, Cambridge 1989, p. 96.

105. Walter Benjamin, 'Imperial Panorama. A Tour of the German Inflation', in *One Way Street and Other Writings*, trans. Edmund Jephcott and Kingsley Shorter, London 1979, p. 58.

106. The video game business is larger than the film industry and many of its customers are adults. David Sheff notes that in 1993 it was worth 10 billion dollars and had very high profit margins. See *Game Over. Nintendo's Battle to Dominate an Industry*, London 1993, pp. 3f, 432.

4

JUST GAMING

'We need a leader. We have many missions to complete. We have to assassinate leaders of our aggressors, we have to destroy heavily guarded installations. We have many enemies, and they are not all human. We need to cross alien landscapes, over rocky surfaces, through vast subterranean caverns and across insect infested swamps. We need help. We need a leader.'[1] Taken from a computer game advertisement, this is the puerile plea of digital characters, a call echoed in hundreds of such games which invite players to become the ghost in the machine, to enter a virtual environment in which they will learn, travel and kill. In looking at the new industry of computer entertainment I shall take up issues of exchange and competition, the character of the commodity, fashion, allegory and objectification. It is also necessary to deal with the issue of simulacra, much beloved by postmodern theorists. However, far from believing that postmodern ideas of simulation adequately describe computer gaming, I shall look at two older cultural models which provide a much more compelling account: Benjamin's writing on allegory and Adorno's theories about aesthetics and the culture industry. There is of course a considerable gap between the perspective and the technology of our time and those of these thinkers, yet there are also parallels, for they witnessed the rise of the electronic mass media, comparable to the current rapid growth in computer gaming. This growth has been a swift, broad flourishing after more than a decade of minority use by a clique of technically minded and – in

3

4

5

6

10

11

popular mythology – socially maladjusted, anorak-wearing males. While Benjamin and Adorno saw the beginnings of the age of television, we have entered a new era of interactive entertainment.

The distinctiveness of computer games lies in interaction: the passivity of cinema and television is replaced by an environment in which the player's actions have a direct, immediate consequence on the virtual world. Players are surrounded by apparatus, in the home by screen, keyboard, joystick and speakers; in the arcade sometimes sitting literally inside the machine, thrown back and forth, shaken in their seats, bombarded by noise; more recently in virtual-reality machines, their heads are encased in helmets which provide an illusion of a fully three-dimensional environment, the views of which change in response to movements of the body. Other devices, such as data gloves, not widely marketed at present, produce tactile feedback and allow an apparently direct interaction with the computer-generated world without the need for arbitrary software interfaces. Whatever the equipment, the aim is to produce an illusion not merely of scene but of action. Games strive for ever greater realism and the envelopment of the player within an immediate, visceral experience. Given the technical means available, and certainly when compared with those of the cinema, this project appears chimerical, yet the experience of even quite crude games can be compelling just because it is interactive. Twitches of joystick and mouse produce great apparent bodily or mechanical movements, rather like driving a car, where the same disparity between movement and effect is apparent. Simulations of flying and driving, where the computer screen becomes a windscreen, directly exploit this effect by producing fantasies of movement and control, counterfeiting speed. Even when the player looks at the scene as on to a stage and the alter-ego appears as one of the characters, the identification remains compelling because this figure is directly controlled. Bodies focused around the tiny actions which operate the controls still attempt to reflect on a larger scale the frantic movements of their digital protagonists; the player winces as the character falls from some precipice, is crushed or otherwise meets its demise. Most of all, in trying to provide a palpable and unified reality in which the player operates, by linking response, vision and sound, the computer game aspires to a phantasmagoric experience of total immersion.[2]

Computer gaming falls readily into genres as rigid as those of nineteenth-century academic painting. Games are often arranged by genre on the shelves of software stores, so buyers may immediately find simulations or puzzles, adventure, arcade or role-playing games. These genres are characterized by game type rather than directly by subject matter but the two are often married in broad tendencies. With the exception of puzzles and to a lesser extent simulations, the genres are dominated by cinema and may be divided broadly into those which emulate film and those which emulate cartoons. Although interaction tends to be of a cartoon type due to limitations in hardware and programming techniques, there is a constant striving for ever greater resolution, smoother animation, more naturalistic movement, more colour and a better rendition of volume and atmosphere. Older games were radically different, tailored to the modest capabilities of the machines on which they ran, and coded with great economy to exploit the tiny amounts of available memory with an ingenuity which was also exercised on their content. These games sought to take advantage of their very limitations: certain formats were established, such as platform games and single-screen space-invader type games, which were particular to the computer. While these are still common, and while some games are still produced (like the Russian *Tetris*) which are very much specific to the computer, in general the medium, with increasing sophistication, is losing any sense of itself, becoming entirely subservient to the conventions of cinematic illusion. The common aim is now the 'interactive movie'. With the rapidly growing use of CD-ROM, game designers have been able to include photographically rendered scenes and passages of video which sometimes feature well-known film actors; the so far insurmountable problem has been to combine such elements with any significant degree of interaction. Dependence on the cinema is expressed in musical scores which accompany the action, introductory screens, rolling credits, cuts and fades, long shots and close-ups. Movie spin-offs, whether of *Indiana Jones* or *Robocop*, are only the most obvious example of an increasing mutual dependence. Flagrant plagiarism and the quoting of cinema plots, motifs and designs are common, a whole sub-genre of games being founded around *Star Wars*.[3] Other subjects are immediately familiar from cinema: sword and sorcery, *Lost Kingdom* scenarios complete with dinosaurs and exotic tribes, detective games and bureaucratic conspiracies.

To some degree separated from cinematic games are a set of Yuppie simulations which take the guise of 'serious' platforms designed to show off the capabilities of expensive computers. Here flight and drive simulations (the latter modelling Porsches and other such toys) compete with golf games. The vain yearning for status of those uninvolved in these real activities is partly compensated for by having a computer of sufficient power to run fast and complex simulations. Occasionally the advertisements for these games dwell overtly on the snobbery and envy which apparently drive their players: 'Ever sat at your desk and thought "great day for golf"? Or winced as you-know-who swaggered off to yet another tournament? No problem. Wait till you get home and go one better. Just pull up a chair and play LINKS: The Challenge of Golf. And enjoy all the thrills of the game in the comfort of your own "clubhouse".'[4] Increasingly, however, the distinction between simulation and the story-based game is blurred as the more sophisticated simulators are built around campaigns, careers or tournaments, while narrative games often involve passages of simulation.

If part of the pleasure of cinematic spectacle is an identification with the protagonist on the screen, an imaginative replay of the action, then computer games seek to make this mental act palpable. In Hollywood film there is already a marked trend towards producing a visceral and enveloping experience, through extreme close-ups, fast cutting and the frequent use of shock, and this is merely in the process of being completed by interactive technology. While the subject matter of computer games is utterly dependent on cinematic genres, cinema itself mimics virtual reality, presaging its arrival as a domestic technology. These games, while posing as first-order simulations of reality, are in fact second-order simulations of scenarios dreamt up in Hollywood.

The basic structure of the game is overlaid with a visual veneer which programmers call 'chrome'. The computer game simulates simulation itself, for – to put it in Hollywood language – beneath its chrome glove lies the iron hand of economy. In early games this structure was visible to the player; elements in the first text-based games appeared as simple characters, and in early line-drawn games transparent opponents were encountered in wire-frame spaces. Here the simple calculations of the program were as transparent as the virtual enemy. Increasing sophistication has clothed these calculations in simulated flesh. There is something familiar about the visual aspect of many games, and while this is partly because we already know their elements from films, comics and advertisements, beyond this they possess a crisp, hallucinatory clarity, the images being constructed from a precise repetition of tiny blocks of which the viewer is often aware. Their ghostly objectivity, their hollowness, is a purer distillation of the generalized forms found in the commodity and the advertisement. To compensate for this lifeless immateriality, the player is distracted by the frequent appearance of glowing objects, flashes, explosions and phantom lights. In this way, the medium simulates aura, not by slowly impressing on the viewer a sense of presence, but rather by making believe something is there, with a glittering, eye-catching display of movement and transience, linked with speed and inconsequentiality, itself mimicking the flow of digital signals.

At first there also seems to be some convergence between the image of computer technology and the shiny, bright, metallic surface of the games themselves, which form a resistant and inhuman glacis. Colours are generally synthetic and perfectly even, shapes are predominantly geometrical, and become more so close up as they are resolved into polygonal surfaces or the differentiated squares of bit-mapped images. Yet games also play on the precise opposite of the glossy sci-fi world rendered by these over-sharp forms, particularly in the numerous dungeon scenarios, where spaces are dark, irregular and confining. The spaceship and the dungeon are two opposing formal and technological ideas of a world which is either a smooth, ordered brushed-steel environment, or its labyrinthine shadow. Between these two extremes, the increasing use of fractals divorces the look of the game from human agency by simulating inhumanly complex natural form.[5] Again, increasing naturalism – and not just fractals but greater resolution and more colours than the human eye can distinguish – means that games are gradually losing their specific look, in favour of a 'style' which is to some degree beyond the control even of their programmers. Nevertheless this glossy complexity is always somehow piercingly clean and sharp, as though seen with a greater intensity than anything in the real world. Specificity begins to find a refuge only in lapses, in the clumsiness of much of the drawing, in the frequent mismatches between the rendering of objects and backgrounds, and in the flattening of virtual space against the screen.

Computer games force a mechanization of the body on their players in which their movements and the image of their alter-ego provide a physical and a simulated image of the self under capital, subject to fragmentation, reification and the play of allegory. Games demand that the players hone their skills to make the body a machine, forging from the uncoordinated and ignorant body of the acolyte an embodiment of the spirit of the game. For Adorno, cinematic images, particularly the mask-like faces of the stars which always adopt a predictable form, are commands to be like them.[6] These masks, freezing mobile life into a still commodity form, are 'emblems of authority' – combinations of image and command.[7] Furthermore, like all the products of the culture industry they anticipate and imitate the required responses of the audience: 'The culture industry is geared to mimetic regression, to the manipulation of repressed impulses to copy. Its method is to anticipate the spectator's imitation of itself, so making it appear as if the agreement already exists which it intends to create.'[8] In computer games, the player not only identifies with the image but controls it in obedience to strict rules of conduct – or else!, and the sanction is usually a virtual death sentence – so conformity has been extended from assent to action.

Computer games are different from films in that players become actors, and they are different from other games because their actions appear to affect a distinct and autonomous world.[9] Action is linked to a fixed narrative structure. In almost every game the alter-ego of the player progresses, at least in obtaining equipment and resistance to damage, if not in more specific skills and even moral qualities. There is a marked liberal and individualist ethic behind such games, for the character develops through intrinsically unrewarding labour. The alter-ego is usually the only character which improves, and this growth is always a matter of trade, the self being constructed from a set of thoroughly independent attributes. Labour or virtual money is traded for weapons and equipment or maybe for wisdom or strength or charisma, but intelligence never has a connection to knowledge or charm, nor strength to dexterity or stamina. Measured by number, self-improvement is always unambiguous. As in the ideal market of economists' models, all players start from the same point and with the same resources. Just as exchange value and aesthetic worth wrap themselves mysteriously around real objects, so an idea of progress is always present in the game, shadowing and interpreting the action.

All digital 'objects' encountered in the game are types, and all are ranked on a common arithmetical scale in which every quality is tradeable. The commodity, with its apparently simple surface concealing metaphysical subtleties and theological niceties, is closely related to computer game elements. Like cast metal sculptures, virtual objects are hollow – code, like air, fills their voids, and their surfaces are a reflective chrome. They are mirror images of undifferentiated, mass-produced consumer goods. Games obsequiously reflect the operation of consumer capital for they are based on exchange, an incessant trading of money, munitions or energy, a shuttling back and forth of goods and blows. Those games where trading plays an important part, like the famous space-exploration game *Elite*, merely make this latent content an explicit theme. Pre-selection screens in which the player chooses character attributes or weapons, all reducible to an expression of number, simulate the deployment of investment capital. The player's performance is of course expressed as a numbered score, while objects when captured or destroyed may become, at the moment of their extinction, a floating number, an economic emblem. Each element of the game, each virtual being or object, acts as a commodity, placed in an extensive metonymic chain in which each link is defined only in relation to the others.

A tyranny of number is the founding principle of these games and to play successfully is to emulate the qualities of the machine: reaction, regulation and economy in discrete, repetitive acts. This substructure is, however, generally concealed beneath a veneer of muscular and spontaneous heroism. The allegorical nature of computer gaming is apparent in this opposition between literal structure and rhetorical gloss, in which the unrepresented – universal fungibility and objectification – is expressed through and simultaneously concealed by the organic, the individualistic, and the absolutes of violence and death. The labour forced on the player is not real, the instrumentalism not really consequential, and nothing (except time) is really consumed. As if previewing cyberspace, this simulation takes the form of a commodification which has arrived at a more rarefied stage, emptied of all materiality. Here in the world of the computer game, use value and exchange value are no longer opposed, but are collapsed into an ideal unity. The game world appears as a perfect, utopian market, in which bright, clear-cut commodities are, for once, all that they seem to be.

In the game, temporal progress is mapped on to spatial projection. Game-time is divided between two types of activity: in some games the player is permitted to stop and think, to work out puzzles or strategies, in others there is an unceasing flow of monsters, as though from a production line. Coordination and timing are all-important in the second type where, as in a time and motion study, a purely mechanical efficiency is demanded. In adventure games there is a mix of slow deliberation and fast reaction, of periods of repetitious, aimless wandering and desultory combat. In both types the action is rigid and episodic. For Benjamin, writing of another allegorical form, German tragic drama of the Baroque period, which he used to illuminate the allegorical aspect of modernism: 'The *Trauerspiel* is [. . .] in no way characterised by immobility, nor indeed by slowness of action [. . .] but by the irregular rhythm of the constant pause, the sudden change of direction, and consolidation into a new rigidity.'[10] It would be hard to arrive at a better description of action in computer games. This is characterized by a discrete series of blows, flashes and sudden plunges into darkness, often accompanied and signalled by disk access: these flashes are like inspirational leaps, suddenly taking the game to a new state in a movement so fast that it borders on the imperceptible. In arcade and adventure games there appears to be a simultaneous unwinding of allegory in time and virtual space. Plot combines the spatial disposition of elements with the hierarchy of progress: it is the allegorical projection of the spatial axis on to the temporal. While the linear unfolding of the plot as actually played is halting and uncertain, with many a wrong turn taken or target missed, the hierarchical structure of the game in virtual space is fixed from the start. In the game of a perfectly coordinated and omniscient player the temporal and the spatial worlds would be brought into harmony, and it is very much the player's task to assure this accord.

The player doggedly follows the plot but, since the computer limits and governs the options, this action tends towards a lightning-fast and almost automatic selection, a switching procedure in which each discrete action mirrors the sudden transitions of the game. Taken together they form a repetitive beat, producing a trance in which all sense of time is lost. A striking feature of these games is their compression of time, both in the world of play, where moments separating action are dramatically foreshortened, and in the real world of the players, who re-emerge to discover that more hours have elapsed than they thought possible. Benjamin claimed that the joy of unrolling Ariadne's ball of thread is deeply related to trance, and to creation. 'We go forward; but in so doing we not only discover the twists and turns of the cave, but also enjoy this pleasure of discovery against the background of the other, rhythmical bliss of unwinding the thread. The certainty of unrolling an artfully wound skein – is that not the joy of all productivity, at least in prose?'[11] Following the trace of the plot through the virtual labyrinth of the game is not a productive activity, but, as a simulation of production, it elicits from the player the same entranced state, and, given the constant repetition of elements, possesses the same structure of discovery against a background of similarity.

Furthermore – and again Benjamin's shade seems to haunt the virtual world – if utopian forms were unconsciously produced in the nineteenth-century architecture of the arcades, an ideal past is a constant feature of these new forms: in computer games the rigidity of the genres, the jerky movements and naivety of the staging (harking back involuntarily to early cinema) and more consciously the simplicity of plot and characterization, all evoke an age of pure belief and a regression to childhood simplicity. In these worlds there is generally little moral complexity or ambiguity, and the binary opposition, 0/1, may serve as a register for the rigid dichotomies of the game. A lost innocence briefly returns in which even knowing parodies and self-referential jokes have an adolescent air, winking at the player. The allure of this early technology is often complemented by its depiction of a childishly romantic, fake medieval or Tolkienesque past. Here games, self-consciously youthful, though so much wanting to grow up, depart a little from the cinema where sword and sorcery scenarios are much less popular. While for Benjamin the utopian aspect of the arcades took the form of a dream, in computer games it is a theme knowingly played on and even mildly mocked, yet at the same time demanding from the player a suspension of disbelief and conformity in action.

Plainly, though, the game world is not simply utopian. One reviewer put the matter candidly: 'computer games have always been about mass carnage on a grand scale and there's nothing quite like a spot of carpet bombing to really make you feel as though you're doing some damage'.[12] In games with modern military scenarios the new medium is found in its most unmasked form. A magazine feature asks, 'What was it really like to fly an American B-17 heavy bomber on dangerous daytime raids over occupied France and Nazi Germany during the Second World War? Microprose [. . .] is busy preparing such a simulation for your playing pleasure.'[13] Despite similarities between the conduct of war and its simulation, the essential difference is fixed on here, that however realistic the game, however capable of inducing fear, vertigo or repulsion, as in watching a horror film, these are always found pleasurable. The contrast between the engaging, repetitive but essentially anodyne activity of the game and the actual experience of the often drunken, short-lived bomber crews – let alone those beneath them – could hardly be greater. This contrast is masked in various ways: an advert for *F117A Stealth Fighter* reads, 'Spectacular night graphics with special HUD [head-up display] features, sprite explosions and smoke, along with cluster bomb explosions will intensify the game's visual appeal.' In the aberrant marriage of gaming and weapons of terror, even so mild an emotion as 'appeal' is qualified by a verb with militaristic connotations. The discord between the scenarios acted out and the players' pleasure is disturbing, even to some manufacturers. The chairman of Sphere Incorporated warns the users of his sophisticated flight simulation, *Falcon 3.0*: 'Unfortunately war is still a reality. We hope you will use this product to gain a better understanding of the dangers our pilots face and the complexity of the systems they must master. We hope you also understand that war is not a game you can simply reset or play again. In war, every truck, tank, plane or building that is destroyed costs human lives. Soldiers and pilots understand this. [. . .] Use this product with respect and keep in mind the differences between fantasy and reality.'[14] It is unclear, of course, how this product could be used with 'respect', for the very purpose of the game is to cause maximum mayhem among those digitized vehicles and buildings. Such replays of military experience are fundamentally false yet take cover behind the realism of their technical details; objectifying their characters and their eternal offer of a rematch, they radically denaturalize acts of mortal violence.

Digitized combat has established a fiction of multiple lives and 'hit-points', which measure the degree of injury a character can sustain. This lack of consequence is indicated by the disappearance of bodies and other debris soon after they fall or even in the act of their anni-hilation so that the arcade machine-gunner may see hundreds of zombies fall before the muzzle, but not a corpse will be left in sight when the smoke clears. Or, if they do remain visible, as in *Doom*, no matter where they were shot or how they fell, all the corpses of a par-ticular monster always look exactly the same. In *Operation Wolf*, and its numerous clones, the player guns down countless foes (and inno-cents if careless), slowly sustaining ever greater damage from enemy bullets and grenades, as if this were mere work, sapping energy. When the player finally succumbs, he finds himself in jail! . . . with the option to continue for another coin. In adventure games characters at death's door can be completely revived by a little food and a good night's sleep. Anyone who has been attacked or injured knows that this is not how it is. Yet the games have to pursue this fiction, largely because of the limitations of the medium and its marketing. In the arcade game there is no time for suspense, and it is unprofitable to kill off the player with a single bullet. Enemies must advance and die in hordes, but for the player nothing can be irrevocable. Here ideo-logy and marketing have arrived at a particularly felicitous marriage. Its single-minded impetus has surprised even those who manufac-tured it. Nolan Bushnell, the founder of Atari, is disappointed with his progeny: 'The repetitive, mindless violence that you see on video games is not anything I want to be associated with. [. . .] I think it's just shit.'[15]

Such fictions have spilled over into other media, including televi-sion, and from there into a hideous reality: in the once popular *A-Team* the side that wins the gun battle is that with the greatest fire-power (usually cobbled-together cannon, mortars and flame-throwers): no one is badly hurt in these fights, the baddies stagger off winded, shaking their heads, and hails of bullets do no more than dishearten the enemy. Similarly, for that children's politician Reagan (in propaganda at least) the arms race was something that could be won – and even survived – by acquiring enough 'hit points' and special shielding. In the Gulf War the bodies of the enemy disappeared from the actual scene and from Western memories as fast as virtual corpses disappear from the screen, bulldozed into the ground, uncounted and unidentified as if they were merely particles of some undifferentiated mass; given this, General Schwarzkopf was right to dub the conflict the 'first Nintendo war'.[16] In such circles, any conception of real harm, of the true nature of violence, is strictly suppressed.

The military-industrial complex strongly influences the world of games, obviously in the general sense that the computing industry has always been heavily subsidized by military expenditure, but also in more specific ways: in the exchange of information and sometimes personnel. The game industry's parasitic relationship to the military-industrial complex may explain why the most over-militarized countries, Britain, France and the United States, have the most successful games industries.[17] Many computer-game scenarios are based on military simulators and war-game programs. Computers which aim to predict the outcome of real military actions perform much the same task as those which take care of the onerous calculations in war games. When a game tracks the path of a virtual missile it simulates a function controlled by a software cousin in real life. Current strategic objectives and political propaganda set the scene for game settings: in flight simulations, for instance, Cold War games involving flashpoints in the East–West conflict have given way to 'low-intensity' operations against drug barons and uncooperative Third World tyrants. Soon after the Gulf War flight simulators started to include Desert Storm scenarios. Nostalgic interests are also catered for, from First World War flying to rewriting history Rambo-style in Vietnam.[18] There is also a chance in some games, especially simulations, to play the forces of 'evil': in *Battle of Britain* the player may take the role of a German pilot and swing the war the other way. Within limits, then, the plots of these games show a degree of amoral lassitude.

Yet if games are allegories, it is reasonable to ask what their demons personify. Aliens, in the broadest sense, take on the guise of demons, whether they are from outer space, politically beyond the law or beyond the pale, perhaps most often being people of the Third World. Vietnam is the genocidal model which lies at the heart of many games, whether they are explicitly based on events there or not. Its vocabulary finds its way into these rewritings of history, where it is of course misused – so 'fragging' in the *Wing Commander* series means simply killing the alien enemy, not assassinating your own officers. Whatever form the enemy takes, whether they are extraterrestrial beings or demons from hell, a subtext relates them to contemporary targets.

As games borrow from the military, so military technology takes on the appearance of becoming more virtual, not in its increasingly destructive consequences, but in its remote manner of delivery, in the judgement of its effect and most of all in the attitudes of those who use it and those who urge them on.[19] Such attitudes are not, of course, new – and a direct line links the low-tech Gulf War media sandpit with its little plastic tanks to the videos tracking 'smart' bombs and Cruise missiles, replayed as prime-time snuff movies – but they are reinforced by such technology. Objectification is the bottom line.

The player of a computer game has the feeling of inhabiting a discrete world where unchangeable truths may be learned. Such learning is not only about plot and scenario, but is also a familiarization with the control system – the interface between player and operating system – which is largely arbitrary. Control systems which are marketed as 'intuitive' merely display some internal consistency. In relation to postmodern theory, it is interesting that this arbitrariness is very much of the sort that Jean Baudrillard describes in his essay 'The Political Economy of the Sign', being inherent in the very act of positing an equivalence between sign and signified. New systems of 'fixed and equational' structures in which all ambivalence is excluded, and where the sign acts as 'discriminant',[20] are regularly invented in the game world and indeed in all programs. Any notion of computing as a postmodern realm of chaos and shifting identifications must account for this founding act of universal reduction which, far from being imposed over an anarchic flux of signals, is built into the physical and virtual architecture of all systems from the very start.

For Adorno, the virtuoso performance in modern culture is achieved not by triumphing over difficulty, but through subordination.

This is highly apparent in computer games, both literally in their agonistic scenarios and also in the way they force a particular form of action on the player, of rhythm, timing and reaction.[21] The player's subordination of the game is achieved through the game's conquest of the player. Computer games perform simulated acts of reification in which slices of immaterial code act as living beings but are arranged and treated as objects. The brutal simplification of these digital figures is a register of objectification. The player, too, is blatantly objectified by the act of playing: this is invoked in a television advertisement for the *Super Nintendo* console in which the player is swiftly transformed part by part into a bio-mechanical being. The player buckles on virtual armour and, in responding to the stimuli of the game, is doubled both in body and on screen as a bio-mechanical being of single mind. Such a construction of the self apes those genetically and mechanically modified warriors of film and comic book, and perhaps prefigures the hideous creations of the military exploitation of genetics, nanotechnology – and computing.

For unsympathetic or bemused onlookers, computer gaming is collapsed into two worrying but possibly contradictory characterizations; of mindless addiction to an alien and impoverished experience, and also the feeling of utter exclusion, that they could not possibly begin to understand or play the game. Both are perhaps based on the hunch that the 'interface' between person and machine is quite unlike that with a tool, that it is somehow mysterious and threatening. Behind these feelings is the correct impression that the interface dehumanizes the user, while (in an equal and opposite reaction) the user tries to humanize the machine. Computers are made more 'personal' by the addition of cute trivia to the screen or keyboard, or by tailoring the operating system with sound patches, pictures, or a particular colour scheme. On the PC, *Windows* users may attach sampled sounds to certain program events,[22] while Macintosh owners have long been able to accompany disk insertion and ejection with moaning and retching noises. User and machine, then, meet halfway in a realm of decorated inhumanity where certainties still hold fast and where each may rely on the other as mere examples of a type.

Another property of the interface is the game's visual presentation. The look of computer game settings is often reminiscent of the stage: the difference between isometric and platform games is only the difference between the views of the stage from the circle and the stalls. The alter-ego may be rendered in first person or third so that the player either sees what the character sees, or directly sees the character. There are also games in which the personification is abstract and invisible, and in which as a result the player merely influences rather than controls aspects of the game. In *Simcity* or *Populous* – which now have numerous offspring – the player becomes respectively a mayor or a mythological deity seeking to influence events, though the game will run quite happily without intervention. Here the player is coextensive with the alter-ego, an immaterial thinking presence, which needs no representation.

In the digital phantasmagoria being dreamed up for us, there may be few points of interruption on to which criticism can latch. For the moment, however, computer games contain many glitches which, again, often echo the charming clumsiness of the first movies, sharing with them unsynchronized sounds, spelling mistakes and continuity errors. Other problems, specific to the computer game, include the difficulty of the character's initial insertion into the virtual world: one of the simplest strategies used to overcome this has the player 'awake' as an amnesiac, and part of the task involves the rediscovery of identity and the recovery of memory. At other times, transport to a different world may be the device but the transition can be awkward, particularly with the presentation of contextual information which the player really ought to know ('Greetings. I am Jessica, your mother', and so on). Another foothold for criticism is provided by the machine itself, for sometimes the game hangs as the disk is accessed, disrupting the player's involvement, while at others what ought to be a surprise event is announced by the flashing of the disk light. Points of critique are also provided by bugs (programming errors) and in the manifestly typical nature of each object encountered. Beyond this, there are ways of finding paths behind the coding, whether by hacking or by chance. Games are generally hacked either to cheat or to get past copy protection. Cheats are generally created by the programmers themselves in order to test the game with ease, and are then discovered by hackers, and these back-door aids, conferring assets or immunity from damage, are often published in games magazines. All of these points of fracture, of which hacking is the most extreme because it is deliberate, are marginal but radical, points at which the phantasmagoria is breached, and the structure of the game peeps through. Increasing technical perfection will perhaps make the glacis of the game ever more slippery for criticism.[23] Such footholds for critical perspectives are, in any case, fleeting and ephemeral, and are certainly no ground for drawing positive conclusions about the medium's development.

Outside the home, computer-game arcades form a digital phantasmagoria, far more menacing and affective than the piped music and plastic trim of the shopping mall. While the wandering consumers of both the nineteenth century and the contemporary arcades effortlessly submerged themselves in a phantasmagoric environment, entering a digitized world often requires commitment and an act of attention, though once this immersion is achieved, virtual wandering is both absorbing and highly controlled. The ambience of these gaming arcades – the noise, the heat, the relative darkness and intense concentrated points of frenetic activity – is insalubrious. They are, for all their puerility, like sex parlours, and in fact often share their locales with sex shops and gambling halls. No wonder that in the tabloid imagination the true aim of virtual reality is 'dildonics' – simulated sex, either using a digitized partner or linked with a real person via a phone line.[24] Arcade play is an essentially solitary, often male activity which involves a tension between public and private spheres. A reflection of the arcades is found in the games themselves. One advert reads: 'You're in the depths of your own worst nightmare . . . but this time there's no waking up. Lost and alone in a dangerous and alien world you must discover where you are, how you got there . . . and how you're going to get out! [. . .] Re-emerging into daylight you race along perfect parallax action scenes, dispatching enemies as you battle ever deeper into the unknown.'[25] This nightmare aspect is common in many games, an enclosing, claustrophobic vision, which evokes the restrictive space of the arcade and the barriers imposed on the player by a digitally constructed world. Dungeons and labyrinths are, of course, traditional places for the exercise of allegory, and the links between scenario, environment and computer architecture may be viewed as allegorical, all referring back to the discrete and enclosed action of commerce which produces them.

These arcades naturally recall Benjamin, for there are various levels on which the computer game conforms to his analysis of bourgeois culture. He wrote of a lithograph showing the occupants of a gambling club, 'the figures presented show us how the mechanism to which the participants in a game of chance entrust themselves seizes them body and soul, so that even in their private sphere, and no matter how agitated they may be, they are capable only of reflex action. [. . .] they live their lives as automatons and resemble Bergson's fictitious characters who have completely liquidated their memories'.[26] Just this combination of automatic action and affective engagement characterizes the playing of computer games. Especially with arcade games, the computer produces in the player a simulacrum of industrial work: the autonomy of each action, its repetition, precise timing and rare completion are all reminiscent of Benjamin's analysis of the gambler's actions. The jerky movement of early games, and even many current ones, clearly presents a progress which takes place in separate steps, and which maintains the idea of a game move. In many slower adventure games, too, play takes the form of labour in which the exploration of highly complex spaces involves repeated sequences of simple actions. Other games punish failure by constantly pushing the player back to the start. As in work, the effect of this endless iteration is dulling. Yet it is only the signs of labour that are apparent in computer gaming, where the physical strain of heavy, repetitive tasks is replaced by the digital twitching demanded by the control system. Because of the medium's intrinsic paucity, emotional attachment to the game is established through labour, emerging out of the Sisyphean nature of the player's task. The arcade, while evoking gambling and sex, is actually a furtive simulacrum of the sweatshop.

Adorno analysed the simulation of work in hobbies and this may be applied to computer games: free time is shackled to modern work which requires useless, disengaged leisure activity to bring about uncritical recuperation. Free time is strictly divided from industry but working habits have become so internalized that 'contraband' modes of behaviour appropriate to work are smuggled into leisure.[27] In the futile tasks set in computer games, as opposed to hobbies, a simulation of this mimicking of working practices is established, for while time is consumed and while the repetition of tiny, discrete tasks and the loss of the self in labour are real enough, the activity is entirely unproductive. Adorno argues:

No fulfilment may be attached to work, which would otherwise lose its functional modesty in the totality of purposes, no spark of reflection is allowed to fall into leisure time, since it might otherwise leap across to the workaday world and set it on fire. While in their structure work and amusement are becoming increasingly alike, they are at the same time being divided ever more rigorously by invisible demarcation lines. Joy and mind have been expelled equally from both. In each, blank-faced seriousness and pseudo-activity hold sway.[28]

The computer game merely makes this simulation literal, being a true pseudo-activity which is nevertheless structured like work. The conceptual demarcation lines between the two even materialize, becoming visible in the borders which outline the screen areas of work and play. Yet this raising of pseudo-activity to a purer, more rarefied level in which no material is ever touched, has been accompanied by a radical shift of scene. Adorno wrote at a time when industrial workers found leisure in hobbies and games which emulated labour. In 'postmodern' Britain and the United States, where manufacturing industry is failing, a population is filling its hours with simulated labour, a fictional activity which gestures towards and mocks the lack of work in the real world.

Another distinction is also apparent. While the actions of the player are fragmented and repeated, the progress of the game taken as a whole is most unlike gambling or factory work, for story lines are constructed, consequences are followed through, and progress can generally be saved (or restored) at any point. Just as shafts of sunlight pick out patterns in floating dust, narrative meaning is born out of a swarm of acts as various elements of continuity are superimposed upon the basic structure of the game. These include thematic music, interventions by a 'narrator', and scenes which comment on or frame the player's performance. Games may be more or less authoritarian in forcing the player to follow sequences of specific acts in order to progress, or in allowing a degree of latitude. Unlike the hackneyed plots of movies, especially those which transparently build up expectations and then seek to surprise, the plots of some computer games are truly polyvalent and non-linear. The player-hero may even end up losing, though this eventuality is usually realized outside the game, when it is abandoned from boredom or frustration. While a huge number of possible worlds are established as each stage is won or lost, and while only a very few of this panoply of a thousand plots lead to final success, the lost game is always discounted in the construction of plot, these branches being forever closed by the restoration of a previously saved position. In the virtual world, the player is usually offered unlimited chances to make good, but for each path to victory there are a hundred diverse ways to fail, most involving some more or less spectacular death. These hundreds of lost or abandoned games for each one completed, their heroes dead or left in digital limbo, echo the fate of billions of lost individuals under the vast play of capital.

As in the *Trauerspiel*, where the chorus represented the world of dreams and meaning, and interpreted the action, so very often there appears in computer games a similar divide (again often established for technical reasons) of action interspersed with animated sequences, dialogue, dreams or visions. These scenes have the function of frames which are placed around the action to make it meaningful, usually by developing the plot. There is also a more literal form where animation is seen inside an ornate frame, or where a screen is framed by hardware. Of course these frames, especially if they cut across the field of vision, like the struts of a cockpit, act as stable reference points and enhance the illusion of movement; in technical terms, they usefully restrict the proportion of the screen that has to be animated. Like a constantly chanting chorus, the elements of the frame (dials, gauges, or numbers) comment on the action.

More connects the computer game and the heritage industry than their use of digital technology to promote kitsch simulations of an idealized past. Many games take the form of a staged, touristic exploration. To complete the game, the player is forced to travel everywhere, and there is a mental compulsion to do this too, a digitized equivalent of the cultural imperative to ubiquity. As with the exploitation of 'heritage' themes, many of the game elements are familiar since childhood and are recognized at once. They are collected, combined and packaged as entertainment, inevitably with a strong flavour of pastiche. The experience is evocative rather than informative, being less the stuff of history than of television series and pulp novels.

Like tourism, computer gaming is largely based on spatial exploration. This is partly because there are several problems with producing temporal development in such games. Actions may obviously be triggered by the player's acts but other characters cannot be permitted to develop independently, or to complete actions autonomously, or the whole plot might collapse. When other characters act, it must be in a circular manner, literally going about their business.[29] The spatial nature of computer gaming means that progress can be expressed only in terms of travel, or, if it is marked as a definite stage, in the breaching of some barrier. Hence the overriding importance of locks and keys, levels, hidden items, secret doors and false walls. The tasks the player must perform to gain entry are often of the boxes-within-boxes type, a way of hierarchically structuring an otherwise free space. Travel, moral progress, the return home, topography and mapping, the distorted spaces of the dream, the dungeon and the labyrinth are all mainstays of allegory.

There is another way of looking at this aspect of the computer game, through the relation between allegory and script. Allegorical writing takes the form of a monogram or hieroglyph.[30] In the earliest games the computer's text characters were used to stand in for fictional characters and objects. More broadly, the inquisition of words and signs in adventure and detective games is allegorical since they are utterly separate from one another and function less as carriers of meaning than as passwords or magical incantations, serving to open doors or motivate actions. Lastly, the whole form of the computer game may be seen as a figure or monogram in which all the characters except the player are tied to specific locations in a strict configuration: the tracing of the figure is the completion of the game.

Although they always have a purpose, computer players act as the flaneurs of the digital realm in their wandering, their detached engagement with virtual objects, and their feeling that nothing really matters. This is the aspect of computing that has endeared it to postmodern theorists: the lack of apparent consequences of action and knowledge, the adoption of multifarious roles, the simulation of phenomena which are already simulations, the self-consciousness of the players and the manifest nature of the fictions. The player is aware of, and even mocks, these game elements, but this does not prevent participation. Yet, unlike the postmodern aspects of plot, role and simulation, the modernist dream of eternal technological progress is not treated ironically. Unlike the aimless flaneur, the computer player (like the shopper, the snapper and the hack) loiters with intent. It might appear that acts of objectification are ameliorated by detachment, but engagement and belief on all levels are hardly necessary for its functioning. Such detachment is partly produced by the current limitations of the medium, and is, in any case, a mere epiphenomenon. To concentrate upon it is to ignore the fundamental features of computer entertainment, most particularly the nature of interaction which not only enforces conformity but does so through the use of a rigid, exclusive sign system.

The operation of desire in these games is simply an acute form of the normal procedure of the market in a fashion-driven culture: there is always a sense of something beyond the present experience, of some unused potential within the machine, of a task never quite finished, of a realism not quite complete. The yearning for completeness in allegory is never satisfied, so details proliferate and plots endlessly lengthen.[31] In computer games, scale, complexity, the number of characters and the size of the playing area are still celebrated as intrinsically positive points, partly because hardware and software restrict these factors, but also because of their allegorical aspect. 'A daemon never tires or changes his nature',[32] claims Angus Fletcher, and so as long as it survives the allegory must continue. Indeed, objects and characters encountered in the game world are generally emblematic, being name-image assemblages and examples of a type. A very literal example of this can be seen in adventure games in which the player may click on some object, causing its name to appear above it. In a game like *Ultima Underworld* the characters encountered are often allegorical expressions of virtues and vices, which can be relied upon to act forever according to their chosen principle, whether it be greed, vanity or pride. The slaughter of the last demon is indeed the only hope for a conclusion. Of course, if it was any different, if expectations were fulfilled or demons took a break, then the game would cease. Computer games have a distinct difficulty in providing an adequate ending: nothing can quite fulfil the expectation of such a long task finished, and indeed the conclusion often jumps up arbitrarily before the player, not as the result of some supremely difficult task, but as the chance consequence of just another combination of key-presses. The ending is longed for but known in advance to be a let-down. The impetus to move on to the next thing is of course an accurate reflection of consumer fashion culture, both in playing the game itself and in the yearning for the next game with its attendant technical advances. A symptom of this is the fixation of the computer leisure magazines on previews, which often dominate coverage of what is actually available.

As the boundaries of illusion are pushed back, and players' expectations follow suit, games very quickly become obsolete. Yesterday's state-of-the-art games are unplayable today since the act of imagination and involvement necessary is intimately tied to the progress of the technology at any particular moment. Constant amazement at the predictable improvement of hardware and software keeps players engaged. As we have seen, the current goal is utter illusionism. As a consequence, games become ever more immediate as – in the interests of realism but also because of their dependence on films and television – words are progressively abandoned in favour of pictures and speech, typing in favour of mouse and joystick movements, even when the former would be more efficient. Yet there are anomalies in this onward march of technical progress. It is ironic that those with sophisticated machines running *Windows* – that most profligate of operating systems – are now treated to a reprise of some of the crudest early games, running in little frames.[33] The advantage of *Windows* for the employee is of course that its multi-tasking system is ideal for playing, say, *Asteroids* at work while pretending to be working on a spreadsheet since the two can be quickly switched between. The increasing dominance of the 'Graphical User Interface' over text-based systems may be partly due to the general trends towards visuality and illiteracy in the culture, but it is comforting that the great popularity of *Windows* may also be owed to the ease with which one can cheat on one's employers.[34] The irony is that employees fool their bosses only to engage in a simulacrum of work. Many of the points of critique which have been examined here, and many of the aspects of computer gaming which are most obviously allegorical, are the product of technical limitations manifested in framing devices, pauses in the action, the fragmentation and repetition of characters and objects. These allegorical forms will probably decay as the medium advances, leaving a seamless, apparently natural face which nevertheless conceals an uncompromising allegorical structure: the mapping of plot on to structure and the disguise of economy behind aggressive heroism.

According to Robert X. Cringely, the documenter of Silicon Valley mores, awkward, alienated adolescents founded the microcomputer industry:

> they split off and started their own culture, based on the completely artificial but totally understandable rules of computer architecture. They defined, built and controlled (and still control) an entire universe in a box – an electronic universe of ideas rather than people – where they made all the rules, and could at last be comfortable.[35]

Social dissatisfaction is certainly inherent in the alternative realities of the game world, and fantasy scenarios often refer to contemporary problems. The well-known *Ultima* games, for instance, definitely have a liberal agenda, confronting problems of pollution, drug addiction, racism and religious fundamentalism. The idea that a single individual is able to rectify such problems is, of course, a deeply ingrained part of Hollywood ideology – and if the real world's problems are too intractable, why not go to a 'place' where they are not? The ambition behind these games is to create a new world and this time to do it right, to make something which is much better, much worse or at least less tedious than reality. The scenario is more often dystopian than utopian, but at least dystopia is not boring. Computer games, whether offering images of heaven or hell, may be seen as the desires for and fears of an imagined history.

Benjamin thought that in games of chance the player empathizes directly with the sums bet, paving the way for an empathy with exchange value itself.[36] Computer games, which, as we have seen, form an ideal image of the market system, obviously serve this same function, but also have a wider ambit. The action of the player is a disturbing reflection of relations which hold true, but remain largely hidden, in the real world. In an ironic simulation of political and military power, the player is accorded an objectifying force and apes those in power, manipulating realistic forms which are actually numbers, rather than manipulating figures which are actually people. Computer games present a precise, reversed reflection of the preoccupations and even the techniques of capitalist power. Marx and Benjamin arrived at widely differing analyses of the nature of phantasmagoria,[37] but the computer game apparently simulates them both. The virtual world is a dream of an alternative, complete and consistent reality in Benjamin's terms, while the cloaking of economy with chrome conforms to Marx's account of the camouflage of actual relations. What, though, is the utopian dream concealed by, if we are to allow the game as phantasmagoria in Benjamin's sense? This is a delicate question, since to the outsider the answer would certainly be: by violence and objectification. So for those looking on, simulated 'real' relations mask utopian dreams, while for the initiate it is the dream which masks economy. Here simulation is the most crucial factor: in the establishment of virtual commodities, exchange and objectification, and even base and superstructure relations, the game creates an ideal structure in which all these elements are harmoniously united.

Computer gaming is no longer the affair of a small minority, nor are the programs written by amateurs in the hours after school. Major companies are involved, deploying substantial development budgets to create games which involve the participation not only of programmers but of writers, actors, artists and musicians. The specific form and ideology of computer games are, then, of much wider concern than the examination of the mores of a narrow and obsessed male-dominated group. Indeed, players are decreasingly defined by gender or even age.[38] The advent of virtual reality, which will have profound effects on our culture, has its basis in the methods and the ethos of computer gaming. Current computer games are already emulating virtuality in their use of first-person perspectives, and their obsessions with space, speed and flight. In their structure and content, computer games are a capitalist and deeply conservative form of culture. Their political content is proscribed by the options open to democracy under contemporary capitalism, that is from those with liberal pretensions to those which are openly fascistic. All of them offer the virtual consumption of empty forms in an ideal market. By confining the ideal forms of work and exchange to the digital world, computer games might appear to offer an implicit critique of post-industrial societies where these ideals are no longer on offer. Actually, they only conform to the views of the propagandists who say that work is always available and that opportunity can always be grasped, that the system is in fact ideal but for the laziness and stupidity of those who people it. Computer games do set out to give the player an escape into a world of certainty and fulfilment, yet they merely echo the past forms of industrial work in an ideal, nostalgic vision of the marketplace.

The technology of computer leisure is not consciously controlled by politicians or captains of industry, but driven by market forces, and conditioned by the parameters of the computer industry's links with the military. Nevertheless, these games exhibit a dialectic of increasing naturalism and objectification which leads to an ever greater concealment of the latter behind the former, to an ever greater blurring of the use of people as instruments in the world and the game. Computer gaming often produces an extreme social atomization of the players; because of the fragmentary and episodic nature of the activity, it is very difficult to relate the experience of it to anyone else – even if they know the game. All that can be recounted are the scores. This is all the more so because forgetting is an essential part of the operation of the market, vital to the rapid obsolescence of any particular game, the unplayability of old games and the impetus of fashion. There is a shadowy ambition behind the concept of the virtual world to have everyone safely confined to their homes, hooked up to sensory feedback devices in an enclosing, interactive environment which will be a far more powerful tool of social control than television.

The aspects of computer gaming I have chosen to examine – allegory, fashion and reification – are all related. Allegory is manifest in a double sense: there is an allegory of plot (where spatial structure is mapped on to temporal progress) and of action (where the absolute of death is laid over with a structure of trading and economy). Allegory is linked to fashion because of its fragmentation of the image into elements, and fashion is like objectification because of the fungibility of its elements, in that there is no restriction on the number or type of combinations allowed. Fashion is an endless and circular process which runs through all the possible sequences of a fragmented ensemble, as in the autonomous rising and falling of hemlines or hair lengths, like the ebb and flow of waves on a shore. Memory and fashion are also linked since, as we have seen, there must be a constant forgetting of meaning which leaves only the husk of forms. There is clearly also a connection between allegory and

objectification, for allegorical characters are empty shells, not creatures but remorseless robots, absolute embodiments of the principle
they serve. Like Max Ernst's painting *The Angel of Hearth and Home,* a
premonition of the demon of Fascism unleashed on Europe, or the
robot in *Terminator,* they proceed inexorably towards their goal, incidentally trampling everything in their path. For Benjamin, dialectical
thinking is embodied in the current epoch dreaming of the next:
'Each epoch not only dreams the next, but also, in dreaming, strives
towards the moment of waking.'[39] While the old arcade culture perhaps produced dreams of the collapse of commodification and an
ideal glass architecture, behind the strained heroics of the computer
game lies another dream, which takes cluster bombing for spectacle
and slaughter for heroics, a dream of the apocalypse, of instrumentalization, of forgetting, and of mechanical stupidity. It contains both
the bright metallic environment of a brave new world and the nightmare spaces of Piranesi's dungeons, identified with utopia and
apocalypse respectively, but each embracing elements of the other. It
also holds a dark fantasy of bio-mechanics, in which the exchange and
manipulability of digital elements are mapped back on to the human
body itself. Finally, it is a dream of dreaming itself, invading subjectivity at a very deep level, and producing manufactured memories and
dreams which are so powerful because they are based on simulated
action.

Adorno, writing of high culture, described how works of art are
'not just allegories, but the catastrophic fulfilment of allegories', in
which the most recent art appears as a shocking 'explosion' which
consumes appearance and the aesthetic itself. Even this form is appro-
priated by computer games which, despite their fake realism, also, 'As
they burn up in appearance, they depart in a glare from empirical
life', being life's antithesis. Adorno concludes, 'Today art is hardly
conceivable except as an orientation anticipating the apocalypse.'[40]
Adorno's pessimistic belief that the cultural means of Fascism were
adopted by those in the West who helped defeat it has obvious relev-
ance to the computer game's militaristic glorification, knowing
employment of myth, and relentless objectification. In these games
there is a tenebrous dance of the utopian and the apocalyptic, an
ambiguity which it is tempting to resolve by saying that they present
the apocalypse as utopia. If this is so, it is because the absolutes of

destruction and death are sought as an escape from the virtuality and artificiality of everyday life. While this is achieved only in a digital simulation, its effects may spill back into the real world. The defining image in all this comes, not from any game, but naturally enough from a blockbuster film, *Terminator 2*: it is the jarring crunch of human skulls under the bright chrome of a robot foot.

NOTES

1. Advert for *Laser Squad*, Krisalis Software Ltd.

2. The term 'phantasmagoria' was invented in the early nineteenth century to describe exhibitions of optical illusions produced by magic lanterns, so its use here seems apt.

3. It was many years between the making of *Star Wars* and LucasArts issuing an 'official' game of the film. This allowed many other companies to program their own space-combat games based loosely on the film.

4. Advert for *Links 386 Pro* published by US Gold.

5. One of the first games to employ fractals for generating landscapes was *Midwinter 2: Flames of Freedom*, produced by Rainbird in 1992.

6. Theodor Adorno, 'The Schema of Mass Culture', *The Culture Industry. Selected Essays on Mass Culture*, London 1991, p. 81.

7. Ibid., p. 82.

8. Adorno, *Minima Moralia. Reflections from Damaged Life*, London 1974, p. 201.

9. In discussing chess Roger Caillois notes that the game takes on an independence in relation to the individual player, who inherits a history and a practice of the game and is aware of their own small part in a continuum of chess playing. In computer gaming there is no comparable formalization or recording, but the autonomy of game from player is solidified and made evident. Caillois, 'L'Imagination rigoureuse', *Cases d'un échiquier*, Paris 1970, p. 39.

10. Walter Benjamin, *The Origin of German Tragic Drama*, trans. John Osborne, London 1977, p. 197.

11. Benjamin, 'Hashish in Marseilles', *Reflections*, New York 1986, p. 142.

12. Paul Presley, review of *B17 Flying Fortress*, *PC Review*, no. 12, October 1992, p. 60.

13. Anon., 'News', *PC Review*, no. 3, January 1992, p. 10.

14. Gilman Louie, 'Foreword: Operation Desert Storm', *Falcon 3.0 Flight Manual*, USA 1991, pp. ix–x.

15. Cited in David Sheff, *Game Over. Nintendo's Battle to Dominate an Industry*, London 1993, p. 375.

16. Ibid., p. 285.

17. The games company Spectrum Holobyte, for example, also makes military simulators.

18. Real history, even when rewritten by the player, is not necessarily sufficient and some games use sci-fi departures from realistic reconstruction. *Secret Weapons of the Luftwaffe*, published by US Gold, for instance, has the player fighting or operating experimental German planes that (thankfully) never flew.

19. Paul Virilio has explored the relationship between visualization techniques and military action in *War and Cinema. The Logistics of Perception*, trans. Patrick Camiller, London 1989. Now computers as well as people 'see' and instantly act on the data they receive. Jean Baudrillard's notorious views on war as simulation, produced in response to events in the Gulf, are dissected by Christopher Norris in *Uncritical Theory. Postmodernism, Intellectuals and the Gulf War*, London 1992.

20. Jean Baudrillard, 'The Political Economy of the Sign', *Selected Essays*, Cambridge 1988, p. 81.

21. There is an ever-lessening engagement of the player in peripheral activities such as note-taking, map-making, even remembering and thinking, which used to be essential to many games. These functions are increasingly taken over by automated facilities, and help keys.

22. See the jokey article about the personalization of computers by Michael Hewitt ('Sounding Off', *Personal Computer World*, November 1992, p. 175). He rightly points out that this phenomenon is seen only with computers and does not extend to toasters or washing machines.

23. A doubt about this point is that, as programs become more complex and the interrelations between modules of code ever more numerous, bugs become much more difficult to detect and control.

24. There are a few sleazy games of a mild character marketed by the major software houses but sex, as opposed to Hollywood romance, is a subject generally avoided.

25. This is for the game *Obitus* published by Psygnosis.

26. Walter Benjamin, *Charles Baudelaire. A Lyric Poet in the Era of High Capitalism*, London 1973, p. 135.

27. Adorno, 'Free Time', *The Culture Industry*, p. 164.

28. Adorno, *Minima Moralia*, pp. 130–31.

29. There is an exception, when a character's action actually ends the game within a certain time limit, which the player generally knows of in advance. Then this character is allegorized into the principle of that act, whether destroying the universe or forcing the princess and, above all, ending the game.

30. See Benjamin, *The Origin of German Tragic Drama*, p. 175.

31. See Angus Fletcher, *Allegory. The Theory of a Symbolic Mode*, New York 1964, pp. 174–5.

32. Ibid., p. 176.

33. At the time of writing the much-hyped *Windows 95* has just appeared which Microsoft claim will run DOS games without crashing and will allow programmers to write advanced games directly for the new system. It is too early to tell whether these claims are justified.

34. There are of course other devices: 'false DOS' keys which apparently return the player to the operating system, programs for hiding entire directories and silencing noisy games.

35. Robert X. Cringely, *Accidental Empires: How the Boys of Silicon Valley Make Their Millions, Battle Foreign Competition, and Still Can't Get a Date*, London 1992, p. 14.

36. Benjamin, letter to Adorno, 9 December 1938, in *Aesthetics and Politics*, London 1977, p. 141.

37. See Rolf Tiedemann, 'Dialectics at a Standstill', in Gary Smith, ed., *On Walter Benjamin. Philosophy, Aesthetics, History*, Chicago 1983, pp. 278–9.

38. Recent studies show little or no gender difference in expressed interest, type of game played or length of playing time among children. See Christine Ward Gailey, 'Mediated Messages. Gender, Class and Cosmos in Home Video Games', *Journal of Popular Culture*, vol. 27, no. 1, Summer 1993, p. 86. Sheff notes that 46 per cent of Western Game Boy players are adults (*Game Over*, p. 339.) Another study, published in 1983, found no significant differences in male and female attitudes to video arcades, though there were markedly more males actually playing the games (see Sidney J. Kaplan, 'The Image of the Amusement Arcades and Differences in Male and Female Video Game Playing', *Journal of Popular Culture*, vol. 17, no. 1, Summer 1983, pp. 93–8). This situation has changed a good deal since, and is still doing so.

39. Benjamin, 'Paris, Capital of the Nineteenth Century', *Reflections*, p. 162.

40. Adorno, *Aesthetic Theory*, trans. C. Lenhardt, London 1984, p. 125.

5

AUTOMOBILE AESTHETICS

In Thomas Pynchon's novel *V*, a character called Profane argues with another, Rachel, about her too intimate relationship with a sports car:

> You know what I always thought? That you were an accessory. That you, flesh, you'd fall apart sooner than the car. That the car would go on, in a junkyard even it would look like it always had, and it would be a thousand years before that thing could rust so you wouldn't recognize it. But old Rachel, she'd be gone. A part, a cheesy part, like a radio, heater, windshield-wiper blade.[1]

It is one thing for people to feel subordinated to a complex machine, which evolves at a terrific rate, giving them glimpses of other worlds, and even of another intelligence, but in fact they have long been expended in favour of a multitude of other machines with none of these qualities. The most notorious and most ubiquitous, the one which affects the everyday texture of our lives more than any other, is the motor car: a crude lump of metal set in motion by perching its passengers on top of an incendiary device; a machine produced by an industry so powerful and hidebound, so entangled with political interests, that it has brought no major technological innovation to mass production for eighty years.

The everyday, material damage the car does is well enough known.

It might be surprising that we are prepared to exchange the increasingly marginal convenience of personal transport for streets which might serve as communal spaces, for our general health, particularly that of children who breathe the air at exhaust-pipe level, for unfettered mental development (in Britain, of course, leaded petrol is still legal), for safety from widespread, arbitrary injury and death, for the fabric of every ancient architectural wonder, and quite possibly for the planet's very environmental balance. What is more surprising, given all this, is that we do not do so a little more grudgingly, shrugging our shoulders at the power of the road lobby to remove the alternatives. Rather, cars are treated by many people with nothing short of love: one man of my acquaintance described his new BMW as the fulfilment of his life, and this devotion is not untypical. So the question is not just practical but cultural: why are cars so loved?

A tempting answer is to look to the power of the propaganda that surrounds them: the considerable weight of the automobile industry is brought to bear on the media, producing constant, inescapable and highly sophisticated propaganda. Such a major source of revenue for television, newspapers and magazines obviously has great sway over owners, editors and producers, encouraging sympathetic 'features' or regular motoring sections and programmes which complement their advertising copy.[2] Yet this is not a complete answer in itself: our amenability to this propaganda also tells us something about ourselves.

It is obvious that the deteriorating situation caused by mass private transport is bad enough to affect drivers almost as much as everybody else. A proportion of the pollutants emitted by their vehicles finds its way into the cab, reducing mental functions and producing nausea in those who are not accustomed to it, again especially children. The transport system is so clogged that it barely functions; these high-speed, high-acceleration vehicles, posing as thoroughbreds – whose performance can supposedly be judged by reading subtle signs inscribed on their steel bodies – these fuel-injected steeds stand idling in herds, or nose their way forward foot by foot.

It was not meant to be like this. From the beginning it was obvious that when pedestrians and motor vehicles came into contact, the result was disastrous: Le Corbusier likened it to throwing dynamite in the street. His solution was totally to segregate people and traffic, but once this was achieved (through radical surgery of the old city), then the outlines of a new aesthetic of speed and geometric purity would be revealed. In 1924, describing his plans for Paris, which involved razing the entire existing city except for a few monuments to be left standing in parkland, Le Corbusier wrote of the experience of driving through the new environment:

> Suppose we are entering the city by way of the Great Park. Our fast car takes the special elevated motor track between the majestic sky-scrapers: as we approach nearer there is seen the repetition against the sky of the twenty-four sky-scrapers [. . .]
> Our car has left the elevated track and has dropped its speed of sixty miles an hour to run gently through the residential quarters. [. . .] There are gardens, games and sports grounds. And sky everywhere, as far as the eye can see.[3]

The car was not merely an efficient means of transport, but would give the driver access to an aesthetic experience of order and geometry, of changing perspectives at high speed. The modern city was a device to lessen distance and increase velocity, being wired for fast, efficient and businesslike mobility, proceeding always in straight lines. At sixty miles an hour, through an awareness of how the zoned, functional parts of the city are linked, social order and efficiency, the harmony of the urban fabric and of society itself, could be experienced as well as known.

The experience of the postmodern motorist is quite another story. Given the manifest failure of such utopian visions of free mobility and aesthetic education for the masses, we might look to a time when the decision to transform Britain into an environment fit only for the motor car was just being made – or at least when the decisions to prevent it from happening were not being made: the sixties. Throughout the decade the pages of the *Architectural Review* were regularly occupied with a debate about roads and transport policy. The journal was of course a defender of functionalist modernism, but of a pragmatic sort that was sensitive to the value of the existing fabric. The growth of private transport was seen as one of the most pressing environmental problems facing the country. It was hardly a matter of dispute, even at this early stage, that streets jammed with cars were both inefficient as transport and also 'a highly efficient lethal barrier to the pedestrian' which 'effectively divide the urban landscape by rivers of metal'.[4] As one of the journal's regular writers, Ian Nairn, put it, 'The apposition here is point blank: you can have unlimited use of unlimited cars in their present form and you can have urban communities but you cannot have both.' Beyond a certain width the road becomes a barrier chopping up the city into insular fragments. In the long term, Nairn thought, communities must prevail over traffic because the desire of humans to congregate is ineradicable.[5] In the long term, as we have seen, there may be other ways around this problem for those who can pay, methods of congregating without leaving home. In the short term, human needs are simply overridden by those of the car economy.

If, by some accident, community failed to sustain itself then it was easy to imagine an automobilist dystopia, which took a modernist, technophile utopia as its disguise:

> With the motor-car as the pre-eminent distress symbol in the forefront of every urban image, one is conditioned into thinking automatically in terms of grade-separated super highways looping and weaving and insinuating themselves in ever more complicated systems, catscradling between high rise buildings that contain thirty-seven storeys of helical ramped parking shelves to serve the top few floors of occupyable space. And for the week-end joy-ride by way of the expressway, onto the thruway, along the freeway to the turnpike, there will have to be designated in what is left of the natural landscape at the end of the parkway some of Frank Lloyd Wright's 'automobile objectives' with, of course, adequate parking facilities, drive-in entertainments, turning circles – and clear signposting to enable the intrepid excursionist to get back into the urban cage, making an easy transition from transistor to hi-fi. It would all go with pre-packaged, pre-digested food and those who prefer their jazz computer cool.[6]

Although the vision of a car-ridden future in this article by Raymond Spurrier must have been already clichéd, its absolutism was used to highlight the supposedly moderate recommendations of the Buchanan Report, 'Traffic in Towns', which suggested tailoring traffic planning to particular environments, matching road building or widening schemes to the existing urban fabric and its use.[7] The 'environmental capacity' for traffic of each particular road was to be judged against the crude maximum traffic flow it was capable of sustaining.[8] The car was not rejected but to be subject to the laws of detailed rational planning. In this the power of the automobile industry was explicitly recognized: 'The increasingly punitive and preventive anti-motor tactics of conventional planning theory threatened, in the end, to drive planners from our towns before they drove cars off the streets.'[9]

The 'little tin goddess' could even be used as a social instrument, encouraging people to move out of old, overcrowded city centres into new, planned settlements where access by private transport would be easier.[10] Of these two scenarios – an extreme vision of a sanitized and unbearable future, and a rational vision of a very British compromise – we have ended up with a bit of both: everyone can point to areas like the Westway in London, where a massive motorway raised on concrete slabs blights a broad swathe of the city and each day brings a tide of cars to a halt at the urban bottleneck which marks its conclusion. Common, too, are new towns and endless suburbs founded on the rule of the automobile. They are served by out-of-town hypermarkets and DIY stores which can be reached only by car, postmodern sheds faced in brick, with picturesque additions of clock towers mocking the past. Around them is laid the sanitized and deserted ornamentation of roundabouts, road-markings and signs, planting used as a barrier, and pedestrian-hostile areas. Surrounding these decorative features are the new housing estates themselves, which exhibit the same faux styles of the shopping hangars, and are equally based on the car, put down arbitrarily on any stretch of land, having no connection to past patterns of settlement and no reason for being there other than their proximity to a road and a store. Extremely tedious for those on foot, these places are sustained partly by the feeling that they are quieter and healthier than city centres, abandoned to the rule of the car and the dangerous poor, but also by the idea that it is easy to get away from them. So our current dystopian situation, a combination of modernist hubris and pragmatic compromise is both more boring and more objectionable than was thought possible in the sixties.

For supporters of urban modernism, the rule of the car would do far more than provide efficient personal transport. There was a great opportunity in the development of the visual apparatus that necessarily had to surround and regulate mass private transport, since it had to be highly functional and, in being so, it was also bound to be beautiful. The benighted taste of the British public would be enlightened by this ubiquitous display of modernist visual beauty gently forced upon it. There was a real hope that this new street furniture would 'restore a fair face to Britain as well as an even traffic flow'.[11] Road signs, for instance, a new standardized set of which was produced in 1963 conforming to conventions already in place on the Continent, were paradigms of modernist thinking. The new signs, claimed the Worboys Committee which designed them, would contribute to the 'reduction of road-side clutter'.[12] Simplicity was a functional imperative but it had the advantage of leading to the removal of popular, picturesque roadside kitsch. As Raymond Spurrier put it:

> It is not for the fun of it that shipping and flying have adopted measures that are aesthetically satisfying; crisp edges, clear colours, bold patterns, and unequivocal signals are vital in these more elemental modes of travel where there is so little room for error.[13]

As more cars filled the roads, so signs, lights and road markings would have to become rigorously functional. The drawings which accompanied Spurrier's article (and they are typical of those in the *Architectural Review*) are tightly linear and selectively but brightly coloured – with green grass and trees, and red, blue and green cars and signs. Here, roads are shown, lightly dotted with cars, gracefully cutting through the countryside, producing satisfying visual contrasts between curves and straight lines, complexity and simplicity, a veritable image of order and harmony.

In street furniture, function and form would be unified in utter economy. Traffic signs should be restricted to symbols without explanatory lettering so that the driver can register them with a cursory glance and without slowing down.[14] Since the red circle in itself stood for prohibition, if a sign also used a red bar through the symbol of, say, a bicycle this was unnecessarily to say the same thing twice over. While, during the education of the public, flexibility was needed, eventually these cancellation bars could be discarded 'in the interests of absolute simplicity'.[15] This is indeed the system we see every day.

Lettering, when necessary, is sparse with well-spaced and -proportioned characters in a sans-serif style and lower case. Symbols are minimal in form, stripped of all detail, reducing the particularities of the layout of the roads and their surroundings to a set of standard situations. Such things tend to be thought of as natural but are determined by a combination of ideology and practical considerations; when you cross into what was East Berlin, one of the first differences you notice is that the rigid, standardized stick figures of the pedestrian stop/go signs have been replaced by the representation of a squat little man in a hat, the green one striding forward with an amusing energy and character. In the apparatus of Western road systems, an absolutely instrumental relationship to the environment is encouraged, and this is particularly true of these signs, not only in their form but in their uniform and ubiquitous placement.

It was not just signs which were to serve as modernist paradigms. So too would the great, spare buildings necessary to house cars:

> Parking structures are terminals; like the great railway sheds of the nineteenth century, they are the points of interchange between two forms of movement – on one side the private motor car, on the other the pedestrian, public transport, lifts, escalators, moving pavements.[16]

Multi-storey car parks are part of an integrated planning of the urban fabric in which traffic and people should harmoniously coexist. The open decks of car parks, fortuitously demanded by their function, are also 'a necessary visual contrast' to the solidity of modern clad buildings with their uniformly opaque or reflective walls: 'Their open skeletal structure requires to be exploited consciously so that they both are, and appear to be, the termini of the open channels of the city that are used for movement.'[17]

In all this, as we have seen, nothing less than the aesthetic and civic education of the public was expected; by the segregation of pedestrian and motor vehicle, each would become an aesthetic spectacle for the delectation of the other. We have already considered the driver's experience through the utopian vision of Le Corbusier. For the pedestrian:

> A swinging curve designed for 30mph in a Ford Consul is meaningless to the pedestrian, unless drunk, but it is fun to watch from above – and

sometimes from below – if the pedestrian has his own separate complex of spaces – angular, irregular, surprising, contrasting.[18]

This segregation did not involve the surrender of traditional urban spaces but was rather an opportunity to make them anew. Even where radical new multi-level complexes were needed, stated the Buchanan Report, it will be possible:

> to re-create, in an even better form, the things that have delighted man for generations in towns – the snug, close, varied atmosphere, the narrow alleys, the contrasting open squares, the effects of light and shade, and the fountains and the sculpture [. . .].[19]

Now it is obvious that this delightful vision, in which British cities were to be endowed with the best of both worlds, fast private transport and lively pedestrian spaces, from which the inhabitants of each would look upon the other admiringly, has not come to pass. Urban traffic moves no faster than it did when it was drawn by horses, yet it invades every street from which it is not actively excluded, producing a ravaged and boring environment which is physically and mentally draining.

What happened to this uplifting vision of twentieth-century automobile monuments? The urban structures devoted to the car exemplify the failure of automobile culture. Multi-storey car parks, far from inspiring the affection produced by the grand architecture of Victorian railway stations, tend to be brutal, cheaply built places, whose leaky facades provide just enough cover for excretion, the writing of graffiti, vandalism and other practices best pursued out of sight. Although these structures are open to the air (so as not to suffocate their clientele) they can never free themselves from that acid, metallic tang which pervades them, which their concrete walls seem to have absorbed into their very fabric.

Likewise, street furniture and 'signage', when seen as an environmental whole, form, against the intention of their makers, a chaotic palimpsest, a jumble of old, new and (thanks to the carelessness of drivers) partially demolished, forever in competition with advertising and commercial signs. The extraordinary system of regulation which surrounds and protects the motorist and which in urban life is rarely absent from the visual field appears especially chaotic from the point of view of the pedestrian who does not have to look at these things instrumentally. When they show scenes shot in the street, old films, even those from the sixties, are endowed with a sparse, unfamiliar beauty, and it takes a little while to realize why: it is the absence of clusters of signs, numerous traffic lights, roundabouts, road-markings regulating lanes and parking, cat's eyes and speed cameras. Stripped of these encumbrances the streets and buildings, and even the space they partially enclose, attract our attention, and repay it, gaining in solidity and particularity. A similar beauty can be found today on roads which go nowhere useful and are unadorned with automobilist garbage. All others, however grand or quaint, are swamped, not just by the apparatus of motoring, but by noise and the moment-to-moment practical attention of those who need to navigate them.

The propagation and extension of a radical and thoroughgoing modernism in the psyches of individuals attached to their cars, which everyone pays a price for, is objectified in the environment of the city and the countryside. The apparatus that surrounds the car has its origins in the basic precepts of pure modernism, in which function would of itself produce beauty, and all the acrobatics of postmodernism have altered this not a jot. This is not hard to figure out: the realm of the most irrational transport system is regulated and salved by the most rational of means. Here, where issues of identity and the aesthetic come up against a real world, which is always threatening to break in upon them with fire and clashing steel, there is no room for intellectual games. After all, accidents, injuries and death, the planners tell themselves, cost money.

Cars are often taken to be very personal possessions and so it is not surprising that driving should raise some curious matters of identity. When drivers are set against each other on the road, then their identities tend to be fixed and hierarchical, bound up with foolish, minor distinctions, largely based upon the precise model of car they are inhabiting.[20] Breaking motorway etiquette, inadvertently or otherwise, can involve one in perilous high-speed games of brinkmanship. Yet, above all, the distinction is between those who are driving (not those who drive, note) and those who are not; between those who are armoured and those who are not, a matter which changes from moment to moment. Identities are certainly fluid in the matter of driving, but this is based not on subjectivity but on pure activity, a matter of thoroughly material modern forces. Drivers take on for a time the guise of hybrid beings who rarely show much tolerance for the softer objects which clutter their routes. Yet, after a while, they have to step out into the street. So while it is not surprising that cyclists are treated badly, since they are, after all, competitors for space on the roads, it is more curious that pedestrians are dealt with so disdainfully, that as soon as the victorious motorist steps from the vehicle, he or she instantly becomes a second-class citizen. Drivers are hybrid, bipolarized identities which reflect the wider splitting of the self under capital into more or less unwitting victims and victimizers. Even off the roads, the lessons of regulating cars are applied to people who are treated as traffic: channelled, confined and processed, in fast-food restaurants, service stations and theme parks.

If there is an element of role-playing in driving, then its affinity with computer games would seem to be the product of a mutual attraction. There are a great many home-computer driving simulations, while the arcades are full of such games involving seats which transmit vibrations and jolts, giant screens and even real car bodies. In the US learners are trained on simulators. The basis for this mutual attraction may be that the road journey is seen as a mini-narrative in which competition, power, obstacles, rules and an eventual destination all play a part. Like games, driving is governed by a set of rules, both those set by the government and those set by other drivers; while the former are generally honoured in the breach, the acceptable limits within which they may be broken are generally set by the latter. The mass production of standardized cars, road signs and traffic cones encourages us to see each element on the road as merely one of a type, composing a complex but somehow standard situation. After a time, all Mercedes drivers, for example, appear to behave the same. Each journey is a pilgrimage full of moral lessons, a microcosm of the journey of life, to which people bring their competitive instincts, unalloyed by bodily and personal modesty, armoured as they are with metal exoskeletons. Although in driving there is a destination but no plot, no graded succession of difficulties to be worked through, in recounting their journeys people often invent one. Most of all, they adopt a role, so that everybody comes to conform to a type: Douglas Browning argues that 'The automobile in the lives of many is a thoroughgoing tool within which the skinned body is absorbed and enjoyed for its functioning and in terms of which one plays at being a self.' Discussing the physical activity of driving, Browning also writes of the new phenomenon which it introduces of an ongoing adaptation to sudden events, of the constant need for fast reactions. Of course, this is also very much a feature of the computer game.[21] Driving prepares us for computer games, and vice versa.

As in games, there is also a great mismatch between the small, separate actions of the driver and their concomitant effects. For Baudrillard:

> Mobility without effort constitutes a kind of unreal happiness, a suspension of existence, an irresponsibility. Speed's effect, by integrating space and time, is one of levelling the world to two dimensions, to an image; it loses its depth and its becoming; in some ways it brings about a sublime immobility and a contemplative state. At more than a hundred miles an hour, there's a presumption of eternity.[22]

So when things go smoothly, the driver is rewarded with a momentary peace in which the span of the world is really shrunk to that of the windscreen. This is definitely the dream that the advertisers insist upon. Yet the world, usually in the form of other drivers, keeps slipping back in. Driving is often taken as an aggressive game of one-upmanship, yet it must be played within strict limits, the most burdensome being the sheer number of players. The mental effects of this exercise in frustration engender exaggerated effects of isolation, competition, instrumentalization and alienation from the body. On the empty road a certain stupidity is encouraged by the instant and effortless gratification of speed and manoeuvre: the disproportion between effort and result is like a gift. When one character from *Repo Man*, a film set in the industrial wastelands of Los Angeles, says: 'the more you drive the less intelligent you are',[23] he has hit on a peculiar truth. While it could be argued that driving makes one faster, brighter, more alert, fostering spatial and tactical judgement, it is its moment-to-moment aspect, matching the repetitive, disconnected actions of Benjamin's gambler, on which these (in any case, modest) skills are lavished. As in games, driving erases memory and, because of its very discontinuity, which there is a tendency to present as narrative, it creates a continuous present. Looking at the ranks of players in arcades, seated side by side in little car bodies, jerking their wheels frantically to avoid some virtual collision, jabbing at the pedals in order to travel nowhere, reveals something about actual behaviour on the roads, where arbitrary lane-swapping and sudden decisions to switch routes because for the next few yards there are no obstacles are so common. To travel is more important than to arrive. In a set of definitions about aspects of our contemporary era, J.G. Ballard puts the point prettily: '**Automobile** All the millions of cars on this planet are stationary, and their apparent motion constitutes mankind's greatest collective dream.'[24] In an odd sense the dominance of the car over our environment is so complete that this is true: cars stay put while the planet revolves around them.

What of the automobile aesthetics which compensates for this long list of depredations? We should try to look at the form of cars insofar as it is not determined by function and economy: their colour, internal styling, decoration and name-plates.

Once cars were strident and unashamed. They sported brash decorations and had aggressive, highly distinctive characters. They were proud of their expense and complexity. Especially in the United States, drivers stared over veritable fields of steel which announced their arrival, while behind them they trailed as much dense matter again. Styling in the fifties and sixties became so governed by fashion that technical matters and even the safety of a car's occupants were sacrificed to its imperatives.[25] These automobiles were prone to extensive damage even from minor accidents and for their size they were over-powered, under-braked and had undersized tyres – though these improved the overall look of the vehicle.[26] Ralph Nader recounts horrific stories of people meeting their deaths on non-functional fins and blade-like bonnet edges.[27] Even economy cars grew to vast dimensions because the manufacturers found that it was more profitable to sell large cars than small ones. The situation led S.I. Hayakawa to complain in 1958 that General Motors, Ford and Chrysler were staging 'an assault on consumer intelligence'.[28]

These cars were not mere road vehicles but in the imagination were transformed into aeroplanes or spaceships. The 1948 Cadillac was inspired by the form of the Lockheed P-38, a Second World War fighter plane, and car design in general aped the look of the plane with pointed noses, long sweeping bumpers, curved windshields, tailfins and, most of all, long, long bodies.[29] Elongated metal fins were often capped with chrome nozzles emitting red plastic flames as though the engines were jet-powered.[30] So the dream of cyberspace, of free flight, was played out for a time, for real, but on the flat of the road. The modernist ideal of uncongested movement, with no restrictions on speed, which may be achieved through the dematerialization of the transport system, was simulated by the upholstered insulation of the driver in a two-ton cage with over-soft suspension. Enthusiasts took even these massive vehicles and adorned them further, sometimes making them sleeker and smoother, sometimes more complex and baroque.[31] Writers like Tom Wolfe assembled texts which matched the hot-rodders' turbo-charged creations (though in his constant references to moribund high art Wolfe was always concerned to show that he celebrated this stuff out of choice, not ignorance, and a snobbish irony is generally lurking behind the overheated prose). Wolfe described the activities of the customizers as sculpture. They eliminated decoration to emphasize pure curvilinear form, lowering bodies between the wheels, lowering roofs, raising fins, and creating shapes with a unitary sense of movement. This led Wolfe to compare their work with that of Brancusi. Of one of George Barris's creations:

> there is an incredible object he built called the XPAK-400 air car. The customizers love all that X jazz. It runs on a cushion of air, which is beside the point, because it is a pure piece of curvilinear abstract sculpture. If Brancusi is any good, then this thing belongs on a pedestal too. There is not a straight line in it, and only one true circle, and those countless planes, and tremendous baroque fins, and yet all in all it's a rigid little piece of solid geometrical harmony.[32]

Another 'utterly baroque' designer's car is described as 'a very Rabelaisian *tour de force*'.[33] Wolfe brings the baroque and the modern into close contact, and despite the loose vocabulary he had a point, for these enthusiasts were carrying the rationalist techniques of engineering to such extremes that the results went well beyond the reasonable. The interesting point is that in the early sixties car manufacturers were funding this activity, taking advice from the customizers and utilizing their ideas in standard mass-produced cars. This is a little difficult to conceive of today.

Compared to these strident creations, contemporary cars have a modest persona, and indeed they have much to be modest about. A particular aesthetic governs their look today, one which is so uniform that almost every car aspires to it, and those that fall short tend to do so only on grounds of economy. The age of the 'individual', mass-produced car, made at a time of glut, appears to have passed; in this age of restriction, buying and running a car, while ever more necessary, has also become so obviously irrational that every financial detail from fuel consumption to insurance costs must be rationally weighed. The irrationalism of the total situation is masked, and slightly mitigated, by an extreme rationalism of its details. Yet once these practical matters are decided, they are then used to form the basis of something aesthetic and affective: aerodynamics, for instance, becomes about far more than fuel economy. The mind is eased by the outward signs of a rationalism which has become aesthetic.

Yet this aesthetic, because it poses as functionalism, is very nearly invisible. This lack of visibility is compounded by other factors: the aesthetic disappears behind the tiny, snobbish distinctions which remain, and which so many people are fixated on, and at the same time it has become so ubiquitous that it takes on the aspect of nature. Furthermore, advertisers, as opposed to manufacturers, still try to imbue these pallid forms with personality – and do in fact succeed in giving them a standardized, mass-produced one. All this is not to say that built-in obsolescence (a matter of durability, reliability and the marketing of parts, but also prominently of style, what indeed from the manufacturers' point of view styling was all about) has fallen out of fashion. This planned obsolescence, first manufactured in automobiles by Alfred P. Sloan, Jr of General Motors as a response to a market increasingly saturated with standardized Fords, is still current but its signs have shrunk, as have the cars themselves, to become discreet little metal numbers on the boot, which can only be read by other drivers when they are close enough to decide whether to overtake. These are discreet signs of distinction which must not ruin by adornment the image of technological efficiency.

Can we find in this aesthetic, in its baroque roots, and even in the undercurrents of its present form, the secret of its irrationality? Let us look briefly at some specific features:

The car as monad: all outer elements are excluded: noise, air and temperature. Vision is flattened on the screen. Music or radio chatter contributes to creating an apparently autonomous micro-climate. Solo driving, ever more prevalent, cuts the driver off from human interaction and regulation, making of car and occupant a melded, hybrid creature. Any assault on the car, intentional or not, is likely to be treated as an assault on the person.[34] In the monad of the car the bourgeois dream of personal autonomy is partially realized; the more the outer world is excluded, the more this dream seems to be realized.

The car as exoskeleton: a locked cage of impact bars surrounds the driver, excluding threatening elements of the outer world, whether persons or objects. The structural cage is hidden, but then is made to appear in signs upon the surface, of solidity and robustness. Drivers are held snugly in place by a belt, and confined by the various controls which are designed around the body, most evidently the steering column on which in an accident they will be impaled. The automobile is a suit of armour and a trap. The more drivers are made to feel safe within it – by the metal frame about them, the belt, the exclusion of the elements, an airbag perhaps – the more risks they are prepared to take: the apparent safety of the driver has a cost which is exacted from the bodies of unprotected pedestrians and cyclists.

Aerodynamics: in the advertiser's dream, the aerodynamic body of the car slips through the environment without contact or disturbance. All parts are fitted flush with the body, indicating their separateness only with the barest of lines, as though nothing about the car is modular, but rather each element is bound together in an organic unity. The glossy paintwork throws back the world like a mirror. In advertisements the glacis of the bodywork appears utterly clean, untouched by the elements, and this is vital to maintaining the distinction between the monad of the car itself and the environment through which it moves. Hence the offence of obviously filthy cars on the street, which quickly attract admonitory graffiti. In advertisements the landscapes through which the car travels (often wildernesses) appear as backdrops, a little less real than the venerated object in the foreground. Since to present the car as natural would be too blatant a lie, nature and technological culture are reconciled by a false separation.

Grille: cars used to grin unashamedly, showing a set of chrome teeth and a glimpse of their innards, giving an idea of the flow of elements across and in their organs, of their inhalation and tainted exhalation.[35] In one road safety advertisement, children were shown these grilles become monstrous mouths, growling at pedestrians. Newer cars are more modest, reducing the size of the aperture, tucking it discreetly down among their black undersides, or shielding it entirely with steel lips. Such cars encase their combustive inner parts as far as possible in a single frame, marrying the passenger compartment and engine housing, as if they were really one, and putting the driving mechanism tidily out of sight and mind.

Demarcation: two narrow bands run around most car bodies. The upper, more prominent one is formed of metal or chrome or sometimes a touch of primary colour, sometimes recessed, sometimes standing slightly proud of the panels; the lower one is a vestigial memory of the running board. The upper line runs about the centre of the body like a plimsoll line, as though the car had been transported briefly from its customary mode of travel to another element, water or air, which has left its mark. The lower, which we hardly see as a line at all, marks the coloured body from the underside, generally painted black. There is no way to keep this area from becoming filthy from the detritus of the road, so it must be dark and recessed, easy to ignore or dismiss as not quite part of the car.

The modern car becomes an expression of the mass-produced personality. People identify with specific makes as being suited to them, or can even say that their car does not suit them.[36] The individuation of models, customization, or the creation merely of a personal environment within the car, all mask from the driver their collective presence as herd animals when seen from the outside. The apparent character a car takes on and the physical alterations it undergoes in prolonged ownership are somehow like that of clothing; it acquires an air, particular patterns of wear, an accumulation of detritus – or not, which is equally telling. Being invited into a car (at least into the front seat) is in itself an experience of slight intimacy; something which Ballard has again explored, this time to perverse extremes, simply by taking the evident cultural connection between automobiles and sexuality literally. Yet even this matter is only part of a wider condition, in which people bored with everyday life find their personalities only in driving. The narrator of *Crash*:

> At the traffic lights I looked across the seat at Catherine. She sat with one hand on the window-sill. The colours of her face and arms revealed themselves in their clearest and richest forms, as if each blood cell and pigment granule, the cartilages of her face, were real for the first time, assembled by the movement of this car.[37]

Many other aspects could be analysed, from the metallic paint in colours which do not quite have the courage to be forthright, to the uniformity of plastic facias and the decoration of hub caps. In all these features there is a calm, rationalist modernism to automobile aesthetics which is utterly deceptive. On the instrument panel everything is placidly marked out with regular precision, the standard intervals on the dials, the digital displays; just as Le Corbusier would have recommended (he enthused over the instrument panels of planes) all is in its place. The even pace of modern engines and the smoothness of the ride, the insulation of the driver from the outside temperature, from noise, from the rushing of the air, the display of the world on the screen, all contribute to this air of rational tranquillity. Yet, as anyone who has stepped into a car after a period of defamiliarization knows, driving is a game of high-speed chicken, of jostling in little metal boxes – each an incendiary bomb personally tailored for its occupants – of hurtling towards one another at combined speeds of over a hundred miles an hour. If accidents happen, well, as Kurt Vonnegut would say, so it goes – we can hardly be surprised.

To this enclosed aesthetic there is an underside of mortality, contingency, dirt, pollution and fire. The contrast between the squeaky-clean form of the car and the degraded environment about it produces this effect: although the car is largely responsible for the filth of its surroundings, it emerges transformed as the only clean, reliable, protecting, even beautiful object in a soiled and dangerous outdoor world. One advertisement asks: 'How do you protect yourself out on the streets?' and then of course proposes the armoured body of its product as the answer.[38]

Furthermore, the car isolates drivers from this degraded environment, by cutting them off from it physically and ensuring that they have little attention to pay to sightseeing. The urban environment then becomes largely imaginary for the driver, constructed from glimpses through a screen during moments of distraction from the insistent task of motoring, rather as television tends to put together a clichéd view of some situation by serving up a collage of instantly recognizable scenes. These glimpses, torn from the fabric of time and context, may easily come to stand as evidence for the standard horror stories recounted in the mass media.

By far the most pernicious social consequence of the car is not effected on those driving, however, but on those not. Cars sweep along thoroughfares which are not merely routes to somewhere else but an essential area of social space. As long as attempts to control drivers' behaviour are confined to (totally ineffectual) exhortations to slow down, watch that child and so on, then this space is made unusable for social interaction, except for the very resilient, or those with no alternatives. Traffic is only one part of a set of attitudes, events and technologies which have led to the breakdown of shared social space. Private telephones, televisions and even washing machines confine people to the home or help forge connections with those outside the area. Cars are perhaps, however, the single most important factor in this fragmentation of local communities, because they alone destroy the street as a place for gathering and produce individualized mobility, so that people can shop in one area, work in another, live in yet another, and pursue a solipsistic existence in each.

As it is said of banging your head against the wall, so with living among traffic: it's nice when you stop. Most people have had the experience of walking by a busy road when that rare moment occurs and suddenly there is no traffic; the noise ceases, and another world is briefly revealed, of space, of air moving the trees, perhaps of bird song. Most of all it is a time when you can listen to yourself. Then after a second or so, a lone car appears in the distance, an outrider for others, and it starts again. The effect of traffic noise is to serve as another ally in the assault on our senses, an auditory adjunct to the advertisers' aim never to allow us any peace, even in our dreams.

So going somewhere where there is very little motor traffic can be a revelation, even when this lack is not so much planned but produced by economic strangulation. There are few places where a major city can be experienced without the assaults of the internal combustion engine, but Cuba is one. Lying awake listening to the sounds of Havana, you have the impression of being in a vast dormitory. Only an occasional engine masks the tapestry of sound woven near and far of peoples' voices and animals' cries. While in most cities the life of the place is blanketed out by the monotonous drone of traffic, here the complex spaces seem alive with incident. The remarks of your neighbours are distinct. Crowing cockerels wake you in the morning, and in the soft light you can feel the city stretch. At night artificial light is scarce. The city has a protective darkness thrown over it, lifted in some areas only by candles and oil lamps from open windows, in others by occasional electric lamps which dramatically highlight some crumbling column or portico, while throwing the area around it into a more profound darkness. Walking down the centre of these streets, it is the people and particular sounds that seize the attention against a background of deep silence.

Daylight reveals a disintegrating city of grand colonial palaces and mansions, impressive in scale and detail, inherited by the poor, who now live in a chaotic and ramshackle splendour. Each doorway is a porch and each workplace is open to the gaze. People treat the street as their home, and it returns their intimacy and warmth. Children wander freely and without fear. They play hide-and-seek in and out of the doorways, or around skips and giant 1950s cars beached on the kerb; or they career down the streets on makeshift go-carts. Even hardships are remade as virtues by these people; petrol shortages have led to the rule of the bicycle, each one precariously carrying two or three people over potholes and obstructions, their warning bells rung assiduously.

Cuba's strong sense of community life is of course based on many other factors besides the lack of motor traffic. Nevertheless it is important that here streets are no longer merely roads, where people pass but do not stop and where no one can afford distraction (on pain of death), but rather a common ground on to which homes exit, a place owned and used by people. In surrendering this to the car, we have unwittingly given up a precious asset, owned by no one and everyone, and in doing so have altered every facet of our lives.

Driving's huge costs are sustained by a still triumphant modernism of smooth speed and fast acceleration, by the even vibration of an engine running efficiently. Yet in masking a situation of utter irrationality, this is a modernism which has come far from its once radical roots. It has become hollow, a mere sign of itself and of reason. This modernism alive, if not well, is paraded everywhere under our noses, invading, indeed, all our senses, and driving out tranquillity. If this is largely ignored as a cultural fact, it is only an illustration of the immense power of the road lobby and the wilful blindness of intellectual apologists for the current culture. Yet, despite this power, there are signs of resistance, especially among the young, whose broad understanding of green issues has opened their eyes to the absolute rule of the automobile: in London some thousands of them have sometimes ventured on to high streets, now major roads, and over a few hours reclaimed them for music, dancing, relaxing and chatting. Such action is a break in the weather, a sign that the cultural hegemony of automobile aesthetics has begun to crack.

In many areas the rule of the automobile is exercised so absolutely that ordinary people are swept from the streets. When the urban fabric is cut into parcels of land bounded by lethal barriers many places become islands, losing all customary life and falling into abandonment. Yet there are people who still frequent them, those with nowhere much to go or much to do, the young, the homeless and the poor. As we shall see in the next chapter, they have often made in these areas their own particular kind of art. These places, no man's land, dangerous to get to and sometimes dangerous to explore, where the low noise of traffic is always in the air and acrid pollution always in the nostrils, are often home to rusting automobile hulks, in ruins but still very much themselves, the stuff of nostalgic legends. In old East Berlin and along the stretches of land where the Wall used to run, people have made sculptures from old cars or used the cavities of their bodies for planting flowers. In one place three armoured cars, covered in graffiti, have been stacked into a triumphal arch; in another, cars are returned to the earth from which they sprang. Long outlasting their owners, they still sport their old aggressive forms and their decorative protuberances on which human flesh was so often sacrificed. These sculptural assemblages, where cars find their proper place, may prefigure a time when the automobile age has passed, when monuments may be raised to the millions who perished, directly or indirectly, at its steel hands. But this is to assume that we survive it at all.

NOTES

1. Thomas Pynchon, *V. A Novel*, Philadelphia 1961, p. 383.
2. For an analysis of advertisers' influence over the media, see Ben H. Bagdikian, *The Media Monopoly*, 4th edition, Boston 1992. The book includes accounts of the influence of large automobile manufacturers.
3. Le Corbusier, *The City of Tomorrow and its Planning*, trans. Frederick Etchells, London 1971, p. 177.
4. Henryk Blachnicki and Kenneth Browne, 'Over and Under. A Survey of Pedestrian/Vehicle Separation', *The Architectural Review*, vol. 129, no. 771, May 1961, p. 321.
5. Ian Nairn, 'The Mindless Masters', *The Architectural Review*, vol. 127, no. 758, April 1960, pp. 229, 231.
6. Raymond Spurrier, 'The Urban Choice. The Architectural Implications of the Buchanan Report', *The Architectural Review*, vol. 135, no. 807, May 1964, p. 355.
7. The Buchanan Report was commissioned by the Minister of Transport and published by HMSO in November 1963.
8. Anon., 'The Environmental Street', *The Architectural Review*, vol. 135, no. 807, May 1964, p. 319.
9. Ibid., p. 320.
10. Spurrier, 'The Urban Choice', p. 357.
11. Spurrier, 'Road-Style on the Motorway', *The Architectural Review*, vol. 128, no. 766, December 1960, p. 408.
12. Anon., 'Traffic Signs', *The Architectural Review*, vol. 134, no. 798, August 1963, p. 84.
13. Spurrier, 'Road-Style', p. 408.
14. Anon., 'Traffic Signs', p. 83.
15. Ibid., p. 84.
16. Michael Brawne, 'Parking Terminals', *The Architectural Review*, vol. 128, no. 762, August 1960, p. 125.
17. Ibid., p. 134.
18. Blachnicki and Browne, 'Over and Under', pp. 321–2.
19. Cited by Spurrier, 'The Urban Choice', p. 355.

20. See Martin Parr and Nicholas Barker, *From A to B. Tales of Modern Motoring*, London 1994.

21. Douglas Browning, 'Some Meanings of Automobiles', in Larry A. Hickman, ed., *Technology as a Human Affair*, New York 1990, pp. 172–7.

22. Jean Baudrillard, *Le système des objets*, Paris 1968, p. 94; cited in English in Kristin Ross, *Fast Cars, Clean Bodies. Decolonization and the Reordering of French Culture*, Cambridge, Mass. 1995, p. 21.

23. Cited in Jon Lewis, 'Punks in L.A.: It's Kiss or Kill', *Journal of Popular Culture*, vol. 22, no. 2, Fall 1988, p. 91.

24. J.G. Ballard, 'Project for a Glossary of the Twentieth Century', in Jonathan Crary and Sandford Kwinter, eds, *Zone 6*, New York 1992, p. 275.

25. See James J. Flink, *The Automobile Age*, Cambridge, Mass. 1988, pp. 286, 290, and also Ralph Nader's justly celebrated book, *Unsafe at Any Speed. The Designed-in Danger of the American Automobile*, New York 1965, chapter 6, 'The Stylists'.

26. James J. Flink, *The Car Culture*, Cambridge, Mass. 1975, p. 196.

27. Nader, *Unsafe at Any Speed*, ch. 6.

28. Cited in Flink, *Car Culture*, p. 194.

29. Flink, *The Automobile Age*, p. 286f. See also Alan Hess, 'Styling the Strip. Cars and Roadside Design in the 1950s', in Martin Wachs and Margaret Crawford, eds, *The Car and the City. The Automobile, the Built Environment and Daily Urban Life*, Ann Arbor 1992, pp. 176–7.

30. See Hess, 'Styling the Strip', p. 177.

31. Early modifications to production cars were generally to do with making them more efficient; in America in the fifties enthusiasts turned to making aesthetic improvements, removing manufacturers' decorations and accentuating smooth lines. See J.T. Borhek, 'Rods, Choppers, and Restorations: the Modification and Re-creation of Production Motor Vehicles in America', *Journal of Popular Culture*, vol. 22, no. 4, Spring 1989, p. 100–1.

32. Tom Wolfe, *The Kandy-Kolored Tangerine-Flake Streamline Baby*, London 1981 (first edition 1966), p. 73.

33. Ibid., p. 85.

34. See Donald D. Hook, 'American and German Driving Habits', *Journal of Popular Culture*, vol. 19, no. 1, Summer 1985, p. 93.

35. Hess describes the Cadillacs of the fifties with their 'air scoops full of clenched teeth'. 'Styling the Strip', p. 177.

36. There are various expression of this in Parr and Barker, *From A to B*. The clearest runs: 'The sooner we get rid of this Mercedes the better. It's too smooth. I think we're more of a rough and ready family. We don't suit this car at all.'

37. J.G. Ballard, *Crash*, London 1985 (first edition 1975), p. 161.

38. Advert for the Fiat Punto, 1995.

6

ADVERTISING THE INVISIBLE

Sometimes it is argued that the illegal actions of graffiti writers, and the vandals with whom they are often associated, are merely a reflection of the wider criminality of planners and speculators who have divided the urban landscape with roads and built inappropriate structures upon the ruins of old communities; who have, in short, always valued immediate commercial gain over every other consideration. Yet the notion that graffiti is a critical comment on the urban environment is extremely ambiguous because sometimes this writing is taken as a form of decoration, of improvement to the alien forms left by speculation, and sometimes it is seen as a further desecration.[1]

In any case, such ideas do not explain the extraordinary prevalence of graffiti. It can hardly be just an urban matter when every village bus stop is so adorned. Graffiti takes many forms which might be seen as a continuum spanning the age-old marking of names, witticisms and scatological messages on walls to organized crews of artists who travel internationally making large-scale, multi-coloured, sophisticated 'pieces'.[2] Between these extremes, there are a great many young writers, working with indelible markers or spraycans to distribute their adopted names as widely and as prominently as possible. While the actions of the crews may be affected by being briefly courted by the art world, or by successful municipal operations against the painting of trains,[3] the broader phenomenon of graffiti, ever prevalent, goes on regardless. Now this very ubiquity makes it

hard to avoid comparison with that other distributor of names, large
and small, in public places and private – advertising. Wherever one
looks, from small object to large, on walls, vehicles, T-shirts, carrier-
bags, pens or pencils, even on dirigibles in the sky, always there are
names and logos. Graffiti and advertising appear to aspire to the
same universal distribution.

Graffiti is made up overwhelmingly of names. The signature of the
individual artist or crew is inflated to become the work itself. Just as
the repetition of some phrase, usually the title, in pop music serves as
an advertisement for the song,[4] so in graffiti there is no distinction
between the advertisement and what is advertised. Graffiti copies the
action of branding and advertising, not only in its insistent repetition
of the name but also in its prominent placement; in the hinterlands
bordering railway tracks, on high buildings and bridges, and around
major roads. In London the broad pillars of raised motorways, in
Westbourne Grove for example, are prime graffiti sites. Although
style and ubiquity are both essential components of graffiti writers'
fame among their peers, ubiquity is the more important.[5] Size, prom-
inence and wide distribution are the basis of the graffiti hierarchy: the
celebrated graffiti writer's tag 'Seen' was exceptionally well chosen,[6]
while 'Hear', whose name is prominent around Paddington station, is
only slightly less literal. As the civilized and populous areas of the city
are comprehensively defaced by the official graffiti writers of advertising, so dangerous and abandoned areas are left to their unofficial
cousins. The identification is strong and conscious: graffiti artists
often take famous brand names as their tags, and having developed
their own style will insist on its originality – often by attaching a © sign,
or ending the name with the letters 'Inc.'. Such writing is a hybrid
practice: like companies, graffiti artists and crews take on corporate
identities behind a brand name; like artists, they sign their works,
signing a signature in effect, and often date them too, sometimes
using Roman numerals as if on memorial plaques.

Graffiti writers' tags generally have little content, or a minimal one,
no more than an allusion, a pun, or a flavour of something, and present themselves, like brand names, as pure presence. The intention in
both advertising and graffiti is to make what is written and how it is
written into an inseparable, organic unit. Unlike brand names, graffiti
is unattached to anything other than the pure renown of the name,

and (often at some remove, for the few in the know) the writer. Graffiti and brand names both buy into the dream of a primordial, undivided language within which 'there would be no knowledge, no infancy, no history', and in which the writer, 'would already be directly one with his linguistic nature and would nowhere find any discontinuity or difference where any history or knowledge might be produced'.[7] In the case of brand names, this unity is employed only for the utilitarian task of manufacturing product loyalty and sales; in the case of graffiti it is much closer to the ideal to which it pretends, for, while the local aim may be a matter of prestige among a small number of peers, the effect upon the environment as a whole is much greater. This is an art which selflessly displays itself before friends and strangers alike. Despite this, the utopian moment of the wish for a direct, natural language has long since evaporated: it is no longer some Edenic bliss but rather the vacant state advertisers encourage in their targets, where neither knowledge nor memory may interrupt the buying mood. Advertising sets out to encourage this vacancy with great calculation, and graffiti, in copying its forms, might appear to do the same; however, graffiti's relationship to the environment is much more intimate than that of the advertisement, and while graffiti might aspire to commercial propaganda's autonomy from its surroundings, its constant failure to achieve this renders it radical.

Despite its claims to organic unity, there is little that is intrinsic to the brand name. We could easily imagine that the Coca-Cola logo might have been written in some modern, sans-serif fashion; as it is, the affective qualities arbitrarily attached to its unchanging, cursive forms have altered greatly over the years according to various marketing strategies. If the form of the successful brand name persists, it is because its greatest assets are its familiarity, repetition and ubiquity: on to this any kind of positive quality may later be attached. The same is oddly true of graffiti, whose practitioners lay great stress on the style, originality and the quality of lettering, but generally have little to say about the different merits of the particulars of different styles. The most important matter, with both graffiti and advertising, is that it is distinct and that it is there.

In its attempt to create a unity of form and meaning, advertising is condemned to constant failure, if only because it is only allowed to say one thing. Indeed, since it must forever repeat that something is good but must find a great variety of means to do so, it produces a complete disjunction between content and expression. In the quest for novelty all sorts of arbitrary links are made between product, word and image which are, however, then falsely presented as integral and organic, so corrupting the meaning of language and imagery together. While there is plenty of other writing and visual imagery which does this, in its imperialistic directive to appropriate all styles and to be present everywhere, advertising is especially pernicious. Advertisements hope to establish a symbolic relation between their brand names and their products, so that the two find an organic unity in the minds of the public. Even successful and persistent brand names and logos, which might appear to have earned this status eternally, have to remake it constantly for fickle and resistant consumers, and in the wake of ever-changing fashion. Allegorical emblems, the arbitrary coupling of a combination of word and image with a meaning, are the typical result. Since the association of name, picture and product must be striking enough to impose itself on the attention, ever more remote charac-teristics of the signifying objects have to be exploited as the mill of fashion grinds on. Its emblems must be provocative and startling, for-ever needing 'fresh infusions of ingenuity'.[8] Failure of reference threatens as meaning collapses under the weight and number of asso-ciations. If the system as a whole continues to function, we might see seeds of its decline in the attitudes of different groups of individuals: think of how the very young and the very old relate to adverts – the former with great interest, joy even, in their novelty and invention; the latter, freighted with memory and with an exponentially exploding number of old and new associations, with irony, weariness and even-tually a defensive confusion.

Every sliver of meaning, or of marketable radicalism, is seized on in an attempt to exploit its spark of authenticity before it is extinguished, in an effort to let some reflection of its glimmer fall on some product. Sometimes it appears as if each hint of originality, even in the moment of its creation, is swiftly settled into a weary, money-spinning domestication. Some advertising in the eighties, responding to such worries no doubt, began to pose as an autonomous cultural product, presenting itself as an art form and awarding its executive teams prizes for creativity. This was only another way of distinguishing itself from more vulgar publicists, a supplementary tactic for grabbing attention and diverting criticism from the parasitic nature of the industry. Graffiti, by contrast, could aspire to the condition of an autonomous discipline, for at least outside the immediate circle of artists and admirers, the name advertises nothing but itself. Writers tend to justify their activities as art, claiming something of its autonomy. Yet even this fails, for people, accustomed to advertisements, want to read messages into graffiti; it cannot avoid its literally material basis, its interaction with an environment and other writing, all of which impart to it, whether it is willing or not, a strong social connotation.

In branding, whereby a product or company is identified with a particular condensed sign or set of words, there is an inherent reduction of process and action to a static, enclosed form which is supposed to be immediately understood, and hopefully associated with nothing other than a positive but essentially empty image. The brand name is designed to exclude a number of important considerations: the idea that anybody actually makes the product with which it is connected, that calculations are constantly made about its design, pricing and marketing, that resources are needed to fabricate it, that it has links with other products and competes with them, and that it is subject to constant action and change. The branded product aspires to become a vacuous constant in an otherwise fluid world.

Similarly, in graffiti identity is a progressively disappearing point, discarding all qualities behind the mask of the sign. Since individuality and its expression in pure differentiation are valued in themselves, all particular attributes of the individual drain away. In this light, the way crews and solo writers present themselves as administrative bodies is no accident. Susan Stewart has argued that 'graffiti promises and indeed depends upon a dream of the individualised masses. It has borrowed from the repetitions of advertising and commercial culture an anti-epitaph: the name's frequent appearance marks the stubborn ghost of individuality and intention in the mass culture, the ironic re-statement of the artist as "brand name".'[9] Sometimes, it is true, the links between graffiti and advertising are recognized in a deliberately ironic fashion; for instance in the way some writers have taken on brand names or company names in order to subvert them – Seen's crew was called 'United Artists'. Yet there is more than mere irony here. Rather there is an identification with the power and the allure of brand names, with commodities themselves finally, which the writers hope will accrue to themselves. As we shall see, this can be seen in the very form of the lettering. Graffiti points towards a secret about identity under capital – the sacrifice of human qualities for renown and tradeability.

For both graffiti and advertising the context and environment in which they are seen have the power to alter the content of their writing. For advertisers this is always a danger and they often seek to place their signs well above the contingent fray of the street, and distinguish them with frames and floodlighting. Adverts rarely become palimpsests, and certainly not when they are properly maintained. Rather they present themselves as discrete events which interrupt the environmental fabric, standing apart because of their size, writing, colour and subject matter. They aspire to control their immediate area, acting as framed points of interest in an otherwise mundane setting.

Generally the aspiration of the more complex graffiti forms is to be similarly distinct and even transcendent, to provide some piece of coloured cursive fluency which will stand out from the general setting of brick and concrete, a panel of brightness and beauty against the filth. Graffiti styles are international, and while there are certainly plenty of local variations, common features can be identified across much writing. Bold designs using large areas of flat colour may be to an extent forced on writers by factors of time and the number of cans they can carry, but they are also often desired in themselves. When spray paint is used and it is not just a single line, graffiti, at its simplest, is merely an outline filled with colour. Lines are usually extremely sharp, emphasizing the form of letters and marking them out against the background. A reversal of the tones of the body of the letters and the line bordering them is common, often black bordering white or vice versa. The idea is to eliminate the surface by creating a form of lettering strong enough to prise itself away from its material base. Certain combinations of colours can make one seem to float free of the other, and graffiti artists are adept at exploiting these contrasts to achieve this spatial separation. The less subtle commonly use gold or silver paint, which outdoors catches the light in different and changing ways from matte paint, to the same purpose. In more elaborate pieces, shadows may be drawn 'behind' the writing, or the letters drawn as if they had three-dimensional form, or backgrounds (often clouds) added, again separating it from the surface.

Letters are often made more attractive by the addition of little stars to their corners as though they were glinting in the light, or with highlights across the top of some curve, as though the letter's glossy surface was shining. The aspiration is to emulate the brilliance of commercial display, of objects and names which glow and glisten within adverts. Furthermore, the forms of graffiti letters tend to be extremely dynamic, the sense of movement inherent in the forms being accentuated by arrows and lines of force thrown off from the main body of the inscription. In cultivating this glossy dynamism, graffiti seems founded on film and television titles, especially perhaps on corporate logos which, at the start of the credits to a film, shoot out fast from the screen to arrange their slick, carefully styled letters before the viewer.

Yet always there are elements which work against this striving to eliminate context. Aspirations to immateriality and a transcendent floating in space are generally denied by the material surface of the wall, incident, weathering and the actions of other writers. New graffiti is regularly written over old out of a sense of competition, or just because suitable sites have been exhausted. Ghosts of older writing and pictures slowly emerge from beneath the surface of new graffiti, while, in overwriting, the prominent forms of the latest layer use the older ones as mere background from which to distinguish themselves. Despite the aspiration of the writers to make sharp edges, spraycans always produce a soft scattered aura of stray paint, and this can be seen when the image is looked at closely, tying lines to their background. Due to weathering, pollution, or the state of the wall itself, the paint or even the very surface on which it is written, starts to lift away from the wall. When pieces break away the illusion of graffiti lettering is revealed in the most brutal way. Above all, graffiti is always at the mercy of its environment; written over bricks, or metal rivets, or over doors, it takes their material into itself; forever present day and night under sunshine or street lighting, it may drastically change its character. It forms a part of a scene, where the grillework of fences, dilapidated buildings, posters or passing cars may all comment on the work, as it comments on them. All these matters bind graffiti to its specific place, despite its aspiration to high-art autonomy or at least the advertising hoarding.

These are the very effects which make graffiti a radical intervention in the environment. The most common experience of graffiti is not of pristine multi-coloured murals, but of scumbled, partially effaced, overlapping letters, of layers of overwriting which have become a complex tangle of indistinguishable lines. Indeed, graffiti seems least itself on official sites where writers have been left at their leisure to make complex pieces on uninterrupted surfaces.[10] It is in the extreme complexity of overwriting that graffiti finds its full significance, in works which are collective by default, with their extraordinary blending of lines and colours that become entirely non-instrumental, abstract paintings. This is not to say that they lack meaning; they are a reaction to branding and advertising, a response akin to interference; they break up the well-marked divisions between walls and hoardings, the bare and the adorned, between that which advertises something and that which advertises only itself, and between different kinds of property.

So when taken together as a collective phenomenon in a particular place, graffiti exceeds the condition of the brand name. Unlike the utterly finished form of commercial imagery on which no trace of process remains, graffiti is always at least the record of its own making. Despite its aspiration to a writing which unifies form and content, large graffiti pieces, unlike advertising, are replete with narrative content, if only because of the difficulties involved in putting them in place. Writers sometimes directly refer to this with little inscriptions in the form of apologies for botched work: 'Too late, too tired'.[11] Sometimes graffiti artists take the opportunity the context provides: their writing may be adapted to comment on or adorn a particular local feature. Their art is given added weight by the material of its support, in what can come to emulate effects of modernist painting and collage. When seen as a palimpsest, against the often neglected environment, graffiti bears the trace of history, of a narrative, of many individual actions and, more broadly, the tale of a building or an area. Of course that work which does not restrict itself to names can tell us of more specific things; of rivalry, love, sex and crime. Local territories may be marked out by names and styles; the police are assiduous readers of graffiti. Collectively, then, graffiti appears as a moral tale, and everyone is anxious to read lessons into it, as they are into any form of name: morals of a degraded urban environment, of radical, spontaneous and creative youth, of popular decoration, or of a benighted underclass governed by crude and dangerous pleasures.

As simple graffiti aspires to the condition of the brand name, so more complicated works often include figures or cars which, in conjunction with the lettering, build up elaborate scenes reminiscent of film posters. Some exciting scenario is shown, but we are unaware of the narrative details, as though these were highly condensed adverts for lives unspoken for. Characters and lettering are often allied in graffiti, where caricatural figures may introduce or draw attention to letters, or flank a piece of writing like decorative statues about a doorway. Figures may even stand in place of letters. These characters, often taken from commercial products, comics or cartoons, are certainly allegorical personifications, participating in the 'branding' of the name. They might be gang-members, partially clad women, cops, graffiti writers themselves or animated spraycans. In all cases, they are very much themselves. The inclusion of these unintegrated characters, so suggestive of narrative, into graffiti is in itself a strong indication of its failure to produce the desired unity between content and form. Instead, like advertising, it emits allegory as a byproduct, like radiation from a decaying particle. Benjamin wrote of script:

> In the context of allegory the image is only a signature, only the monogram of an essence, not the essence itself in a mask. But there is nothing subordinate about written script; it is not cast away in reading, like dross. It is absorbed along with what is read, as its 'pattern'.[12]

Graffiti fails as symbol because of the mismatch between real identities and the tags which are supposed to stand in for them but end up only representing themselves. The temporary adoption of an identity by a writer is sometimes signalled by script of the form, 'Frankie as the Monster'.[13] The identities which writers take on must be partially dehumanized in order to be present as script or caricature which is not cast away in reading. Lastly, it fails because the public generally reads graffiti as a collective, homogeneous whole: perhaps as meaningless, or as vandalism, as symptom, rarely on the terms of the writers.

Graffiti is, however, a consciously oppositional art. It is a 'criminal' act, made in defiance of commercial and governmental authorities. Artists take considerable personal risks in dedicating their gifts to the public. Subway writers in New York and elsewhere risk not only electrocution and being hit by trains but also the violence of the police. Graffiti artists everywhere accept, at the very least, the dangers of trespass and the possibility of arrest. As one New York graffiti crew puts it (writing in the first person):

> To me, the essence of Graffiti is working hard, developing style and being able to pull it off under extreme pressure. Only then do you earn the real rewards of recognition from people who know the difficulties, seeing your piece run where you managed to retain style in near complete darkness, hanging off a rusty pipe or standing on a rickety crate inches from a live rail; and of course while you're doing all this you're shit scared that you're gonna be raided by mad cops and thrown in jail.[14]

Furthermore the economy of this art is very far from that of the high-art market and has generally avoided assimilation. Despite the stress placed on finding an original style, graffiti-writing tends to be a collective, though competitive, activity based on apprenticeship and extensive copying from many different sources, including other writers and comic books. Its products, particularly the most prestigious, are necessarily short-lived. When New York writers covered trains from top to bottom, including the windows, this was the most ambitious form their graffiti took, but also the most transient, since the authorities would be sure to remove the paint quickly. A painful glory was attached to these brief, often extraordinary creations as a result. Most of all, and this is something the art market finds particularly hard to understand, these works are given freely and anonymously to the public – who may of course not necessarily want such a gift.[15]

Despite these differences, there has been some intersection of graffiti and high art, which until recently was a matter of artists appropriating either the look or sometimes the material of graffiti into their work; Brassaï photographed graffiti which was scratched into walls, while Dubuffet drew on its look. More recently certain graffiti artists, such as Keith Haring, have broken into the high-art scene directly, sometimes by using writing as a direct form of self-advertisement on streets near galleries. There are certain similarities between the fine artist and the graffiti writer, both looking for a distinctive and original style, which will achieve recognition by supposedly expressing their identity. The appropriation of graffiti writers was confined naturally to those who had made a reputation doing major pieces; relatively common in the eighties, particularly in Holland, it was dropped as the fashion changed and recession bit. More assimilation might have taken place, but for the fact that the worlds of graffiti and high art do not mix well, particularly because writers often explicitly reject the commercial values of the art market.[16]

Nevertheless, it is apparently paradoxical that the content, as opposed to the practice, of graffiti art is better understood as part of a mass-produced culture than in opposition to it. Although the economy of graffiti is about cost (of time and materials at least) and hardly ever about price, it does not escape a close relation to the commodity. Wolfgang Haug has argued that the 'body' of the commodity itself carries meaning: as a signifier, it is peculiar because its referent is actually present. Commodities do not so much represent use value as present it within their material form. The object, he writes, '(re)doubles itself aesthetically into the object and its appearance'.[17] This collapse of the signifier and the signified within objects echoes that of the brand names which advertise them. Similarly, in graffiti signifier and referent are literally identical. Graffiti, although it has no price tag attached, is a useless commodity which is consumed through its very production.

The writers' rejection of commercial values and the colonization of their creations by the forms of advertising is only an apparent contradiction: what these artists fix on are the broken promises of commodity culture – of an integral, joyful and meaningful life, of a better place than the council estates and motorway flyovers where the work is often found, somewhere which can be glimpsed in their writing. For within the lettering of the more elaborate graffiti there can often be seen bright patterns (sometimes abstract, sometimes stars or more significantly dollar signs) which seem to continue beyond the limits of their borders, as if they had been cut out of a roll of wallpaper, or rather, as if, instead of being painted on the wall, these letters allowed the viewer to look through it, to gain a shifting vision of another world of indeterminate and brilliantly coloured forms.

Lacan, Derrida and many of their followers attack the notion of a purely ideographic writing as a symptom of nostalgia for a lost immediacy. Both find the generation of the signifier hidden behind ideographic writing or images – for Lacan in the dream, for Derrida in arguing that the spatiality of writing resists instantaneous, totalizing perception.[18] Such arguments may equally be directed against the pretensions of advertising, and the similar yearning for the recovery of identity, direct expression and the creation of a like-minded audience in graffiti. The post-structuralist argument works against advertising and graffiti indiscriminately, however, and refuses to recognize the positive moment which corresponds to real needs, in the activity of the graffiti artists. Most of all, it cannot allow, as Martha Cooper's wonderful photographs of painted subway trains passing through New York City clearly show, that momentarily these exceptional artists can succeed in their aims; that the browns and greys of the urban landscape may be briefly illuminated by a gift of abstract brilliance. The largest of these works, covering the entire train, are surely among the most accomplished *conceptual* works of art; the writers risk their very lives to make them, expending much time and material in raising an image which will travel around the city for some few hours or days only, and will be glimpsed by thousands, as it flies through the urban landscape en route to its inevitable erasure. Lee, of the crew Fabulous Five, describes painting their first whole train piece, then riding the train on its route through many neighbourhoods, and the reactions of the people who saw it: 'That was the greatest thing we ever did [. . .] It was a big show stopper and I think those people who saw it went home that night and didn't watch TV. They talked about the train they saw.'[19]

These are, however, exceptional moments which stand on the shoulders of a much broader, failed collective practice. It is in the nature of graffiti art to be built up as a palimpsest, as generations of adolescents efface their predecessors' scrawlings. The contribution of the photographer incidentally (and it is sometimes the writers themselves) is to add another layer of comment, and at the same time to fix a particular ensemble of writing and material support seen under a particular light against change, decay and effacement. In the experience of the average viewer, each name is barely read separately, but participates in a general fabric which constitutes the experience of the city. Each individual presence, expressed however cursorily in writing or by a cartoon figure, in the face of the rigours of the physical and cultural environment, is slowly erased.

As we have seen, both graffiti and advertising strive towards a script which unifies form and meaning. Their failure to achieve it partly accounts for their compulsion to repeat their 'tags', individual or commercial, which alter and are altered by numerous different environments, forever changing and being changed by context. Graffiti thus becomes an allegory for many contemporary problems. For conservatives, its scrawlings are emblematic of urban and moral decay; for radicals, of protest. We may, rather, take the message from overwriting, which is very often a deliberate act of rivalry, challenging the claim to fame left by another writer.[20] In the subsequent combat of lines and forms, the competition is so intense that each individual name is sunk in a tangle of signatures. Graffiti may then be seen as an expression and a critical comment on fragmentation, the loss of meaning and the decline of writing under commercial culture. As Stewart has argued, 'It is precisely graffiti's mere surface, repetition, lack of use, meaninglessness, and negativity that give us the paradox of insight with regard to the billboard of commodity culture. And this is exactly the point: that graffiti has no lasting value, no transcendent significance.'[21]

Advertisements advertise not only particular brands but consumption in itself, and not only consumption in itself, but the very idea of advertising. The same is true of graffiti, whose very ubiquity becomes a debility. Both advertisements and graffiti compete in an environment already saturated with visual signs. Both rightly assume that the viewer is distracted, disinterested or resistant and present themselves ever more boldly and brightly as a consequence – in this way, both anticipate the viewer's activity.[22] As with advertising, the more individual writers try to distinguish themselves, the more their productions appear uniform; the style becomes one of a baroque and finally unreadable exaggeration, an extreme mannerism. The highly condensed combination of economy and complexity in individual writing styles – the complexity being necessary for competition, the economy for reasons of time and expense – echo the similar conjunction of television advertisements, which must cram their message into the least possible time. This compressed complexity becomes, especially for the wider public beyond the writers themselves, the identifying universal characteristic of graffiti. Advertising and graffiti travel together towards a total completion, in which total saturation and total powerlessness will be simultaneously achieved. While advertising as a whole, as a presence, advertises itself and consumption as a way of life, graffiti as a collective project of simultaneous decoration and desecration, a spontaneous community art, serves to advertise the invisible.

Graffiti writers recast themselves as commodities in order to achieve a certain notoriety, to leave a mark and to armour themselves against transience. Only by making their identities empty can they hope for their lettering to work as organic symbol. This is the basis of graffiti's transcendent aspect, expressed in the prising of script from degraded surface. In remaking themselves as brand names, these artists (sometimes ironically) adopt a reduced form of identity, exchanging humanity for fame, flesh for the small hope of immortality. Tied so intimately to identity, graffiti's transience is painfully felt. Again the very intensity of competition undermines the assertion of identity as individual graffiti are buried beneath tangles of names, and even 'pieces' made by internationally renowned crews are defaced by junior practitioners. The allegory of graffiti tells a story all right: of particular identities, male or less often female, of all racial groups, of those largely disenfranchised, who participate in a fellowship which crosses the usual boundaries.[23] They sign the environment, as though it were their masterpiece. In the blighted areas in which they are often found, their works adorn in order to desecrate, like the dentist who threatens to polish only every other one of a child's uncared-for teeth. Writers are people who refuse to be anonymous, who create alternative identities and glimpses of other, better worlds, which burn on walls, momentarily, uncertainly, before being effaced by the environment, the authorities, or simply the aspirations of thousands of others who write over the dreams of their precursors; but while they do persist, they burn brightly.

NOTES

1. Many graffiti writers believe that they beautify the environment with their painting and consider this a public service. See Craig Castleman, *Getting Up. Subway Graffiti in New York*, Cambridge, Mass. 1982, p. 71.

13

16

17

22

2. 'Piece' is short for masterpiece in graffiti jargon. The literature on graffiti which looks on it as an aesthetic phenomenon tends to concentrate on large works by these crews. See for instance Martha Cooper and Henry Chalfant, *Subway Art*, London 1984, and Henry Chalfant and James Prigoff, *Spraycan Art*, London 1987.

3. See Martha Cooper and Joseph Sciorra, *R.I.P. New York Spraycan Memorials*, London 1994, p. 11.

4. Theodor W. Adorno, *The Culture Industry. Selected Essays on Mass Culture*, ed. J.M. Bernstein, London 1991, p. 33.

5. See Susan Stewart, 'Ceci Tuera Cela: Graffiti as Crime and Art', in John Fekete, ed., *Life After Postmodernism. Essays on Value and Culture*, London 1988, p. 166, and Castleman, *Getting Up*, pp. 19–20.

6. For accounts of Seen's remarkable career, see Cooper and Chalfant, *Subway Art*, pp. 67, 70, and Chalfant and Prigoff, *Spraycan Art*, pp. 32–3.

7. See Giorgio Agamben, *Infancy and History. Essays on the Destruction of Experience*, trans. Liz Heron, London 1993, pp. 6–7. By infancy Agamben means a stage at which language becomes split between the signifier and the signified.

8. For a discussion of this point in relation to allegorical emblems, see John McCole, *Walter Benjamin and the Antimonies of Tradition*, Ithaca 1993, p. 143.

9. See Susan Stewart, 'Ceci Tuera Cela', pp. 174–5.

10. There are official or at least officially tolerated 'Halls of Fame' in many cities where crews may practise relatively free from interruption.

11. For this and other examples, see Cooper and Chalfant, *Subway Art*, p. 38.

12. Walter Benjamin, *The Origin of German Tragic Drama*, trans. John Osborne, London 1977, pp. 214–15.

13. See Herbert Kohl, 'Names, Graffiti, and Culture', in Thomas Kochman, ed., *Rappin' and Stylin' Out. Communication in Urban Black America*, Urbana 1972, pp. 116–17.

14. Prime, 'Prime Time', *Graphotism*, no. 3, 1993, n.p.

15. There are artists who have also done this; some are radical and marginal figures who find themselves in opposition to the mainstream art world. Others, like Barbara Kruger and Jenny Holzer, make art which is seen as advertisements are seen, though this is on the basis of a wider practice, seen in museums, and receiving acclaim and rewards from the high-art establishment.

16. For spats with the art world in which the rejection of art-world values is explicit, see the anonymous article, 'The Downlow on the ILC Exhibition, N'Ham '93', *Graphotism*, no. 5, 1994, n.p.; for a view on commercial assimilation, see Drax, 'Maybe it's because I'm a Londoner . . .', *Graphotism*, no. 3, 1993, n.p.

17. Wolfgang Haug, *Commodity Aesthetics, Ideology and Culture*, New York 1987, p. 148.

18. See Peter Dews, *The Logics of Disintegration. Post-Structuralist Thought and the Claims of Critical Theory*, London 1987, p. 93.

19. Castleman, *Getting Up*, p. 15.

20. See Herbert Kohl, 'Names, Graffiti, and Culture', pp. 111, 127–8.

21. Stewart, 'Ceci Tuera Cela', p. 176.

22. See Theodor W. Adorno, *Prisms*, trans. Samuel and Shierry Weber, Cambridge, Mass. 1981, p. 163.

23. Cooper and Chalfant note the racial mix of the crews and that they transcend usual neighbourhood boundaries. *Subway Art*, p. 50. Castleman describes the same mix and also claims that there is variation even in the writers' economic fortunes. *Getting Up*, pp. 67–8.

7

THE DUTY TO CONSUME

It is in the interests of manufacturers and retailers to present shopping as a leisure activity rather than a chore. This is not only because people may more willingly devote their free time to shopping if they see it as opposed to work, but also because in leisure time it is easier to encourage a relaxed rather than a calculating mood – it is easier to sell. Much academic work on shopping and consumer culture has blithely followed this interest, concentrating on consumption as leisure, rather than as work and duty, and on buying leisure clothes or decorative knick-knacks rather than the regular cycle of food and household shopping. This is partly why so much more attention has been paid to the shopping centre or mall than to the supermarket, although even in the latter managers are doing their best to blur the distinctions between more durable luxuries and transient, everyday goods.[1] There is one way in which this focus on consumption as leisure makes sense: as societies or groups of people get richer, they spend a greater proportion of their income on non-essentials.[2] If there is a scale of shopping activities with pure hedonism at one end and pure necessity at the other, then most things are of course a mixture, but nevertheless the chore aspect is increasingly concealed. To concentrate on the hedonistic or leisure aspect alone is not only to mistake the nature of the whole activity, but to cut out of consideration all those who can rarely or never shop for pleasure, the many impoverished individuals in the First World and the great majority in the Third.

If the postmodern era is supposed to announce 'a virtual delirium of the consumption of the very idea of consumption',[3] then the concentration of purpose in the mall is extremely important, for here there is a literal staging of consumption and nothing else. It is as though commodities are delicate things which within the mall's enveloping environment seek protection from rough contingency. This enclosure is also necessary to the presentation of shopping in itself as a leisure activity: to the idea that people go there not to shop for something but merely to shop. The mall must close itself off from the outside world in order to sustain this illusion and remove the thought of alternatives. These centres for consumption turn in on themselves, generally excluding daylight, controlling temperature and the circulation of air, confronting consumers, when their gazes stray from the shop windows, with expanses of bare material, or mirrors in which to see themselves. Although some more recently built malls have opened themselves to natural light, this has only been via the roof; aside from the sky, the scene is closely controlled. Any contingency which might disrupt the activity of buying is excluded. Shoppers, who always trail something of the outer world in with them, are of course an unavoidable anomaly inhabiting this supposedly seamless illusion.

The creation of a small, self-contained world within the mall compensates for the exclusion of the real one, especially by providing little bits of 'nature' in the form of water and plants. Shopping centres are in many ways modernist palaces: their bare exposure of sleek materials juxtaposed with fountains and greenery, and their air-conditioning – something much recommended by Le Corbusier to standardize the climate of interiors everywhere. They form a neutral utopia against which a diverse range of goods can display their characters to the full, just as the white boxes of modern rooms were supposed to act as blank foils against which occupants would exercise their individual taste with books, flowers and pictures. In the mall, nothing is allowed to intrude which might interfere with a particular marketing pitch. Each type of good generally dwells within its own little unit, a form of micrological zoning, so that each does not infect the other by contrast. This is very different from the old department store, where one might feel a little disoriented when walking, for instance, straight from the over-stuffed and over-embroidered offerings of the furniture department into the clean blacks and silvers of the electronics section, from an upholstered silence to bright noises of piercing clarity.

Theoretical study has tended to concentrate not merely on the mall as opposed to other stores, but often on the very largest malls of all. These spaces, more than any other, are where postmodern culture should be found in a confusion of commodities, cultural artefacts, images, signs and mirrors. No unitary meaning may be discovered there, no coherence found, but the consumer may drift pleasurably across the range of goods and services on offer, choosing whatever appeals to their particular mood, or just looking. Malls are commonly dubbed the cathedrals of contemporary culture.[4] Although this is by now a cliché of the theory of consumption, it should be treated with great suspicion. First, the enclosed environment of the shopping centre is generally not so different from the area surrounding it: the display of goods, the ubiquitous ads, chain stores and much of the decor are highly familiar. It is certainly not on a par with the contrast between a medieval cathedral and the surrounding town, where the former may have been one of the few stone buildings and certainly would have dominated the area with its sheer scale. The cathedral was also likely to have had a local monopoly on painted and sculpted images of any quality. Secondly, there is no evidence that people treat malls with much reverence or generally assign much importance to them beyond mere convenience. In fact, there is some evidence of the reverse, given the 'subversive' uses people find to make of them, whether stealing, boozing or necking. Children and adolescents, of course, sometimes find a special attachment to the mall, but this could be said of any environment where they can escape parental supervision. So malls can be seen as aspects and symbols of consumerism, and as condensed arenas for consumption, but not as central icons, let alone temples.

Naturally, when the most massive malls are considered, it is not surprising that component theme parks, video arcades, waterfalls and so on can be found within them, and the conclusion can then be reached that there is little distinction to be made between the experiences of the shopping centre and the museum, or that so many diverse environments are on offer that 'cultural disorder and stylistic eclecticism become common features of spaces in which consumption and leisure are meant to be constructed as "experiences".'[5] Actually, when other elements are put into the environment of the mall, such as popular themed displays or arenas in which you can shoot at your fellow consumers with lasers, they are rigorously separated from the shops, usually by a frontage which conceals what is inside. Rather than concentrating on the largest malls, we might think about some more typical places. Where there are riches, the illusion of universal consumption can be sustained. In shopping centres which serve the wealthier parts of London, for example, the interior of the mall is clothed in marble and every metal surface gleams under intense but carefully controlled lighting. Each shop window displays equally exclusive goods. Here the customers contribute to the image of wealth, well-being and good taste. Even disaffected youth is at least expensively dressed and security is discreet. Then, at the other extreme, think of those malls in the further reaches of North or East London, where gentrification is unlikely ever to reach. In such shopping centres, the exclusion of the outer world often means a gloomy interior, especially in those service areas where there are no shops, and the buildings often present a forbidding façade reminiscent of a mausoleum or bunker. In recession, the empty, boarded-up units form a highly visible and painful punctuation of the supposed consumerist phantasmagoria. The weighty security guards strolling among the shoppers and the cameras at every corner inform the consumer that they are not yet in utopia. Here people's appearances often match the paucity and the shoddiness of many of the goods. There are closing-down sales with poor, unwanted objects thrown into cardboard boxes for bargain hunters. Always, though, there are the same advertising images reminding shoppers of what they should aspire to and how far they fall short. The parade of shoppers often contrasts dramatically with the mannequins and the immaculate idols who stare down from hoardings. Far from being seamless displays of postmodern diversity, a shallow juxtaposition of multivalent signs, most shopping centres are far more banal, and much easier to 'read': they are a mix of riches and poverty, openness and control, illusion and blatant pretension.

If instead of thinking of North American 'mega-malls', like the one in West Edmonton with its sixty-four-acre entertainment centre, golf range and indoor lake containing dolphins,[6] we look at the shopping centre in Edmonton Green, North London, a different idea of these consumer palaces may emerge. The centre in Edmonton Green is situated around a covered square formed by the placement of a number of tall blocks of flats. It is a pedestrian area which people come to straight from their homes. The design is purely modernist, with the dramatic, bare open space of the square faced in unadorned concrete and toplit from a glass roof; a balcony runs around the edge of the entire space, giving access to a second level of shops and views which are meant to be of architectural interest. The shops proper are confined to the edges of the square and the open corridors which run off it, while the square itself is filled with a busy market selling mostly fruit and vegetables, but also with stalls bearing anything from framed pictures to pet food. Obviously people come here for many reasons; although the area is not rich, it is also not so poor that people cannot do some shopping for leisure. The square encourages more than this, however; it is plainly a meeting place and wherever you look, you can see people chatting in groups. This is a centre which turns its back on the outer world in order to provide a pedestrian haven for locals. It is an example of an older, more idealistic modernism which believed in trying to provide facilities other than those related to pure selling. More than that, it has done so modestly but successfully. There is nothing very mysterious about this place; it is friendly and a little run-down, a mundane area where people come to talk, and buy their food, shoes or music.

Now Edmonton Green shopping centre may be a little unusual in some respects, but its modernist origins are highly typical. The calming and neutral environment of malls is quietly aestheticized; if it can be described as postmodern, this is because it has sometimes become a perverse realization of idealist modern dreams. The basis of mall design is, surprisingly enough, a thoroughgoing functionalism. The first parameter to be calculated is the ratio between the ground areas of the shops and the car park. Internal layout is often designed for the manoeuvre of the shopping trolley, not mere strolling. Such factors mean that the mall, when compared with the more phantasmagoric department store, 'adventitiously recreates the illusion of the rational shopper determinedly exercising her or his [. . .] "choice" in the market-place'.[7] Now this is more than adventitious: when it comes down to selling, rational planning will always win out over postmodern fantasy.

Some of these instrumental factors are well known; for example, the notorious benches which are designed so that no one can sit comfortably on them for long. Most malls are built around a plan which encourages an endless circling, as if for prey.

Furthermore, if the mall presents itself as a spectacle, this is not so much a postmodern form of self-reference as an instrumental factor in creating the buying mood. Vistas are created over the whole space from various vantage points, while mobile views from escalators or glass lifts create a consumerist version of Le Corbusier's *promenade architecturale*. In large, open spaces, atria, and open-plan cafés and restaurants the customers become exhibits and participants in a moving spectacle. Like the commodity, the mall presents itself as a picture. It is a self-contained unit, a monad, which also exhibits the image of its enclosed nature.

Just because malls are designed functionally does not mean that people cannot use them subversively. Much has been written about the supposedly radical nature of hanging about a shopping centre, without buying.[8] Yet seen from the point of view of shopping as a leisure activity, this is an essential part of the shopping-centre experience for all concerned. Those with every intent to buy must first circle the mall, look around, compare goods and prices, before settling on some purchase or moving elsewhere. Those intending to steal must do the same, with slightly different criteria in mind. The youths who hang about the halls and passageways, meeting others, may not buy every time they visit, but they are surely customers, of drinks and sweets if nothing else. Their observation, circulation and boredom are different only in degree from those of their older counterparts: they are consumers in training.

Much ink has also been spilt on the 'liminal' or 'phantasmagoric' aspect of consumer spaces, on their dizzying and confusing nature, on the complex shallowness of their assembly of diverse signs. Now it is perfectly understandable that certain professors of literature or cultural studies should be confused by these places, but it is rather important to realize that most people are not, and, even as they participate in the environment, are quite capable of understanding the particular combinations of signs and the instrumental manipulation of shoppers. This, then, is the mall, supposedly that most postmodern of shopping experiences; we have not even considered those hangars with postmodern skins which attach themselves to motorways and ring-roads, which in one huge space devote themselves to a single task: the selling of food, or clothes, or DIY or toys.

Like the shopping centre which encloses it, the commodity presents itself as a monad. There is a link between the masking of social relations in the commodity form and its adoption of an apparently aesthetic meaning as an autonomous object. The commodity, like Athena, appears to be born fully formed and armed, without process and without manufacture. Its appearance is a miracle, the material-ization of an ideal in which all marks of its making have been effaced. Like the reflective, uniform bodies of cars, contemporary commod-ities aspire to a seamless, resistant surface. The thing has its life because of labour but, since this labour is hidden, life seems to inhere in the object itself, as a mystic, aesthetic glow, which speaks directly to the beholder.

While labour is obliterated, a myth of origin, a whiff of exoticism or a hint of the social may remain. So a nicely coloured drawing of peas-ant tea-pickers might appear on a box of teabags. The producing nation, if it is capable of summoning up some idyllic image or the idea of a friendly essentialist character, may be prominently advertised. The actual history of production and consumption relations, tied to the legacies of a bloody and unjust past, and an equally unpalatable present which determines pricing, is entirely concealed. Rather, and again for the wealthy few, commodities are sometimes displayed as though they were exhibits at a gallery:

> the supermarket is something of a postmodern museum of the third world, whose displays of exotic fruits and vegetables, such as breadfruit, cactus apples, passion fruit, star fruit and horn melons often include museum-like inscriptions [. . .][9]

So the commodity becomes like a work of art, auratic and mysterious. Yet, unlike the museum, all the exhibits here can be pawed, picked up, taken home and consumed. The aura of the commodity is transit-ory, except for those without the means to pay.

The material bodies of commodities are mere vehicles for a higher harmony which runs through the world, the object and the consumer, and will bring them to peaceful unity. Commodities aspire to a condition of transfiguration in which they become radiant, glowing or beaming like a 'face transformed by bliss' in which 'spiritual essence shines forth through earthly appearances'.[10] They may cease to glow after we get them home, but they surely do in adverts, and often in shop windows, selectively and brightly illuminated by spots. Like symbols they seek to embody 'momentary totality', being self-contained, concentrated and steadfastly remaining themselves. The promise of this symbolism is vague but insistent; that there is a natural and organic connection, re-established in the purchase of the commodity, between its consumption and some form of the good life; whether it be attractiveness, companionship, power, success or just plain wealth. When it trades on the promise of warm, direct human relationships, the commodity posits the very thing which it is responsible for destroying. This symbolic idealization is of course false, and behind it, as we have already seen in relation to adverts, lies the far more mundane and contradictory operation of allegory, with its 'discontinuous structure of a series of moments, failed attempts to capture meaning'.[11] The point of this attempted symbolism is always to conceal utility, and therefore labour, behind the image of utility.

As we have seen in the previous chapter, Wolfgang Haug has argued that the commodity must not only have use value, but must also have its appearance; it is this latter quality which is fixed on by the apparatus of marketing and advertising. So the commodity is brought very close to the ideology of television (where appearance is everything) and, indeed, to the core of the visual bias of the culture as a whole. With the presentation of identity on television, too, what is crucial is not to have a quality but to appear to have it, or rather that appearing to have it is the same as actually having it. Commodities, particularly those for children, are often animated as television characters, these being personifications of the supposed qualities of the product. As such, they can only be allegorical robots or demons of an unchanging principle. So Guinness becomes the image of an unfeasibly cool genius; a fizzy orange drink becomes a fast-moving imp which mugs its victims (its customers of course) in the twinkling of an eye; or in Sega's advert for *Virtua Racing*, the game becomes an animated figure of death, with a skull for a face, and a sense of humour, racing lightning fast cars against mere humans.

In *The Origin of German Tragic Drama*, Benjamin argues that allegory always points from its ostensible object to something else, thus conferring on the object 'a power which makes them appear no longer commensurable with profane things, which raises them onto a higher plane, and which can, indeed, sanctify them. Considered in allegorical terms, then, the profane world is both elevated and devalued.'[12] The ambiguous nature of the commodity is in part captured by this description, for its impoverished body becomes the vehicle of a valorizing spirit, sanctified by social distinction. When the commodity has been consumed, or has failed to deliver its promise, its body becomes a mere material husk which must be swiftly discarded or tucked away out of sight.

If commodities act allegorically, then the control of their meanings can become a problem. For those spinning the arbitrary connections made in marketing commodities, the play of significance cannot be called to a halt. As Terry Eagleton has argued, allegory is symbolism 'run riot, pressed to self-undoing extreme; if anything can now fulfil the role of a "concrete universal", then nothing is particularly remarkable'.[13] If everything takes on an aesthetic cast, then nothing is particularly aesthetic. In the signification of the commodity form, as in advertising, there is a tendency to self-defeat. Fashion is one way around it, through the momentary creation and reinforcement of new connections, but it also finally contributes to the decline of meaning by bringing people to an awareness of the very transience of these associations. The mass-production of the commodity and the display of multiple examples works against its uniqueness, which is supposed to speak to the individual purchaser. Andy Warhol, forever playing on the tension between the aesthetic of the unique object and the repetition of mass production, wrote of works using series of representations: 'I want it to be exactly the same. Because the more you look at the same exact thing, the more meaning goes away, and the better and emptier you feel'.[14] This attitude may be related to his obsessive buying of many exemplars of the same object. Blankness and a lack of affect are a consequence of commodity culture but not exactly the one desired by the advertisers for it has a tendency to irony, which, though it is not immediately threatening, admits of defeat and possible reaction. It applies just as much to the 'progress' of consumer goods as it does to their mass-production:

The cult of the new, and thus the idea of modernity, is a rebellion against the fact that there is no longer anything new. The never-changing quality of machine-produced goods, the lattice of socialisation that enmeshes and assimilates equally objects and the view of them, converts everything encountered into what always was, a fortuitous specimen of a species, the *doppel-gänger* of a model.[15]

Commodity and mass-produced identity, then, may be produced together, if this rebellion is not realized.

Concealment takes place from two ends at once: as we have already seen, the social relations of work which create the product are concealed from the purchaser; at the same time, the very activity of purchasing is also made mysterious by being made as much as possible a matter of leisure, the acquiring of some small piece of aura – never anything so vulgar as the purchase of a mere thing. There is, as we have seen, some sense in which the dematerialization of the commodity may be realized in cyberspace, and this may augment its mysterious aesthetic aura; it may also be able quasi-intelligently to tailor its products to individual preferences, rather than presenting a wide range of multiples from which we select. Yet we should not get too carried away by this possibility for it applies only to information in a broad sense: the material basis must continue bloodily to sustain itself.

Since the appeal of the commodity is increasingly geared to the subjectivity of the buyer, we should look at the effects of this concealment of labour and the duty of consumption on the identity of the consumer. The supposedly liberating effect of catering to subjectivity becomes the opposite when it is universal, colonizing, as it were, the objective. Adorno wrote of this matter:

> Absolute subjectivity is also subjectless. The self lives solely through transformation into otherness; as the secure residue of the subject which cuts itself off from everything alien it becomes the blind residue of the world. The more the I of expressionism is thrown back upon itself, the more like the excluded world of things it becomes. [. . .] pure subjectivity, being of necessity estranged from itself as well and having become a thing, assumes the dimensions of objectivity which expresses itself through its own estrangement. The boundary between what is human and the world of things becomes blurred.[16]

In the world of commodities, where everything ideally conforms to every wrinkle of the subjective personality, the subject loses itself within an ideal objective. Practically, the constraints of marketing and knowledge of the consumer mean that does not quite happen but the construction of a utopia of subjectivity in cyberspace promises and threatens just this, to produce identity as a pure monad. In the meantime, without this technological fix, the tendency is still strongly present.

Advertisers would have us believe that people express themselves through the purchase of commodities which make statements about their character. Sometimes the commodity as sign may be read in quite a specific manner, for it is plainly possible to make statements about the image one wishes to present through the goods one chooses to display. In the choice of clothing, for instance, a peasant-style dress might, alongside other clues, be read as a statement of solidarity with Third World people. Yet prior to any such matters of detail, what such clothes say is this: that the wearer is a person who chooses to make statements about their personality through the display of ready-made, purchased signs. As in the personifications of commodities themselves, there is the same congruence of image and character. The acting out of an image in masquerade, highly convenient to the fashion industry, just pushes the identification back a step: this is the kind of person who chooses to make statements about their personality by temporarily adopting such an image. What is advertised before anything else is consumption itself.

It is not supposed to be easy – or on some accounts even possible – to step out of this world of signs, but actually people do it all the time, if only by sending out contradictory or incoherent signals (inadvertently or not) or by raising the noise to signal ratio. Further, we should never forget that many people do not have the opportunity to make statements through consumer choices; think of the clothes of the very poor, which in their disrepair and arbitrary matching simply make the statement that they have had few options in their selection. This says something about that person's situation, but nothing whatever about their desired image or actual character. Things do slip – or are pushed – out of the interstices of signification all the time.

When a personal image is produced through the selection of commodities, an evening out of idiosyncrasies is often the result. The serial production of identical commodities, even for niche markets, leads to the homogenization of the identity of consumers. As Martin Davidson, in his book on advertising, has argued, 'To "respond" to an ad is necessarily to respond *as* a stereotype. The logic of branding includes the consumer who brands him or herself in the art of "consuming" the ad.'[17] The commodity, as we have seen, is branded with a particular unitary identity, a name or image in which form and content are supposed to be fused. In assembling a unitary ensemble of identifying commodities, consumers produce themselves as the commodities' stock. As at election time, consumers select from what is on offer, but cannot make choices about what is available. The promise of fulfilment is eternally offered and eternally withdrawn, as indeed it must be if the selling process is to continue. Adorno's controversial arguments about innovation in jazz music may be applied far more widely. While jazz must always promise its listeners something new:

> it is not allowed to leave the beaten path; it must always be new and always the same. Hence, the deviations are just as standardised as the standards and in effect revoke themselves the instant they appear. Jazz, like everything else in the culture industry, gratifies desires only to frustrate them at the same time.[18]

Since the system of fashion and selling must perpetuate itself, such restrictions are absolutely integral to its functioning. The diverse identities produced by marketing conform to a strict standard.

There is a tendency for the process of branding, while proceeding to produce ever finer distinctions between niche markets, also to produce the illusion of a certain equality. As Lauren Langman has put it, writing of people in the mall:

> Whatever one's status or job in the world of work or even without job, there is an equality of just being there and looking at the shows of decor, goods and other people. Malls appear democratic and open to all, rich or poor, young or old. Age is often the only visible marker of difference given androgynous fashions, embourgeoisement of the masses and affluent slumming. This is the realm where the goods of the good life promised in the magazine ads and television commercials can be found.[19]

This is a very important point, though overplayed when the difference between different malls is considered. In presenting different images as choices, rather than fixed social identities, certain profound distinctions are rendered harder to see. While there may be a certain equality within malls, even this is only in appearance, for their inhabitants are far from equal in the terms which really matter there; of cash and credit rating.

In the process by which consumption has come to assume the hegemony it now enjoys, older hierarchies were of course sometimes actually subsumed, rather than just buried under diverse images, and their remnants continue to decline. Some theorists have taken these fallen distinctions and assumed that their downfall was fundamental to the process as a whole. So consumer culture appears as a liberating force. It is evident, for instance, that the rise of consumption has empowered some women, since their choices over the management of resources have become more complex and more important. Now it is quite true that if you have nothing, then such empowerment might seem liberating for a time, but this is a poor form of equality. The tendency is egalitarian only in the negative sense that it is blind to the identity of buyers.

There are other powerful tendencies to homogenization. The link of person and product in advertising is supposed to function to secure an admiration of the product because it is used by such an admirable person, and eventually vice versa. It is hardly necessary to say that there is an overwhelming predominance of particular types of people used for this purpose: young, professional models of great beauty, aided by the considerable skills of make-up artists, lighting specialists, photographers and retouchers. These models are humans remade as commodities whose only significant features are surface qualities open to the gaze. Their uniformly unblemished features and skinny bodies hardly work for the fragmentation of identity through consumption. Rather these types, and the aspiration to be like them, remain relatively constant against an ever-changing panoply of goods and fashions. The tyranny of these stereotypes has often had appalling effects, particularly on the young and on women. This at least is slowly changing; in the brave new postmodern world of universal consumer choice anyone can be objectified and, as we might expect, there is an increasing incidence of, for instance, anorexia among males.

The mall is a unified display of such conventions, with advertisements and mannequins constantly reminding the consumer of the
diverse but somehow standard set of charismatic images they should
be inhabiting. Here mirrors do not so much serve the purpose of dis-
orienting the shopper by making the space appear more complex, but
simply provide an adjunct to the spectacle of consumption, in which
consumers can check out their appearance against the recommended
ideals. It may of course cut both ways, for although it is designed as a
spur to consumption, it may become a form of critique if the contrast
between model and actuality is too wide.

Homogenization is the method and the purpose of market
research, motivational research and advertising. Such disciplines sub-
scribe to a well-funded positivism in which volunteer squads of
psychologists, sociologists, specialists in physiology and perception
calculate the effects of particular products and their marketing. They
are based on the idea of the consumer as a passive and suggestible
being, and this is backed up among market researchers with many a
tale of success among the gullible.[20] This positivism is of course partial; these researchers are paid to be effective and must propagandize
their effectiveness. Yet it is also based on sales, which are an objective
measure, independent of this partiality. If marketing can never establish itself on a fully scientific basis, this is not only because the
conditions for its experiments can never be controlled, nor placebos
tested for comparison, but also because the widespread dissemination
of any marketing technique alters its recipients. Yet this does not
mean that marketing eschews an experimental methodology, nor that
it is not tested on success and failure in the only terms that matter.
Those who argue that, since a large proportion of new products fail,
the ones that succeed must be those which people really want, miss
the point in a truly spectacular fashion, as the consumer market continues to perpetuate itself and grow.[21] Since Vance Packard's day it has
been clear that advertisers and market researchers have been appealing increasingly to unconscious and irrational elements in people's
psychological make-up. In such circumstances, criticism of theories
which are supposed to model people as 'dupes' rather miss the point.
For instance muzak, widely loathed when people are asked to express
a conscious opinion about it, is often played in supermarkets because
it has been shown to increase sales. Many shoppers are unaware even

of its presence.[22] The question, then, is not so much about our gulli-
bility, but about our ability to resist pervasive and ubiquitous
environments, created with the particulars of our physiology and psychology in mind, and geared to giving coherence to only certain
kinds of activity. The complex and effective pseudo-science of marketing is a rejoinder to postmodern scepticism and to radical theories
of consumer resistance.

We should not forget, however, that most advertising and marketing appeals to the consumer in a straightforward, self-conscious
fashion. The postmodern disintegration of identity is supposed to be
based partly on unconscious responses to the competing blandish-
ments of the culture industry. Advertising and marketing are always
about changing people's minds, and this has led some to argue that
this means that there can never be any question of their appealing to
an immutable, self-contained consciousness.[23] This is a category error
between thinking about identity or character as such and about the
many little decisions which are made on its basis each day. While it is
trivially true that these decisions taken together alter character, the
real question is to what degree and in what direction. The style of
advertising must change, and it must respond to social forces and
changes in fashion, but the basis of selling remains remarkably constant – and more often than not biological. There may be elements of
these marketing pitches which are geared to the unconscious, but
the conscious message is hardly subtle and is readily understood.
Adverts for jeans forthrightly tell you that if you wear this particular
brand you will get laid: people understand them perfectly on a conscious level. The promise of sex is probably the most commonly used
marketing technique, and also the most basic. Mediated through varying circumstances of social distinction, fashion and varying sexual
mores, it is a constant which is based on the appeal to and the marketing of our biological imperatives. As such, it is unlikely to change.

Homogeneous and instrumental identities are then constantly
forged through marketing. At the same time, the system is delicate,
founded as it is on the continuance of widespread affluence and the
repetition of broken promises. There is always some chance that
people might learn from their experiences. Indeed, this might be
one reason why the young are the best-behaved consumers, and why
many advertisers shun the old. Advertisements sometimes even try to

thematize these dangers to commodity culture within their content. Davidson writes of an advert for vodka, in which a couple are caught in a compromising situation, that 'Behind this ad is a whole new sense of social value, that in guilt, precisely in guilt, lies pleasure.'[24] Of course this applies to the marketing of much else. Advertisements are skating close to the edge here; in displacing guilt about consumption from essentials to trivia (the consumption of cream cakes or hard liquor and illicit affairs) they seek to make of personal responsibility only a matter of the consequences of consumption for the person.

In thinking about the fragility of this situation, we should remember the role played by mediation in Lukács's theory of class consciousness where through mediation the frozen and fragmentary nature of reality is recognized and raises itself to self-consciousness. There are immanent tendencies within it which lead towards self-realization. So illusory appearances are recognized, are detached from their immediate context (just as a photograph does by framing them) and are then related to the social whole. For Lukács the working class have a particular stake in this process because, when they recognize themselves as commodities, as the object of the capitalist system, they take the first step towards liberating themselves.[25] Now to apply this scheme to consumers might seem perverse: there is after all a very great difference between the exploitation of those who make goods and those who buy them. Nevertheless, it is usually necessary to do one in order to do the other, and consumers are likewise constituted as fragmentary identities through marketing and are used instrumentally.

The relation between production and consumption is of course very close. Marx wrote of their utter entanglement, arguing that the production of the commodity is completed only in consumption, and that most consumption is in itself undertaken for the production of something else, if only the continued existence of the workforce. Furthermore:

> Consumption accomplishes the act of production only in completing the product as product by dissolving it, by consuming its independently material form, by raising the inclination developed in the first act of production, through the need for repetition, to its finished form; it is

thus not only the concluding act in which the product becomes product, but also that in which the producer becomes producer.[26]

The idea that the two worlds can be separated is nonsense, as is the notion that somehow the world economy has shifted from being driven by production to consumption: in this very first step, much postmodern theory is perpetuating the most fundamental mystification, from which a great many more must follow. When consumption is necessary for survival or to further production, then consumption itself can be seen as labour. Even consumption which we are not forced into takes effort. The splitting of the self between work and leisure conceals a deeper unity, in which work determines the forms of a leisure which is more and more founded on the duty to consume. This must be concealed behind a glittering façade of mirrors and shiny surfaces, of products and stores, all brilliantly lit. Sometimes, watching shoppers struggle around the circuit of the mall, laden with goods, or trying to keep children out of trouble, we may be reminded of those old painted fantasies of lands of plenty, where exhaustion finally overcomes those who pursue excessive consumption, who gorge themselves until they drop.

If workers have an interest in recognizing their status as objects of use for capital, then curiously consumers find themselves in a similar situation – though less urgent in times of affluence. People take on the role of branded goods and goods become characters, somehow more solid than the people around them. By trying to efface the distinction between shopping for necessities and shopping as a leisure activity, there is a tendency to make all purchasing into a chore to which the consumer is driven by marketing imperatives. In selling culture, capital has extended its homogenizing imperatives to the very base of our subjectivities. The world comes to take on the character of the mall, a monad but, thankfully, a leaky one. If the world is a mall, at least from the perspective of the comfortable classes, then this mall should be seen not as a cathedral but as a factory, where the round of consumption and production grinds on, not to the sound of machinery, but to muzak and the smell of cappuccino. In the mall which is the wider world, the same cycle also runs, and outside the direct environment of the affluent, it is fuelled by hard labour and little reward, and maintained by repression and constant bloodletting.

We have seen that the aura surrounding the commodity is a delicate and transient matter. It may be subsumed under competing
meanings or damaged by the lightest wear. For Benjamin, under allegory, objects 'submit to its purposes, surrendering any claims of their
own'. These objects are 'exposed', 'made soulless', 'drained of life'
and 'dismembered'.[27] We may take allegory seriously, bending it to
our own purposes in order to mire the commodity with labour. When
looked at critically, commodities have the potential to become signs of
the past and present of imperialism and class difference, while their
transport over borders may reflect the often tragic transport of
people. As Raymond Williams noted, the earliest uses of the word
'consume' meant to destroy, to use up, exhaust or waste.[28] When the
commodity appears natural, at once auratically mysterious but at
home in the world, then this is the product of a very specific amnesia.
If all reification is a forgetting,[29] and if the reified form of commodities obscures their origins and the process of their creation, then
perhaps around objects which have been drained of the appearance
of use, there may be opportunity for remembering.

In a celebrated passage from his 'Theses on the Philosophy of
History', Benjamin uses a painting by Paul Klee, *Angelus Novus* (1920)
to make a point about progress:

> An angel is presented in it who looks as if he were about to move away
> from something at which he is staring. His eyes are wide open, mouth
> agape, wings spread. The angel of history must look like that. His face
> is turned toward the past. Where a chain of events appears to *us*, *he* sees
> one single catastrophe which relentlessly piles wreckage upon wreck-
> age, and hurls them before his feet. [. . .] The storm drives him
> irresistibly into the future to which his back is turned, while the pile of
> debris before him grows towards the sky. That which we call progress is
> the storm.[30]

The storm still blows, and the catastrophes continue to pile up,
although many fewer than in Benjamin's time would now so simply
describe this as progress. There also grows before our eyes another
pile – of cultural tat, a vast production of toys, knick-knacks, consumer magazines and gimmicks quickly worn out and thrown on to
the streets, and for which the countryside is hollowed out in vast pits

to accommodate the resultant debris. In the comfortable West, however, faces are often turned away from the consequences of its production, bedazzled as we are by the overwhelming apparatus of its advertisement and display. Sometimes, though, we can catch sight of our own reflection, along with Benjamin's angel, in a shop window perhaps, flying backwards before a rising mountain of disasters and rapidly discarded kitsch.

NOTES

1. See Peter K. Lunt and Sonia M. Livingstone, *Mass Consumption and Personal Identity. Everyday Economic Experience*, Buckingham 1992, p. 97.

2. This point is made by Lunt and Livingstone, p. 96.

3. Fredric Jameson, *Postmodernism or, the Cultural Logic of Late Capitalism*, London 1991, p. 269.

4. 'The New Cathedral' is the title of the chapter devoted to shopping centres by Carl Gardner and Julie Sheppard in *Consuming Passion. The Rise of Retail Culture*, London 1989. John Fiske also begins an essay on shopping by stating that 'malls are cathedrals of consumption', dubbing this a cliché but then subscribing to it, at least in part. Fiske, *Reading the Popular*, London 1989, p. 13.

5. Mike Featherstone, *Consumer Culture and Postmodernism*, London 1991, p. 103.

6. The literature on malls is reviewed by Featherstone, *Consumer Culture and Postmodernism*, pp. 103–4. Rob Shields has written about the West Edmonton mall in 'Social Spatialisation and the Built Environment: the case of West Edmonton Mall', *Environment and Planning D: Society and Space*, vol. 7, no. 2, 1989, pp. 147–64. See also Gardner and Sheppard, *Consuming Passion*, p. 109.

7. Harvie Ferguson, 'Watching the World Go Round. Atrium Culture and the Psychology of Shopping', in Rob Shields, ed., *Lifestyle Shopping. The Subject of Consumption*, London 1992, p. 32.

8. See for instance John Fiske, 'Shopping for Pleasure' in *Reading the Popular*.

9. Susan Willis, *A Primer for Daily Life*, London 1991, p. 17.

10. See John McCole's analysis of Benjamin's use of the concept *Verklärung* in *Walter Benjamin and the Antimonies of Tradition*, Ithaca 1993, pp. 136–7.

11. Ibid., p. 133.

12. Walter Benjamin, *The Origin of German Tragic Drama*, trans. John Osborne, London 1977, p. 175.

13. Terry Eagleton, *The Ideology of the Aesthetic*, Oxford 1990, p. 320.

14. Cited in Peter Wollen, *Raiding the Icebox. Reflections on Twentieth-Century Culture*, London 1993, p. 169.

15. Theodor W. Adorno, *Minima Moralia. Reflections from Damaged Life*, trans. E.F.N. Jephcott, London 1974, p. 235.

16. Adorno, 'Notes on Kafka', *Prisms*, trans. Samuel and Shierry Weber, Cambridge, Mass. 1981, p. 262.

17. Martin P. Davidson, *The Consumerist Manifesto. Advertising in Postmodern Times*, London 1992, p. 162.

18. Adorno, 'Perennial Fashion – Jazz', in *Prisms*, p. 126.

19. Lauren Langman, 'Goffman meets Marx at the Shopping Mall', paper presented at the ASA Annual Conference, 1991; cited in Rob Shields, 'Spaces for the Subject of Consumption', in Shields, ed., *Lifestyle Shopping*, p. 5.

20. See Daniel Miller, *Material Culture and Mass Consumption*, Oxford 1987, p. 144.

21. See Fiske, *Reading the Popular*, p. 14.

22. See Mary Yelanjian, 'Rhythms of Consumption', *Cultural Studies*, vol. 5, no. 1, January 1991, p. 93.

23. See for instance Rachel Bowlby, *Shopping with Freud*, London 1993, p. 100.

24. Davidson, *Consumerist Manifesto*, p. 68.

25. As discussed by Arato in 'Esthetic Theory and Cultural Criticism', in Andrew Arato and Eike Gebhardt, eds., *The Essential Frankfurt School Reader*, New York 1982, p. 198.

26. Karl Marx, *Grundrisse. Foundations of the Critique of Political Economy (Rough Draft)*, trans. Martin Nicolaus, Harmondsworth 1973, p. 93.

27. Benjamin, *Gesammelte Schriften*, vol. I, pp. 360–61. Cited in McCole, *Walter Benjamin*, pp. 145–6.

28. Raymond Williams, *Keywords. A Vocabulary of Culture and Society*, revised edition, London 1983, p. 78.

29. Theodor Adorno and Max Horkheimer, *Dialectic of Enlightenment*, trans. John Cumming, London 1973, p. 230.

30. Susan Buck-Morss, *The Dialectics of Seeing. Walter Benjamin and the Arcades Project*, Cambridge, Mass. 1989, p. 95; for a slightly different translation, see *Illuminations*, pp. 259–60.

8

TRASH

This is William Gibson's description of the reactions of a visitor to a virtual world:

> She took her place beside him and peered down at the dirty pavement between the scuffed toes of her black Paris boots. She saw a chip of pale gravel, a rusted paperclip, the small dusty corpse of a bee or hornet. 'It's amazingly detailed . . .'[1]

Cyberspace, as we have seen, may come to concern itself largely with the strict control of the contingent, binding every aspect of the real to concepts. In trying to indicate the extent of the resources brought to bear to produce one rich man's consensual hallucination, it is natural, then, that Gibson should point to the inclusion of the useless and the neglected – to trash. Here the attention paid to rubbish, for so many people a matter of absolute necessity, becomes the expensive whim of the fantastically wealthy. In a world where concept and object are brought into perfect unison, the meaningless is the only area left for the exercise of conspicuous consumption.

While technotopia remains forever just over the horizon, it is as well to look at trash as it actually appears in our environment. Perhaps because it is so omnipresent, in greater or lesser concentrations, trash as such tends to be left unregarded, edited out of vision (and generally of photographs), ignored except as a practical problem, and deplored from an 'aesthetic' point of view, which repudiates it so as not to see it.

Trash is of course the direct product of the 'consumption' (in the sense of the early history of the word which Raymond Williams traced) of commodities. For Marx:

> a product becomes a real product only by being consumed. For example, a garment becomes a real garment only in the act of being worn; a house where no one lives is in fact not a real house; thus the product, unlike a mere natural object, proves itself to be, *becomes*, a product only through consumption. Only by decomposing the product does consumption give the product the finishing touch [. . .].[2]

It is a truism that as commodities acquired more of a character, as marketing decked them out as lavishly as models, then more and more packaging – immediate trash – surrounded them, while their passage from commodity to rubbish was ever shortened by the pace of fashion.[3] So the commodity and trash are as closely linked as production and consumption. It may even be that we can think of commodities as deferred trash.

I want to look at the afterlife of commodities closely for a while, to examine it as advertisements would have us look at new products, to see if it might yield narratives or express identities; to see, in short, if it is possible to salvage from it, unlike commodity culture, some 'true stories'. One of the constant claims of this book has been that grounds for critique may be found in mistakes and contingencies, whether in the bugs of computer coding, the inane techniques of the amateur photographer or the accidental effects of overwriting in graffiti. It might be strange to call it culture, but a great and subversive work of art, an immensely complex collage, is made and remade every day on the street and everyone participates in its fabrication. Trash, like graffiti, is something which people make collectively, and not quite inadvertently. Its form and the manner of its making are closely tied to the materials of our commercial culture and our attitudes to its products and the environment. Such a treatment of this subject can be relevant only in rich capitalist societies where the material from which broken commodities is made is not endlessly reused, bricolaged into intricate and ingenious devices, but is simply thrown away.

There are certain precedents for such an analysis: Adorno wrote of Siegfried Kracaeur, for instance, who concentrated on objects as a compensation for the lack of meaningful relationships with people and attempted to turn reification against itself, by taking its claims seriously:

> To a consciousness that suspects it has been abandoned by human beings, objects are superior. In them thought makes reparations for what human beings have done to the living. The state of innocence would be the condition of needy objects, shabby, despised objects alienated from their purposes. For Kracaeur they alone embody something that would be other than the universal functional complex, and his idea of philosophy would be to lure their indiscernible life from them.[4]

It was also, of course, a part of Benjamin's project to make history from its refuse, and Adorno wrote of him in similar terms: 'Philosophy appropriates the fetishization of commodities for itself: everything must metamorphose into a thing in order to break the catastrophic spell of things'.[5] An apparently redundant beauty, particular only to trash, is certainly a frequent feature of its appearance in the street and by the roadside – anywhere, in fact, where it is not meant to be. Sometimes in the country a storm will catch the top layers of some landfill site, and suddenly, when calm has returned, the bare trees will be full of strange new flowers in bright primary colours, twisting and rustling in the breeze. These plastic bags hang on the branches for months, slowly becoming more soiled, faded and ripped until they take on the appearance of glossy rags. The meaning of trash would seem to lie in a surreal absurdity, but by taking it seriously, this very quality may come to illuminate the real absurdity of the situation in which it is produced.

There are a shrinking number of everyday spaces which do not construct eternal presents, where memory is not discarded from moment to moment – we have looked at the computer screen and driving, and will look at television. The street is one of the few environments which do not at least aspire to phantasmagoria; here incident is constantly thrown into competition with commercial propaganda. The Walkman is of course an attempt to seal off the street from the pedestrian, but its effect is very incomplete and may end up organizing the incident of sights, other sounds, jostling and the feel of the pavement into a narrative by providing it with a sound track. It can load trivia with significance, thus ironically increasing its sense of particularity. As far as rubbish goes, strenuous attempts are of course made, particularly in the wealthier areas, to keep this displaced matter hidden from sight. These municipal measures are pitted against the constant torrent of packaged goods which pours out on to the streets in the hands of millions every hour of the day, and they constantly fail.

To inquire about rubbish is to ask what happens to commodities when they cease to be commodities, but which for a time retain their form as objects. For Marx, as we have seen, only when the object is consumed does it shed its material nature and become a product; when its use value, or at least the appearance of its use value, is exhausted, the product should become once more a merely material husk. Yet there hangs about it a certain air of embarrassment, a reminder of some vague promise unredeemed. Such objects, when abandoned in the streets, first allow their material natures to step out from behind the form of use value. They seem lost, like children who have strayed. Thrown into combination with other objects or with dirt, they comment ironically on themselves. Unmade, their polished unitary surfaces fall away, reinscribing in them for a time the labour that went into their making. As they begin to disintegrate, their mixing and eventual merging with other diverse products reveals for a time their differentiated identity as matter, and when they are finally ground into the unity of filth, their graded identities as commodities, unified only by the universal typology of money, become apparent. Somehow, during this process, their allure is not lost but, loosed from exchange and use value, it takes on an apparently more genuine aesthetic air.

While the puns and subversive gestures of Cubist and Dada collage have long since lost their power for radicalism, hanging on the walls of public museums and exclusive galleries, the collage of filth in the street retains its effect precisely because it really is impermanent (rather than merely looking it) and because it really does register something of the constantly changing forces which surround us. Indeed this collective, unconscious action on cultural products (writing, pictures, packaging, commodities all) amounts to an act of criticism of the culture as a whole, a tearing of it into equal fragments and their random disposal, followed by a promiscuous mixing and blending. Habermas's comments about the role of criticism in relation to allegorical works of art are relevant here: 'the critique practices this mortification of the work of art only to transpose what is worth knowing from the medium of the beautiful into that of the true and thereby to rescue it'.[6] Disposal then may be seen as a form of criticism; the way in which objects are thrown down in the street reveals a certain contempt, and it may be witnessed often enough in that singular, abrupt gesture in which people toss something down on the pavement, or let it fly in a little arc from a car window. Truth does not lie in the disciplined gardens and the scrubbed streets of the rich, where anything disposed of is kept in containers sealed away from sight and then quickly whisked away: the poor have a near monopoly on this non-commodity. The allegorical nature of criticism itself is here entirely appropriate for we are already dealing with the fragmentary remains of dead objects.

Objects gain and lose something when they are abandoned as rubbish. What they lose is related to their presentation by advertising as desirable commodities: newness, utility, wholeness, a distinction from other objects, or at least a resistance to arbitrary merging. The presentation of the commodity in advertising photography has been, almost from its origin, to stress these qualities, to mark the object as highly distinct from its surroundings – however appropriate they might be – to stress its cleanliness, to light it in order to emphasize the clarity of its borders. If it is brought into contact with other objects, or even transformed into them, this only happens after the most meticulous research into their symbolic suitability. In becoming rubbish the object, stripped of this mystification, gains a doleful truthfulness, as though confessing: it becomes a reminder that commodities, despite all their tricks, are just stuff; little combinations of plastics or metal or paper. The stripping away of branding and its attendant emotive attachments reveals the matter of the object behind the veneer imposed by a manufactured desire.

Abandoned objects have crossed a great divide from which they can never return. Commodities are of course signs in a system of value, both monetary and social, which is lost when they are abandoned. When objects are seen together as trash, relationships of a more poetic and intrinsic interest emerge. The qualities of the thing itself begin to appear in sharp relief like pictures in a developing tray. We see them for the first time with clarity, which is the same as that clear-sighted ridicule with which we greet old adverts and the particularities and idiosyncrasies of design in old commodities: their arbitrariness and alien nature are suddenly revealed. With the ever more rapid cycling of products into obsolescence, the whole process of manufacture and discarding becomes an accelerated archaeology.

The uniqueness and materiality of commodities are false projections or fetishes which are nonetheless realized when the individual commodity begins to acquire a history in its consumption: when objects finally cease to be of commercial use, these qualities are realized and released. Aside from its dishonourable history in the service of advertising, photography has long had a role in making this latent content manifest: we might think, for instance, of the work of Bernd and Hilla Becher, who photograph derelict industrial architecture. The sharpness of their photographs and the weight of presence of each peculiarity in the buildings they represent suggest that we can only see these structures as themselves, or rather that they only become suitable for aesthetic appropriation, when they have ceased to function. Just as the product only becomes real in being consumed, so Hilla Becher has claimed that their work is only complete when its subject has been destroyed.[7]

Trash is often present as writing or images as well as mere matter. When packaging is discarded the bright, slick company logos, deformed by buckled paper or plastic, finally find their proper place. Because the brand name is an attempt to forge form and signification into an inseparable unit, when the material of the brand name falls as trash, its content must follow. Commodities – and let us think of those which most often end up underfoot, soft drinks, confectionery, fast food – are literally mired with filth. This trash writing may be seen as another form of graffiti, omnipresent like its wall-bound counterpart, critical, and, unlike brand-name graffiti, full of content. Pictures and words disintegrate as water dissolves the fabric of the paper, or under the wear of feet and tyres, producing an image of the decline of reading and expression. Accidental meanings in collages of trash sometimes emerge, often as inadvertent puns and jokes. When language is so governed by commerce and a specious equivalence of signifier and signified has been established, the dissolution of words, of language itself, can seem positive. The simultaneous destruction of fabric and the content it supports may serve as a comment on the deleterious effects of the false unity of form and content on meaning. In commodified language, when taken as a whole as an elaborate collage of text and advertising, the significance of content falls away and a uniformity of form holds sway: we can generally spot a hobbyist's magazine or a newspaper supplement well before being able to read the title, or identify any of the predictable content. In the street, where this discarded material loses its content and is transformed into matter, its form at last takes on something of the truth of its content, being turned slowly into pulp. Of course in the original photographs and often in texts there is some residue of the particular, something which in its fragmented state exceeds commodification, and this suffers from material degradation as much as everything else. To look to destruction for the positive, and for critique in garbage, is one way of saying how bad things are.

It is important to realize that what we are examining here is filth, not stuff disposed of in rubbish dumps where it can be safely ignored, but rather trash on the streets or by roadsides: it is not merely redundant, but out of place, reacting against the unitary phantasmagoria of capital. As Mary Douglas famously put it in 'Purity and Danger', 'Where there is dirt there is system.'[8] Dirt is an omnibus category for matter out of place. Each displaced object is collaged with others and with a mismatched environment, whether rural, industrial or urban. In all cases an allegorical aesthetic of the fragment is opened up which may be read as revelatory of the operation of capitalism. The advert attempts to present its product as an autonomous and vaguely significant symbol, while in trash, commodities, having passed out of the hierarchies and false associations of exchange, are revealed as specific allegories.

Photography may bring out the allegorical potential of lost objects by framing, dematerializing and arranging them within the frame of the picture, thus presenting them as something to be read. Advertisements and the more generalized use of photography to make narratives prepare us for such a reading. In taking rubbish as an allegory of contemporary capital we are simply using the devices of commerce and turning them on other objects which lie all about us. This is certainly not to claim, as the propagandists of commercial culture constantly do, that there are symbolic or organic connections between these things. Trash, breaking with the false unity of the consumer object, reveals its allegorical potential by unmasking the symbolic pose of the commodity as a sham. Torn, dirtied or broken, thrown into combination with other fragmentary objects, while it remains itself, it becomes a broken shell, its meaning reaching out to its partners in a forlorn but telling narrative.

In making an image of the dissolution of our dominant systems, trash finds forms which reflect various aspects of high art – or they, drawn by certain affinities, sometimes come to reflect its appearance. The straightforward presentation of such objects in photographs may be open to Adorno's critique of Benjamin's methods in 'The Paris of the Second Empire in Baudelaire'. Adorno argued that motifs can be explained only by the overall social and economic tendency of the age, by an analysis of the commodity form, and that, for instance, 'The direct inference from the duty on wine to *L'Ame du vin* imputes to phenomena precisely that kind of spontaneity, palpability and density which they have lost in capitalism.' He continues that a lack of mediation, a wide-eyed presentation of the facts (and this is photography exactly) lends to empirical evidence a 'deceptively epic character', placing it solely in the realm of the subjective so ignoring its 'historico-philosophical weight'.[9] The rejoinder here, of course, is that in looking at ex-commodities, there may be some occasional return of a palpability and density which are still present as an ideal in our minds, that they may cling to certain residues of object and thought alike. The predilection of photography, though, to construct a false epic, one much used by advertisers, must be admitted. The question is whether this tendency can be turned.

Benjamin's reply to Adorno was that his practice of philology was a prelude to critique and was itself an implicit critique of philology.[10] While Douglas warns us that 'We should not force ourselves to focus on dirt',[11] to look seriously at trash is a similar activity: a means to critique, and an implicit condemnation of the readings of those who peddle commercial culture. In literary allegory there is an apparent excess of detail which alerts the reader to the operation of a structure beyond the norms of realism; this cannot be expected to operate in the real, where there are no expectations of reading, however literal the combinations of trash sometimes appear to be. The presentation of this subject in photographs, however, creates expectations, especially in its parasitic operation against customary commercial readings.

We should also recall, from the first chapter, Benjamin's criticism of a photography which makes enjoyment out of abject poverty and transfigures even a 'refuse heap'.[12] Yet there is also a positive side to this recognition of beauty in the world, one closely related to the practice of amateur photography, of working against the evidence in the hope of transforming the world. Arcadian images spoilt by the presence of trash show how beauty survives the transformation, if only by contrast, and how ruination provides an indication of the possibility of something better.

The image of trash is perfectly suited to allegory for 'it is as something incomplete and imperfect that the objects stare out from the allegorical structure'. By separating image and meaning, allegory rejects the false appearance of artistic unity and presents itself as a ruin.[13] In this it has an honesty which utopian symbolism can no longer claim. As a form, allegory contains a critique within itself, since in its presentation of itself in ruins and decay it becomes an expression of the experience of 'the passionate, the oppressed, the unreconciled and the failed'.[14] The fragment, torn from a false totality, becomes the ground for a totalizing critique, if only because its symbolic connection to the whole has not been completely shed in its transformation into allegory. The links are still felt, but are now manifestly arbitrary and so the natural appearance of the system of commercial symbols is broken. Allegory, in showing us images of death and of a mortified nature, also reveals the fixed and arbitrary systems which are responsible.

While allegory has often been associated with decaying objects and petrified nature, advertisements, though they inadvertently take allegory as their form, shy away from such subjects, very nearly without exception. In such marketing all is the exact opposite in a display of pristine objects and an absolute, mandatory liveliness. More than anything else, trash reveals the broken utopian promise of the commodity.

The lesson of the obsolete gives the lie to the promise of ultimate satisfaction. It is all the more powerful at a time when there is rising disaffection with materialism and the price that must be paid for mass-produced idiocy, when green issues are rightly seen to be ever more urgent. The capitalist 'answer' to this is a move to encouraging the increased consumption of software. There is no trash in cyberspace because there is nothing material to be disposed of and indeed because everything may be kept. This technological fix is of course insufficient, for many reasons which we have already considered, but also because, until the rich are transfigured as digital angels, they will retain their current material and bodily needs and whims.

Maybe there are other things that trash can say. It is of course a powerful reminder of the West's profligacy in consumption, of the extraordinary engines of waste that are our economies, sacrificing vast quantities of matter and human labour on rubbish dumps. In this way trash rightly becomes a matter of guilt because of the despoliation of the environment, because of conspicuous wastage flaunted in the face of those who do not have enough, and because of our own indulgence, carefully fostered by corporations.

In commodities, as we have seen, branding is the identification of the object as quasi-human, the embodiment of a principle, a demon which is fixed and faithful, inexorable in its cheerfulness, reliability, protectiveness, or whatever quality is at that moment being marketed. When they are thrown out as rubbish, commodities lose this character but gain a semblance of a 'real' personality, that is, something fluid which alters and is altered by the things around it, and which, as groups, forever create and destroy each other. Where commodities have taken on the guise of persons in branding, and when they are thrown away, then this action and their fall into the gutter are the equivalent of discarding persons, and indeed there they accompany the real outcasts. As if seeing their companionship, some of the homeless collect trash, using it to help clothe and shelter them. Some carry their own fantastical trash collages in old supermarket trolleys. Occasionally one sees, as in a vision, scraps of plastic, paper and cloth, bound together with string, rising again from the street in human form, shuffling down the street, an animated stumpy tower of trash, a hybrid human-object. Only when the commodity is done with can it assume human form. Both brands and workers are imperfect

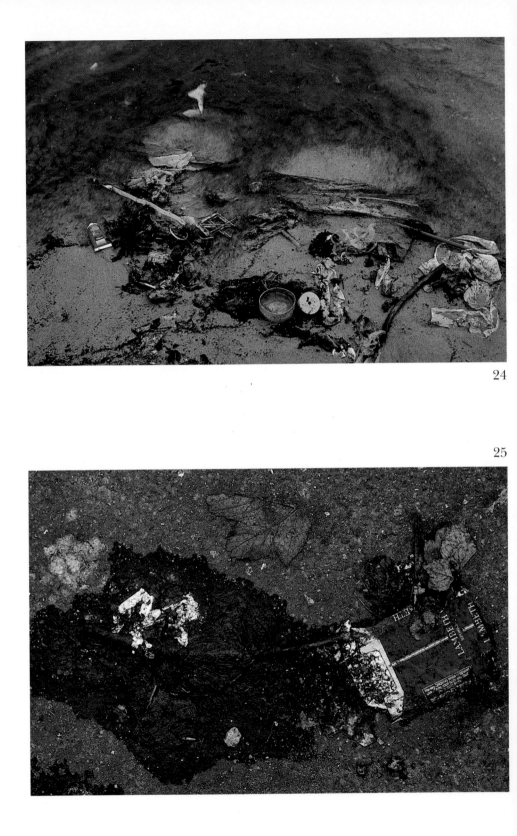

26

27

persons, being carefully graded types matched to markets and tasks respectively. As with Lukács's self-recognition of reification, there is some poignant self-recognition to be found in trash, when it is torn from its usual context and presented in the light of the social totality. When the commodity form is stripped away, something may be revealed of the social relations which are immanent in the objects and which bind people and their fates.

Benjamin wrote of children:

> They are irresistibly drawn by the detritus generated by building, gar-
> dening, housework, tailoring, or carpentry. In waste products they
> recognize that the world of things turns directly and solely to them. In
> using these things they do not so much imitate the work of adults as
> bring together, in the artifact produced in play, materials of widely dif-
> fering kinds in a new, intuitive relationship.[15]

So there is a certain freedom revealed in children's relation to objects, which is not governed by instrumentality, in which all qualities of their playthings are treated equally. This is surely an aesthetic attitude; in their innocence, children may still have unmediated access to the playful, light-hearted aspect of art, which is essential to it, but which adults of the twentieth century may have to repudiate.[16] It is doubly true of an art which is non-commercial, by accident or design, which may serve as a refuge, however fragile, against the unremitting instrumentality of the market.[17] When something has been required to throw into opposition to the commodity, the work of art has often been cast in the role. Lukács, for instance, argued that art provides features that the commodity cannot: a form irreducible from content, an enriching objectification of the subjective, and a deconstruction of the opposition between freedom and necessity, since each element of the work of art seems both autonomous and subordinated to the whole.[18] Now many of these factors have changed as a result of modernism, which has affected the work of art and the commodity alike, especially as commodities and the marketing which surrounds them have aspired to the condition of art. However, some of these qualities can be looked for in trash. For Adorno the modernist work of art produced a dialectic of particularity and aesthetic integration, the latter formed by a progressive emptying of content from the elements of a work. So, 'The particular, the very life element of the work, flees the viewing subject, its concreteness evaporates under the micrological gaze'. Amorphous elements, when combined in a composition, find in this organization a 'natural moment' in which the 'not yet formed' and 'unarticulated' return in strength. Taken separately, they evaporate.[19] While subsuming each element to its overall scheme, the work of art must recognize and exploit some intrinsic quality of that element with which to order it in relation to the others, so in the composition each element finds its particularity understood.

Now, ironically, this is something like the operation of the metonymic field of differentiated commodities which as a whole forms that structure which presents itself as an aesthetic unit, the consumer market. Each element is empty except in relation to each other and the appearance of the whole is as of nature, an inevitable form. As in the modernist work of art, the same dialectic of integration and particularity is established. The grounds of this operation are the single, apparently universal typology of monetary value, just as in art it is the aesthetic.

It may be, then, that a certain liberation can be found in aspects of trash which is no longer present in the thoroughly colonized ground of high art. Commodification and much contemporary art seek to subjectify the objective, while trash activates the opposite process, muddying the subjective with the objective and revealing something of the former's vanity. The elements of commodities are subject to false instrumental unities, while the random collage of trash allows each element its own voice for as long as it survives, yet seems governed by the necessity of a higher power. The constant flux of objects on to and through the streets, and their removal or disintegration, has a rhythm which is usually too slow and disjointed to grasp, although we might get an impression of it when papers are blown about in high winds, or carrier bags lifted into the air like balloons. When snorkelling once I caught sight of something which seemed to summarize this process: swimming between two narrowing rock faces, I saw that the sea-bed at their foot was carpeted with garbage and unidentifiable detritus forming a thick mass which shifted in and out with each tug and push of the waves, changing its form subtly as it did so. In such scenes there appears a vision of an emergent order, gathering rubbish, and governing its disposition and the rate of its disintegration. Such an order, better than that of immaterial cyberspace, may serve as an image of an otherwise unrepresentable capital.

While in modernist high art, elements may lose all qualities other than those which sustain them within an order, photography starts from the opposite position. In 'straight' photographs, where the photographer finds rather than creates subject matter, each element of the picture retains a large portion of its autonomy and particularity, for they are integrated mostly through the selection of a viewpoint. It is a form of composition in which elements are arranged rather than altered. It is when integration is at the point of disappearing (for the more subtle it is, the more retiring) that the meaning of the particular steps out from behind it. Photography's loose compositional structure and respect for contingency may then be allied with the allegorical form of trash.

Adorno, writing of a desperate historical situation, but one no worse than our own, stated grimly, 'there is no longer beauty or consolation except in the gaze falling on horror, withstanding it, and in unalleviated consciousness of negativity holding fast to the possibility of what is better'.[20] Unmanipulated photography may for the moment allow an unalleviated gaze of this kind. There might be a sense in which commodities, represented in photographs and stripped of specious attractions, acquire something of a true aesthetic charge as trash. They become a complex of contradictory, oppositional and negative forces. If a 'true' aesthetic is to be found in trash then the art-historical references which it unwittingly produces (and which a viewer may construct) assume a particular importance as an 'unconscious' construction of a tradition, and as a mark of trash's artistry. Of these art-historical 'references' in trash, the connection between still life and allegory, particularly the memento mori, is the most striking.

There is no sense in which this merely aesthetic recuperation is more than the starting point for a critique which must be material and social as well as affective. It is no more than an illustration. In itself such aestheticism is a highly marginalized, elite and powerless kind of radicalism. Yet even this carries its own dangers. The most immediately obvious is that this concentration on the fragment and on allegory is seen as a mere gesture against the total system of capital rather than a specific critique of a set of particular circumstances, however persistent. Nevertheless, Adorno is surely right that such a totalizing critique, while being a form of untruth, is a necessary consequence of and response to a totalizing system.[21]

There is also a danger that in too specifically spelling out the other side of homogenization and domination, and particularly in bringing it to representation, we might make it fixed enough to be reified as an object for consumption in its turn. This brings us to the matter of whether there are things which capital cannot assimilate. As we have seen, Terry Eagleton has argued that it can only fail to assimilate its own defeat,[22] but is this strictly the case? While high art is in part defined by the freedom which it is permitted, its sphere of operation is strictly proscribed. Is it really true that everything has been levelled, everything commercialized, that there is nothing that cannot be assimilated into the chat and the image of the advertisement? As Bataille understood, there are certain aspects of uncleanliness and filth that do seem resistant to this treatment. Advertisements may deal sometimes with disturbing or even horrific imagery, but it is more difficult to imagine them dealing with something which is their precise obverse: with fragmented, aged, dirty and chaotically combined objects – with the discarded. The filth in the street is radical because it informs us of the fate of commodities, a destination which is carefully repressed in all adverts: it is impossible to imagine advertisements for chocolate bars turning from their predictable references to fellatio to reminding the customer of the final destination of their product. Commodity culture is certainly bound by rigid exclusions and the regular censorship of the mainstream media for political and commercial purposes points to matters which go beyond assimilation. So there is plenty that capitalism must suppress, at least for the consumption of those outside the elite. At the same time commercial culture is voracious in its appropriation of the new, the radical and the potentially dangerous: the Benetton advertisements are only the most notorious recent example of this, illustrating precisely the need of a certain kind of advertising to push back the boundaries of assimilation. Any marked tendency that tries to put itself beyond the pale, especially if it labels itself as marginal, is inviting this treatment.

In looking at the negative, the problem is of course how to avoid turning shock into schlock, for any form of represented or mediated horror is immediately absorbed as part of the culture industry. Fallen objects resist such assimilation in the brief time of their existence, but works of art in their travel through time cannot: the photographs in this book, then, must serve as mere illustrations, as evidence for an argument. As we have seen, photography tends to say the same thing over and over again: this is the way things are. Here photographs serve a more explicit purpose, being governed by their relationship to the text.[23] It is worth asking, though, what photography itself contributes.

In their presentation of sheer surface, trash and photography have a certain affinity for one another. Roland Barthes has written of the way Dutch still life concentrates on surface, on 'the secondary vibrations of appearance', particularly on sheen. Is this, asks Barthes, so as 'to lubricate man's gaze amid his domain, to facilitate his daily business among objects whose riddle is dissolved and which are no longer anything but easy surfaces?'[24] Here, at the origins of the capitalist world, is a type of painting which tries to make objects easier to handle and trade by glossing over them with the unitary brush of the aesthetic. In photography, as we have seen, surface is all, yet, in some occult fashion, it is supposed to give us access to some universal essence. With the representation of trash, however, things are a little different; here any sheen is not the product of some advertiser's skill, but is the gloss formed by a layer of liquid over the object, or of some corruption breaking its surface. In wet climes, at any rate, trash carries its own aura of dampness about it, as though it had bled evenly on to the pavement. It is in the process of breaking down surface and progressively revealing its insides until there is no longer a rigorous distinction between them. So where the surface of trash is expressive of the nature of the object and the processes which it undergoes, then photography can assume its superficial role without dissimulation or guilt.

Context is everything in the construction of critical meanings. Irving Penn made refined black and white platinum prints of pieces of trash which he had picked up and then shot in the studio against pristine white backgrounds. Torn from the company of the environment and their fellow objects, they lost the largest part of their significance. These isolated fragments were treated just like new commodities by this successful commercial photographer, becoming renewed as abstractions, and most of all revealed themselves as discrete objects and as prints for purchase. No photography, however, can avoid beginning to embark along this road of abstraction, if only through the selection, framing and disposing of objects within a pictorial configuration. Such a practice is bound up with modern and postmodern scrutiny of the street, with sniffing about in the place where some vestigial community might be found, in the hope of picking up some scent of significance, which may then be marketed to distinguish some product. This is especially true also of a photography which searches, isolates and to an extent fabricates meaning in the street. If context disappears, and all that is left is a typically masculine view of the urban environment, where a flaneur wanders, selecting fragments for aesthetic delectation, and understanding nothing of people's interactions or the fitting together of elements, then this is not accidental. The aesthetic appears only as functions shrivel, and the operation of commodity culture and all its products acts to sever people from one another, leaving the poorest to dwell among its discarded goods.

All this is not of course been to claim that there is some radical, popular power to littering. It is merely a symptom which may be activated by criticism. Photography acts as another layer of subject matter, a comment fixing and laid over what is temporarily there and what will continue to be transformed after the shutter blades have closed. It freezes the temporal unfolding of allegorical decay producing dialectics at a standstill, a snapshot of a conflicting process under way, revealing past, present and future. In its rarest and very best moments, photography may also indicate a point in the historical process where the tensions are greatest, the point of phase change.

As we have seen, Benjamin's angel flies backwards into the future, looking to the past as an ever greater pile of catastrophes mounts at its feet. Our life in the developed world, too, is a constant process of discarding, of consigning ever greater piles of material to waste, and with it, often all values which are not based on continuing this renewal and disposal, all sense of continuity. The grounds for criticism are literally in front of our eyes. In the next chapter, and this will be the final case study of visual culture, we shall turn from the 'unconscious' display of critique in trash to the highly self-conscious self-critique of television; or, from real to electronic trash.

NOTES

1. William Gibson, *Count Zero*, London 1986, p. 26.

2. Karl Marx, *Grundrisse. Foundations of the Critique of Political Economy (Rough Draft)*, trans. Martin Nicolaus, Harmondsworth 1973, p. 91.

3. For a curious account of this process, and the way in which rubbish can eventually acquire a new kind of value as a non-disposable artefact, see Michael Thompson, *Rubbish Theory. The Creation and Destruction of Value*, Oxford 1979.

4. Theodor W. Adorno, 'The Curious Realist: On Siegfried Kracaeur', *Notes to Literature*, ed. Rolf Tiedemann, trans. Shierry Weber Nicholsen, New York 1992, vol. II, p. 75.

5. Adorno, *Prisms*, trans. Samuel and Shierry Weber, Cambridge, Mass. 1981, p. 233.

6. Jürgen Habermas, 'Walter Benjmain: Consciousness-Raising or Rescuing Critique', in Gary Smith, ed., *On Walter Benjamin. Critical Essays and Recollections*, Cambridge, Mass. 1988, p. 99.

7. Paris, Centre National des Arts Plastiques/Prato, Museo d'Arte Contemporanea Luigi Pecci, *Un'altra obiettività/Another Objectivity*, curated by Jean François Chevrier and James Lingwood, Milan 1989, p. 57.

8. Mary Douglas, 'Purity and Danger', in Robert Bocock and Kenneth Thompson, *Religion and Ideology*, Manchester 1985, p. 111.

9. Theodor Adorno, Walter Benjamin, Ernst Bloch, Bertolt Brecht and Georg Lukács, *Aesthetics and Politics*, London 1980, p. 129.

10. Ibid., p. 136.

11. Douglas, 'Purity and Danger', p. 111.

12. Benjamin, 'The Author as Producer', in Andrew Arato and Eike Gebhardt, eds., *The Essential Frankfurt School Reader*, New York 1982, p. 262.

13. Benjamin, *Trauerspiel*, p. 186; cited and analysed by Charles Rosen, 'The Ruins of Walter Benjamin', in Gary Smith, ed., *On Walter Benjamin*, pp. 150–51.

14. Habermas, 'Walter Benjamin', p. 96.

15. Benjamin, *One Way Street and Other Writings*, trans. Edmund Jephcott and Kingsley Shorter, London 1979, pp. 52–3.

16. See Adorno, 'Is Art Lighthearted?', in *Notes to Literature*.

17. See Adorno, *Minima Moralia. Reflections from Damaged Life*, trans. E.F.N. Jephcott, London 1974, p. 68.

18. As discussed by Eagleton in *The Ideology of the Aesthetic*, Oxford 1990, p. 324.

19. Adorno, *Aesthetic Theory*, trans. C. Lenhardt, London 1984, pp. 148–9.

20. Adorno, *Minima Moralia*, p. 25.

21. See Adorno, *Negative Dialectics*, trans. E.B. Ashton, London 1973, pp. 5–6.

22. Eagleton, *The Ideology of the Aesthetic*, p. 372.

23. Benjamin's answer to the uncontrolled aestheticization of subject matter by photography was of course to unify it with writing, so controlling the context of each. Benjamin, 'The Author as Producer', in Arato and Gebhardt, eds, *The Essential Frankfurt School Reader*, p. 263.

24. Barthes, 'The World as Object', in Susan Sontag, ed., *A Barthes Reader*, London 1982, p. 64.

9

LOOKING-GLASS TV

In the flight from contingency the most effective vehicle is still television. In many homes and places of leisure its constant, diverting presence, light emitting, ever mobile, ever noisy, attempts to fill distracted consciousness to the brim. Fear of the vacuum and of silence is banished. Much has rightly been made of television's ideological import and, more recently, much more of people's varied responses to its one-way communication. Less has been said, except very generally, about the effects of its constant presence on lives, activities and conversations. Some of the best analyses of this are found not in academic writing but in novels, particularly in the work of John Updike, whose character Rabbit walks 'under television aerials raking the same four o'clock garbage from the sky'.[1] Elsewhere in the Rabbit tetralogy the fragmented conversations in front of television, the divided attention between screen and fellow viewers, and the invasion of subjective habits and ways of thinking by the fake mores of television acting are dissected in detail.

The style of television programming has been shifting due to the impetus of new technologies, competition from new media, marketing devices and modes of delivery. Television documentary, and indeed its presentation of most information, is an already jaded preview of virtual reality, a simulation of the experience of actually being there, in which the aim is always to conjure an atmosphere, as if this could serve as a context for facts, as if understanding, bypassing the mind, were absorbed through the skin. In this it pretends always to be at the service of the subjective.

Against this apparent address to subjectivity, aspects of the human interior are usually expressed on the surface. To use an example given by Stanley Aronowitz in an essay about the impact of the visual media on interpretation, social class is indicated through clothing or accent, but what it means from the subjective point of view is rarely explored, being rather merely gestured towards, as if somehow the viewer already understood.[2] Television documentary has adapted a metonymic way of illustrating themes taken from narrative film and television drama. It well exemplifies the old argument about bourgeois vision being passive and distanced, suspending time and action and striving, not to explain the functional connections between things, but to evoke their essence or flavour. So if the 1920s are mentioned, then inevitably we hear some jazz music and are shown sepia-tinted film of a desk with a bakelite phone or an Art Deco paperweight. This is not just to identify the era by reminding people of clichés about the decade which they have at the back of their minds, but is supposed to invoke a subjective, aestheticized experience of being there – in short, a simulation.[3] The unspoken ideological basis of such techniques is an extreme phenomenological position which is very much connected to the primacy of sight. By stimulating the senses with the sights and sounds of an experience, its inner feeling – and thus its meaning, inevitably dragged in its wake – can be raised within the viewer like a ghost. If it is true that people actually respond to these images in different ways – or sometimes not at all – then one would never know it from the medium itself, which remains singularly unitary. A postmodern diversity of views is generally confined to words while the visual basis of the broadcast is straightforward stimulus–response. Advertisements exploit these now customary readings in an even more condensed fashion. This economical means of expression has a tendency to reinforce cliché through a series of standard images, collaged together. Viewers come to expect that surfaces are directly expressive of essences and that complex social situations can be condensed within a single, telling image.

So, while television takes as its target the subjective experience of the individual, its forms of expression undermine subjectivity and interiority. Aronowitz argues:

The attempt to go beyond bourgeois subjectivity to the things themselves is entirely consistent with the tendency of modern thought to
transform everything into a measurable object in order to dominate it.
Yet the activity of abolishing the interiority is undertaken in the name
of freedom from domination.[4]

The abolition is taken over from film and television into the mores
of everyday life, where it is ever more readily assumed that people
will wear their hearts on their sleeves, defining themselves by dress,
and interchangeably bearing political slogans and brand names on
their shirts. Adorno and Horkheimer, writing of mass culture in
general at a time when television was still in its infancy, nevertheless
anticipated this abolition of the individual and its replacement by
the pseudo-originality of the personality which must always be
expressed in signs on the surface: 'The peculiarity of the self is a
monopoly commodity determined by society; it is falsely represented
as natural.'[5]

This has consequences both for the viewer's self-image and for the
way in which information is conveyed. Like much documentary photography (although for reasons much more to do with approach than
the restrictions of the medium itself) television only occasionally conveys evidence; more often it illustrates something which we are
supposed to assent to or already know. In this way its commercial
symbiosis with other media is matched by its intellectually parasitic
relation to books, magazines, newspapers and, at the base of it all,
school learning; on the very thing, in fact, which the ubiquity of television and its associated technologies helps to undermine. A vicious
circle is established in which broadcasters' falling expectations of
people's attention span and general knowledge contribute to their
decline.

The conventional wisdom of recent writing about television in cultural studies has been to challenge such views. As David Morley put it
in a comprehensive overview of academic studies of the medium:

As we all know, in the bad old days television audiences were considered
as passive consumers, to whom things happened as television's miracu-
lous powers affected them. According to choice, these (always other)

people were turned into zombies, transfixed by bourgeois ideology or filled with consumerist desires. Happily, so the story goes, it was then discovered that this was an inaccurate picture, because in fact these people were out there, in front of the set, being active in all kinds of ways – making critical/oppositional readings of dominant cultural forms, perceiving ideological messages selectively/subversively, etc., etc. So, it seems, we needn't worry – the passively consuming audience is a thing of the past.[6]

Somehow, Morley further claims, as this shift of view took place, the political issue of media power slipped off the academic agenda. Various assumptions underlie these influential theories: the semiotic process is romanticized and divorced from all considerations of the social to the extent that it is assumed that the range of readings open to the trained critic are also open to all other viewers.[7] When such readings have been based on psychoanalysis, they have deduced audience responses wholly from the structure of the 'text' and have taken as their subject only the relation between an isolated, preconceived subject and a single programme.[8] It is curious that views which support the polysemic reading of television are generally predicated on the autonomous, bourgeois individual constructing an identity from diverse components. Any reading, however complex or arcane, has the same status as any other. Indeed, although most of us find watching television all too easy, the 'skills' brought to 'reading' television are constantly described as though they were hard-won academic competencies:

> Cultural competence involves a critical understanding of the text and the conventions by which it is constructed, it involves the bringing of both textual and social experience to bear upon the program at the moment of reading, and it involves a constant and subtle negotiation and renegotiation of the relationship between the textual and the social.[9]

Now this all sounds very impressive, but we should be aware of the difference between actions which are highly complex but which we find easy (like walking and chewing gum at the same time) and those which are intellectually difficult. If we conflate the two, anything can

seem like academic work. As Meaghan Morris sharply put it, referring
to the work of John Fiske and others: '"the people" have no necessary
defining characteristics – except an indomitable capacity to "negoti-
ate" readings, generate new interpretations, and remake the materials
of culture [. . .]'.[10] In this contradictory theoretical fabric, the conclusion turns out to be the very task of cultural studies itself: these
academics look to the viewing habits of ordinary people and find
only their own reflection.[11]

Now of course different groups of people do look at television in
different ways: for instance, convincing studies unsurprisingly show
that in conventional nuclear families, men generally watch television
with fixed attention and without brooking interruption, while women
do so more episodically and combine it with various domestic tasks.[12]
Such diverse types of viewing and 'reading' should not blind one to
the general effects of television as a presence, or to its overwhelmingly
middle-class outlook, which is highly apparent, for instance, in the
characters depicted and the agendas set in drama.[13] Populist, working-
class entertainment does of course have a prominent place on the
main channels, but it is set within a rigid hierarchy of high and low,
serious and light, tragic and comic. The alternation of high drama
and light comedy, of series which depict the lives of middle-class professionals and popular game shows is the product of an ordering so
durable that it can be found in much the same form in the alternation
of scenes involving noble and vulgar characters in Shakespeare.
Everybody knows where they stand in this scheme, and the very rare
exceptions break over us like a cold wave and trail controversy with
them. Set against this tide of middle-class mores, then, there are some
radical and resistant individual viewers but the statistical effect of television on the political views of the audience as a whole can be
gauged.[14]

Reader-response theorists who wish to defend the medium from its
elitist enemies need to show, then, not merely that different readings
are possible, but that they are prevalent, and that they tend to undermine the dominant ideology of the producers of television. For Fiske,
perhaps the most influential of these theorists, the crucial argument
runs as follows: 'Pleasure for the subordinate is produced by the assertion of one's social identity in resistance to, in independence of, or in
negotiation with, the structure of domination. There is no pleasure in

being a "cultural dope" [. . .]'.[15] There is no pleasure, then, in day-dreaming or fantasizing about the lifestyles, power or sexual attractiveness of the characters on television, only in reading these matters against the grain. For the disenfranchised and the marginal – a concept which encompasses a good many departures from the norm – all pleasurable readings must be in opposition to the domin-ant middle-class values prevalent in television; they must detect the subterranean clues integral to the medium to produce their own subversive script. Watching television for all but the conservative, white, male, heterosexual, able-bodied, middle-class viewer (the list of qualifiers could be greatly extended – add your own) is a very strenu-ous matter.

More fundamental even than this view is the assumption that people watch television for pleasure; that if they did not derive pleas-ure from it, they would cease to watch. This is a curiously utilitarian view. In reading surveys of the consumption of television, and par-ticularly Morley's work, *Family Television*, one of the most striking features is the uniformity of viewing habits and of people's self-descriptions of their viewing.[16] In most of the households in Morley's study the television is turned on for every waking hour, although a few might switch it off if visitors call round. The people in his sample commonly describe themselves as television addicts, and they do not feel happy with the situation: one husband describes himself and his family as 'telemaniacs, I admit', another as 'addicted' to television, 'it's like a dope to me'.[17] He expands, thinking of his wife's reading habits: 'I've never read a book in my life. I've not got the patience to read a book. I've got the patience to sit and watch telly. I ain't got the patience to do anything else, like painting. I don't do anything really.'[18] Another who reads the paper while others watch: 'I'm not really an addict of TV. It's just that I'm captured. I get tired and sit down, so I'm a captive audience [. . .]'.[19] Similarly a wife and daugh-ter are rather embarrassed about their enthusiasm for soaps: '*Crossroads, Coronation Street*. We watch all the soap operas. It's only because we haven't got much else to do.'[20] Many of them are painfully aware, at least when they are forced to reflect before a researcher, that the programmes they watch are trash. Morley is acute about the gen-der struggles that are waged over the television which often lead female viewers to dismiss their tastes as trivial or foolish. What this does not explain is the generalized, male and female distaste and guilt about television viewing, and the regular mismatch between expressed tastes and actual viewing. Morley recounts one domestic tiff (complete with Freudian slip) in which the male is defensive about his taste for light drama and comedy:

> Man: 'I'm not keen on that sort of programme.'
> Woman: 'Well, it's on now.'
> Man: 'Yes, I watch it, but – The thing I can't stand is the quiz programmes. *The Price is Right* and the other thing is *This is Your Wife* [sic].'
> Woman: '*This is Your Life.* We watched it last night.'[21]

Now it might be easy to think that, if we are saddened or made uncomfortable by these accounts, then this is just an arousal of educated, middle-class prejudice against the mores of another way of life. It is true of course that there is some determination of class here: middle-class nuclear families who have been through higher education tend to be more selective in their viewing and plan what they are going to watch.[22] Yet the problem with such relativism is that these telly addicts, of whatever class, plainly realize that most of what they watch is worthless, and that they are in some obscure way forced into it; in describing the situation they readily use the metaphor of addiction, of a force, in other words, which goes beyond their will. And, as many a compulsive bourgeois viewer knows, this is a matter which is quite capable of transcending class.

Television as a whole must be the subject of consideration. The cultural resources and possibilities open to different sets of viewers vary according to time and circumstance but the omnipresence of television and its associated products must never be forgotten. It is this integration of television into daily life which 'has somehow slipped through the net of academic enquiry'.[23] There are of course some exceptions: Joke Hermes, for example, argues that much engagement with media is strictly meaningless just because people cannot stop and think about everything they are exposed to: 'Life is largely organised around routines which do not allow for elaborate self-reflection.'[24] These forms still have an effect, however distracted their viewers, or perhaps because of their very distraction.

Character is by far the most saleable of television commodities, to the extent that the most successful ones may break away from the contexts of their invention to found new shows, and may also lead a highly profitable afterlife among advertisements.[25] The identities promised in mass culture are already fully formed and fulfilled: in them, there is rarely any possibility for change, development or learning.[26] This is taken so far that in serials (rather than soaps) any romantic involvement between the main characters must remain forever latent and never consummated. The stasis of character is partly enforced by the repetition of standard programmes at standard times which means that the character must be preserved intact in the interim.[27] In the dead week between episodes, children may wonder whether the hero, always on the point of death, will be affected by this anguishing limbo; but after the correct passage of time, there he is again, Batman or whoever, suddenly quickening from a still frame, and just the same as ever. Due to commercial pressures, television characters must adopt a purely allegorical nature:

> The finger is always poised near the dial, so all salient elements have to be established with breathtaking haste. In network logic, it follows that characters have to be stripped down to unequivocal moral emblems; their troubles spotlit; their traits, like trademarks, leaping out of the screen.[28]

Temporal development is of course a crucial aspect of individuality and it is just this which is generally edited out of television, with its presentation of never-changing 'characters' and autonomous events, both leading to constant repetition. These charismatic, beautiful characters, like commodities, appear from nowhere perfectly formed without history except of the most perfunctory, imagistic sort: a failed marriage, a bereavement, a past addiction. As character and event are frozen together into a series of fixed moments, historical process is denigrated in favour of fetishized, autonomous events and strictly delineated zeitgeists typically based, at least for recent history, on decades.

This collage effect, where vignettes which are supposed to carry meaning on their surfaces are arbitrarily juxtaposed, has been celebrated as nothing less than the aesthetic of a new era. In the age of television, argues David Harvey, listing some of the features of a postmodern aesthetics, an attachment to cultural surface, collage, superimposed quoted images and a collapsed sense of time and space are hardly surprising.[29] To go back, then, to Aronowitz's argument, film (and we may append television) tends to depict only 'the outer shell of the social character'. As we have seen, this is determined by the predominance accorded to the visual in the media, but is also due to 'the ideological predispositions of the producers faced with a mass audience for whom interiority as a psychic category was at least problematic'. He argues that the literalness of film has achieved a hegemonic position in the arts which has led to the abandonment of subjectivity where 'literalism dissolves the subject–object split into object relations'.[30] Indeed, given that television, unlike silent cinema, is not confined to the visual, its priority is probably to do with some deeper social requirement. Even where the ostensible subject is a matter of the inner being (in the depiction of emotions, for example) the faces of American actors tend to assume fixed sets of discrete expressions, separated from one another by barriers as definitive as the black bars dividing one frame of film from another, but when run fast enough, or before a distracted audience, giving the illusion of transition. As allegorical figures responding to the actions of others, they must take up a series of immediately identifiable actions and masks which stand in for internal states.

This abandonment of interiority is reinforced by television techniques of framing and cutting. Again some theorists celebrate these techniques of rigid separation of moments as heralding a new, popular aesthetic. For Fiske:

> The close-ups in soap opera may produce *jouissance*. The intense materiality of emotion in the magnified quiver of the mouth's corner, the narrowing of the eyes, the breathy wetness of the voice may produce tears in the viewer quite independent of, or even counter to, the narrative of what is said, or even what is felt, and the way that they work in the subjectivity.[31]

Such pleasures, we may note, are not much to do with 'reading'. The function and cause of these discrete and unconnected visions are in themselves extremely banal, not so much a matter of the zeitgeist but of pure commercial expediency. It has long been recognized that:

The assembly-line character of the culture industry, the synthetic, planned method of turning out its products (factory-like not only in the studio but, more or less, in the compilation of cheap biographies, pseudodocumentary novels, and hit songs) is very suited to advertising: the important individual points, by becoming detachable, inter-changeable, and even technically alienated from any connected meaning, lend themselves to ends external to the work.[32]

Their effect, however, is to reinforce the notion of an ever-changing and ever-repeating present over which we have no intellectual grasp or power. The present appears as a great, arbitrary collation of alle-gorical fragments. Some have seen zapping as a liberating activity.[33] But does it really make a great deal of difference whether viewers watch the assembled fragments of a programme put together for them, or zap from one fragment to another of the limited options on offer? As relativism has come into vogue among programme-makers, more and more shows and even documentaries are constructed to look like zapping anyhow. Zapping may make fragmentation con-scious but awareness in itself is insufficient for critique or action.

Television is surely a major factor in the homogenization of iden-tity. If art is reduced to consumption, then the audience must be reduced to a functioning part of its mechanism. From the point of view of the manufacturers and purveyors of television programmes, the participation of the audience is reduced to a simple on/off deci-sion: to watch or not to watch. The nuanced studies of diverse readings pursued by academics of popular culture are relevant to this view only insofar as multiple viewer responses are desired by produ-cers and advertisers as a way of appealing to a broad cross-section of the population. It is also important to remind ourselves that, for those who make the programmes and those who advertise alongside them, there is no question of the equality of different groups or different readings: rather, they are carefully graded by their ability and willing-ness to spend.

The audience are written into the programmes in many ways, of which canned laughter and applause are the most obvious. This is an old device which has developed from the simulation of hearty com-pany to a self-advertisement for the programme. The canned audience no longer responds only to a joke made but in anticipation of jokes about to be made or at the appearance of some favourite character or guest celebrity. This way the remote actual audience are told how to react even before the event has taken place. The same kind of naked self-advertising is seen in the overwhelming majority of pop videos: in a medium which is supposed to be about entertainment and escapism, the viewer is increasingly referred to and reified in every act.

Homogenizing effects are multiplied as people begin to refer their actual behaviour not to the other groups or individuals but to the pre-eminent fabrications of television programmes and commercials. Raymond Williams has argued that the precarious and desperate images of early modernism, of fragmentation and loss of identity, and of the grounds of communication made by artists who were often exiles, have been transformed into a modernist and post-modernist establishment:

> This, near the centres of corporate power, takes human inadequacy, self-deception, role-playing, the confusion and substitution of individuals in temporary relationships, and even the lying paradox of the communication of the fact of non-communication, as self-evident routine data.[34]

Television enforces this not only in its messages, but also in the developed fabric of the medium, which has become ever more dumbly visual, and telegraphic in its conveyance of spoken meaning. This reflects and reinforces broader social change in the character of individuals. Peter Dews has analysed Adorno's work on the erosion of the distinction between the ego and the unconscious in contemporary capitalist society, this process conforming to the deepest requirements of the 'total socialized society' in which 'the mediating instance of the ego, which contains a kernel of spontaneity and autonomy is no longer required'. The predominant social character becomes a 'subjectless subject', marked by a 'scattered, disconnected, interchangeable and ephemeral state of "informedness", which one can see will be erased by the very next moment to be replaced by new information'.[35] This is a fine description of the construction of the television viewer in which the decline of the autonomous, bourgeois subject is highly evident. Postmodern attacks upon the autonomy of the individual are accurate when they are taken as descriptions of social tendencies, but mistaken when they pretend to describe an essentialized and unchangeable condition. Behind the latter there is an assumption that the masses at any rate – if not the self-conscious theorist, who at least has the poor awareness of how easy it is to be mistaken – are incapable of mature individuality. The saving grace of this situation is supposed to be multiple, autonomous subjectivities which people inhabit and switch between. Such subjectivity must be founded, never on class, but on ever smaller, ever more separate micro-identities. If as individuals we have the power to act, to learn and to develop, then it is obvious that we should have the opportunity to do so. If various forms of 'marginality' are seen, by contrast, as a condition or an essential state, then change is hardly warranted.

This brings us to the central problem of reader-response theories in their dealings with television: they rarely take account of how television as a whole, as a ubiquitous, everyday phenomenon, affects the self which is doing the 'reading'. Active interpretations can take place, and may be fostered and brought to consciousness by academics who are out to look for them, but this should not blind us to the boredom which television caters to and the distraction it offers. Sometimes a subjective account, which fixes on interiority, best characterizes such matters:

> Television has mutilated our capacity for solitude. It has violated our most intimate, private, and secret dimension. Enslaved by an invading ritual, we fix our gaze on a bright screen which casts up billions of things that annul one another in a dizzying spiral. Peace only comes when we turn it off. At eleven o'clock or midnight great fatigue descends upon us. We go to bed with an uneasy conscience, and in the night, with closed eyes, we try to renew, like a broken thread, the inner silence that was ours.[36]

Television has a relentless one-way character. Think of the experience of first coming back to television after a break of some weeks or months, and the sharp critical attention which results. The conventions, the switches of scene and strange juxtapositions of the small screen are newly impressed on the mind, and we may marvel for a while at its ridiculous nature. To do this is to bring one's character and experience to television. But television never responds, and after some hours or days of much watching and doing little else, when you are tired or your mind is on something else, television brings its character to you.

There have been many studies of television programmes which address people as family members differentiated by gender, as citizens of a nation, as hobbyists or adherents to a religion. What, though, of those programmes which address people primarily as viewers of television? It is obvious that the makers of television generally treat their audience as though they were extraordinarily stupid. Todd Gitlin has described some of the ways in which programmers behave towards the audience as you would towards children, spelling out the plot and patiently repeating the salient points.[37] More generally he has argued that the flattened and simplified social content of many programmes is not simply political propaganda, but is a result of programmers trying not to upset the expectations of an audience who are taken to be 'uneducated, distracted, and easily bewildered'.[38] The constant injunctions of television stars, whether heroes of cop series or cartoon, models or game-show hosts, to be like themselves assumes that the audience is childishly unformed and eager to adapt. Above all, television addresses people in their unity as consumers through the constant display of goods in advertisements, game shows, consumer programmes, features and fiction – the latter by product placement. The screen becomes a shop window.[39] Beyond such broad considerations, many programmes use a mode of direct address which is designed to constitute as the object of its statements the television audience as such. The remarkable thing about much of this material, particularly in light entertainment, is the extent of its self-recognition and self-criticism.

There is a striking and quite conscious contrast between the characters generally presented on television and the construction of its viewers. Television characters, fictional heroes or presenters or the characters in advertisements, overwhelmingly conform to a positive and homogeneous ideal: whether male or female, they seem charismatic, attractive, young, and successful, at least in terms of lifestyle if not merely material wealth. They are the 'classless' middle class, independent, asocial beings who are ruled only by their (impeccable) tastes. Compulsive television viewers can only take up an ironic distance from such images, fully aware that they, far from exercising their individual tastes in the construction of an autonomous bourgeois paradise, are being governed by the taste of the programmers, consuming their lives in the contemplation of fake heroism and charisma. There is a marked and perhaps painful contrast between this manufactured utopian, hedonistic ideal and its human products.

Yet there is a form of criticism even in living as a couch potato. It is to say that you do not believe in the fakery of television identities strongly enough to try and manufacture one for yourself. Television takes up this critique as a theme of entertainment. In so many of the programmes which address viewers as viewers, there is a marked strain of both self-criticism and a critique of the audience, as though to say, 'We know this programme is trash, and we think that you are worthless individuals for watching it, but we also know that you know this, and we both know that it is pretentious and futile to try for anything better.' In programmes like *Noel Edmonds' House Party*, this attitude is played out as a specific theme: cameras are secreted in the living-rooms of couch potatoes, who find that suddenly their television is acting as a looking glass, reflecting their image back at them and, even worse, that it is talking back. This is a momentous event of which the early propagandists of television dreamt; after all those years, finally the box listens to what the viewer says and even responds – but it does so only to take the piss. Viewers are sarcastically asked about their weekend activities and made to perform some poor party turn in front of a silent audience of millions. All good, clean fun. Before the age of television, Adorno and Horkheimer wrote that:

> Conciliatory laughter is heard as the echo of an escape from power; the wrong kind overcomes fear by capitulating to the forces which are to be feared. It is the echo of power as something inescapable. Fun is a medicinal bath. The pleasure industry never fails to prescribe it.[40]

In such shows the laughter is turned directly against its consumers. This attitude to the television audience is quite general and is accompanied with a cold and knowing sneer that Wyndham Lewis, that universal satirist, would have found highly familiar.

Other more extreme examples involve their audiences only

implicitly in a display of self-conscious, craven stupidity and philistin-ism. *Beavis and Butthead* is a direct critique and simultaneous endorsement of what has been dubbed 'yob culture'. These cartoon adolescents spend most of their time watching television and – unless you really are endowed with the mental equipment of the protag-onists – the link between their viewing habits and their ignorance, smuttiness and arbitrary acts of violence is obvious. Such shows are ironic celebrations of their subjects and their audience in which cel-ebration and irony have become absolutely inseparable. This reflexive irony is linked with the increasingly fragile structure of the use of the media itself: television is facing serious challenges from interactive media including computer games, and from video 'shops' which may shortly go online. In this situation, television pre-empts criticism of itself by using it as an important element of entertainment, an old diversionary trick.

Such self-referential material is of course a great mainstay of post-modern theory: when the medium smirkingly refers to itself, revealing its own artifice, this is supposed to be a liberating experi-ence for the viewer. *Thirtysomething*, a programme with certain intellectual pretensions, regularly did this in a highly self-conscious fashion. Its self-reference, however ironic, acts as a sign of its quality, a postmodern validation in terms of complexity. Ava Collins describes one scenario where the protagonists are looking at the making of an advertisement. The set for this creation looks very much as if it could be the set for *Thirtysomething* itself and its characters could have come from the show. Naturally, the onlookers hate the advert, and criticize it in just the terms in which *Thirtysomething* had been condemned: 'the characters are whiny yuppies without real problems, the men don't act like men, there is too much male-bonding crap'. And significantly: 'I enjoyed it – I enjoyed hating it.' Collins correctly surmises that, like real viewers, these characters cannot move beyond this position of cri-tique to any further analysis or action; that television is the medium which they love to hate and even to condemn, but can never aban-don.[41] Awareness of the partiality and the shoddiness of a particular programme does not lead to action or stop people watching. Again, what clearly emerges from Morley's work is that people know that what they are watching is worthless. One woman cries out under the stress of being quizzed about her family's viewing habits: 'What will people think when they read this? They'll think us morons!'[42] Television's self-critical references to itself are only radical if it is assumed that people believe in what they are watching in the first place and think it valuable. If this is not the case, when a programme refers to its own qualities, this is a reminder to those who watch that they are being short-changed, that they know it, that the programme-makers know it, and that each knows that the other knows it.[43] Far from being a liberation, it is pointing to the jailhouse bars.

It is not just particular programmes which do this: rather there is an increasing tendency for programmes to trail others within themselves; soap operas, for instance, may take stories from the news – and occasionally vice versa. Furthermore, programmes must establish themselves in the viewer's attention quickly, preferably before the first advertising break: the first part of a programme thus becomes a trailer for itself.[44] This is seen explicitly in the credits of many an American series. With the growth of cable and satellite television the amount of this material has much increased, if only because there are so many more programming hours to fill. Programmes are padded out with self-referential material: trailers, self-advertisements, nostalgia television, retro advertisements (an economically determined matter which leads to a knowing, ironic effect) and the rebirth of the directly sponsored television programme in which content and product are directly identified. At its bluntest, a video may be framed by a picture of a television monitor. All these elements foreground the artificiality of the medium and make the viewer more aware both that they are watching a 'simulation' and of themselves as watchers of television. Again, some see this as radical and as a problem for theories of mystification.[45] Yet this is merely the typical tactic of thematizing an anxiety as entertainment, of salving a worry not by concealment but display. The greatest power is wielded when people know that they are being conned, but no longer care.

Some academics have argued that the autonomous material of television culture is a liberation from the grim, restrictive Enlightenment standards of rationality which are so caught up with orders of white, masculine power. Mark Poster, for instance, rejects criticism of television advertisements which evaluates them from a rationalist point of view, because this judgement has been based on an assessment of their forms as a feminine mode of consuming irrationalism which could easily shift from condemning the adverts to condemning the largely female audience at which they were aimed. This is a fair point to raise when such a shift has been actually made by a critic (as it was occasionally by Vance Packard for example), but Poster then proceeds, performing rather an amazing shift himself, as though this description of the advertisement as essentially feminine were actually true. So, 'When a man watches a TV ad, his autonomy is threatened by feminine irrationality.'[46] The argument, and it is a symptomatic one, is carried further:

> If the TV ad is read through the representational mode of signification, it is interpreted as an offence, a manipulation, a set of falsehoods, deeply disgusting and even morally dangerous. And so it is if the world is constituted with reference to the adult, white, male metanarrative of reason.
>
> But it is difficult day after day to sustain such a reading of the TV ad and it is important to investigate why it is so difficult. As ad after ad is viewed, the representational critic gradually loses interest, becomes lulled into a noncritical stance, is bored and gradually receives the communication differently. My argument is that the ads constitute the viewer in a nonrepresentational, noninstrumental communications mode, one different from reading print.[47]

So the advertisement, which of course has no instrumental purpose, allows the uptight, white, male academic to cast aside his critical faculties and reach out towards the other side of himself, to become a child once more. Its constant repetition and ubiquity, designed to quiet critique and moral objections, become servants of radicalism, although, as Poster admits, it forms a threat to the status quo which somehow has 'little direct political impact at this time'. On the principle that the enemy of my enemy must be my friend, anything that opposes the rationalist 'languages of domination' must be embraced.[48]

Against this sort of nonsense, we may juxtapose a telling convergence of Enlightenment methods and postmodern theory in television which Wolfgang Haug has analysed. He rightly relates the dissolution of the object to that of the subject, which finds its apotheosis in television. He cites Descartes: 'I will consider myself as someone who has no hands and no eyes, neither flesh nor blood nor any sense organ, but only a consciousness falsified by an overwhelming technique.' Haug comments that there is a logic in the fact that Descartes, the theoretician of abstract thinking, should use aesthetic abstraction as 'the technique to introduce the derealization of the sensuous-real world', as if in a central television programme.[49] Descartes, founder of Enlightenment thinking and of the bourgeois ratio which seeks to turn all quality into quantity, reappears in the guise of a postmodern slayer of reality. The dissolution of subject, object and concept produces not liberation but capitulation to a universal, highly instrumental technique.

As we have seen, the way information is conveyed on television does not merely degrade the real, it also constructs a specific type of viewing subject. In the atomization and fragmentation of industrial work, labourers are finally reduced to a single, partial operation, a fragment of a person, and reduced also to mere spectatorship of their own estranged activity.[50] Similarly the television viewer is constituted as a type governed largely by the imperative to sell and is aware that only a part of the self is engaged by this medium, and may attempt in collaboration with it to shut down the other sides. Awareness, though, is always ready to push its way back in. Sometimes, on those days when sunlight emerges sporadically from behind clouds only to fade again a moment later, the viewer is left with the intermittent spectacle of their own image appearing reflected in the screen, of a figure seated and still, blocking out for a moment the eternal procession of images.

Television culture is inescapable, even for those who do not have a set. Todd Gitlin has made a fine analysis of its peculiar combination of accessibility and fascination which flies in the face of much reader-response theory:

> when a television set is switched on for almost seven hours a day in the average American household, the curious power of this electronic machinery begins with the fact it requires so little of us. Turning a single set off seems almost beside the point. While we nod off, or get up to go to the refrigerator or the bathroom, the images go on living their strangely insubstantial yet ubiquitous lives. We hear about them at work, or from our children, or parents, or friends, or encounter them transfigured into the styles of people in the street.[51]

The television, this 'piece of talking furniture',[52] becomes a constant accompaniment to existence; switched on forever like a light, the most mobile element in the living-room, kitchen or bedroom, from which it is hard to drag the eyes away to attend to a person or a book. This fascination goes beyond choice or differential reading: even those programmes which are disliked are 'something to look at'.[53] The ubiquity of television, and the culture which surrounds it, is connected with the apparent contradiction between the extreme diversity of the material displayed on the small screen and the fact that, after a while, it all comes to seem the same. Barbara Kruger has written of the bizarre nature of television's flow from one set of images to another. She has just seen an oily close-up of a bicep:

> It is then quickly replaced by a talking roll of toilet tissue which pleads with members of a family to 'touch' it. The rotund glob of needy, animated paper gives way to an anchorman, a somber talking head who reports a catastrophic plane crash. We look at images of emergency medical teams packaging the dead in yellow body bags. The runway is littered with blood and spare body parts. This segment is immediately followed by a shot of a kitten in sunglasses propped under a beach umbrella.[54]

This diversity which produces similarity may not only be connected with television's universality, its attempt to colonize each corner of our existence, but also to a fascination with the medium itself. Postmodern cultural critics tend to assume that people watch television for seven hours a day simply because they find pleasure in it: as we have seen, this is a utilitarian view which runs counter to many of the opinions of the viewers themselves. Perhaps there is also another kind of fascination, the kind which makes people stop and watch the screens in shop windows, looking not so much at the set but at the dumb images displayed. Or the way that it draws the eye in any room or when seen through someone's window: a point of light and of constantly flickering movement, a parade of sharp but roughly drawn forms and bright, crude colour. Raymond Williams raised this question in a chapter of his book on television which examined in turn the way the medium treated drama, documentary, sports and so forth, but ended with a short section on television itself, which Williams claimed was encouraging new ways of looking:

To get this kind of attention it is often necessary to turn off the sound
[. . .]. What can then happen, in some surprising ways, is an experience
of visual mobility, of contrast of angle, of variation of focus, which is
often very beautiful. [. . .] I see it as one of the primary processes of the
technology itself, and one that may come to have an increasing importance. And when, in the past, I have tried to describe and explain this,
I have found it significant that the only people who ever agreed with
me were painters.[55]

Of course Williams was quite correct to think that this aspect
would assume greater importance: fragmentation, fast cutting and
unusual visual forms have become the standard devices of much
advertising, pop videos and the 'cutting-edge' shows which emulate
them. There is a utopian moment in this celebration of the visual as
such, which can indeed only be seen when the sound is turned down,
when the music which imparts the appearance of unity to the fragmented assemblage of scenes is no longer heard and when at least
part of the instrumental message of these fascinating, hypnotic
images is avoided. Yet what also becomes apparent, when the sound
is turned down, or when one happens to see television in a language
one does not understand, is the unitary nature of the medium as a
whole; how advertisements, programmes and linking material are
all part of a piece, very often manufacturing the same feel-good
atmosphere, always sporting the same forced smiles, and occasionally
showing the tremendous strain of achieving this mandatory cheerfulness. Again Williams put his finger on the fundamental issue by
writing of the 'flow' of television, which effaced boundaries, operated
without transitions and was bound together by the unifying elements
of news magazines and bulletins.[56] This effect is absolutely deliberate:
Gitlin has described the US networks' calculations about audience
flow which is designed to keep people tuned to the same channel
over as many programmes as possible, and how inertia does indeed
keep many people fixed like this for hours on end.[57] Self-referential
material is highly necessary for this effect, so programmes are less discrete entities than the links of a chain, constantly referring
backwards and, more importantly, forwards. Blandness is the
inevitable product because, in serving this system, the important
thing is to avoid driving an audience away, and for this only the least

objectionable programming is required.[58] Television and its audience, then, are constantly flirting with boredom.

In moving from the practice of amateur photography to watching television, we have proceeded from analysing an activity of exploration, in which objects and the relations between them may be unearthed, to a largely passive matter of confirmation, and we have done so by way of the mixed activities involved in looking at and interacting with the computer screen, the windscreen, the wall, the shop window and the pavement.

This chapter, more than any other, has analysed aspects of our contemporary *trahison des clercs* in which those who are most privileged and most aware, those who have, to use Bourdieu's term, the most 'cultural capital', have taken consolation in the idea that radical misreadings of mass culture are possible, while some have even convinced themselves that they are widespread. Yet the terms of these supposedly creative misreadings are highly abstract, even metaphysical, and are defined negatively against a straw-man figure of rationalism. They are, most of all, an excuse for inaction, at least outside of advancing careers and publishing in accredited journals.

The old cultural criticism sometimes accused people of being cultural dupes. The new criticism has rightly abandoned this position and it is at least evident that, if people are duped, they knowingly succumb. Television's adopted role is to give people a quasi-visceral experience of the things portrayed; in this way it potentially transforms the relations between rich and poor, near and far, making them more immediate and personal, bypassing the bureaucratic and economic apparatus which distances people from the consequences of their actions. In a world as unjust and inequitable as this, other kinds of false consciousness must be manufactured if this perception is not to become unbearable. One of the most powerful is the tendency of this presentation of the immediate to be broken into meaningless, atomistic fragments; to be convinced of the absurdity or perversity of the world is also to be convinced of one's own powerlessness. Another is to claim that there are just many points of view, each as valid as the other, and that it is an illusion to think there can be any deciding between them. Television, with its rapidly displayed and vanishing succession of images, seems to present an argument for this: 'Very frequently, I watch television as a postmodernist, caught up in the flow of signification, looking for diversion. But sometimes I watch television under the illusion – so widespread – that it will give me information about the world.'[59]

The enlightened intellectual knows that this is an illusion; that pictures of Tiananmen Square or the beating of Rodney King are mere points of view and have nothing to tell us about the behaviour of the Beijing government or the Los Angeles Police Department. Yet, despite the sophisticated art of the programme-makers which is directed towards relativism and a dwelling on the surface, towards the mere look of an event, the lumpen masses persist in the primitive idea that television has a relation to the world; they frequently criticize even drama for not being true to life,[60] or refuse to watch the news because it is too upsetting. There are certain limits, then, to the intellectual obfuscation that television and its apologists can spin.

The admission that one watches worthless programmes is often accompanied by the claim that, unlike everyone else, one is not taken in by them:

> People often compare their own television watching to that of the imagined mass audience, one that is more interested, more duped, more entertained, more gullible than they are. Academics as television viewers are no exception to this rule.[61]

While the viewing masses may knowingly turn their backs on the tragedies which television at once reveals and constantly disposes of, the same cannot be claimed of the academic critics who take refuge in relativism or even present themselves as fans: if they find radical political ground in television advertisements or experience *jouissance* when watching soap operas, then they have been fooled, pure and simple.

NOTES

1. John Updike, *Rabbit Redux*, London 1972, p. 199.
2. Stanley Aronowitz, *Dead Artists, Live Theories and Other Cultural Problems*, New York 1994, p. 52.
3. For an analysis of this phenomenon in relation to renditions of fifties

America on film see Fredric Jameson, *Postmodernism or, the Cultural Logic of Late Capitalism*, London 1991.

4. Aronowitz, *Dead Artists*, p. 64.

5. Theodor Adorno and Max Horkheimer, *Dialectic of Enlightenment*, trans. John Cumming, London 1973, p. 154.

6. David Morley, *Television, Audiences and Cultural Studies*, London 1992, p. 18.

7. Ibid., pp. 32–3.

8. Ibid., pp. 59–60. He also notes various recent critiques of these views, particularly on the grounds that they endorse commercial products claiming that if they are popular then they must be good. See p. 273.

9. John Fiske, *TV Culture*, London 1987, p. 19.

10. Meaghan Morris, 'Banality in Cultural Studies', *Block*, no. 14, Autumn 1988, p. 20.

11. For some suggestions about the sociological roots of such views, see Jopstein Gripsrud, '"High Culture" Revisited', *Cultural Studies*, vol. 3, no. 2, May 1989, pp. 196f.

12. Morley, *Television, Audiences and Cultural Studies*, pp. 145f. See also his cavil that this distinction should not be taken in isolation from other social determinants such as age and class (p. 160).

13. Some writers who privilege readers' power are quite happy to concede this point. See Fiske's analysis of the repugnant crime series *Hart to Hart* in *TV Culture*, pp. 8ff.

14. See George Gerbner, Larry Gross, Michael Morgan and Nancy Signorielli, 'Charting the Mainstream: Television's Contributions to Political Organizations', in Donald Lazere, ed., *American Media and Mass Culture. New Perspectives*, Berkeley 1987.

15. Fiske, *TV Culture*, p. 19.

16. Some of this uniformity may be a product of Morley's sample, which was composed of white, mostly lower-middle-class and working-class, nuclear families from a particular area of South London. See David Morley, *Family Television. Cultural Power and Domestic Leisure*, London 1986, pp. 52–3.

17. Morley, *Family Television*, pp. 62, 68.

18. Ibid., p. 74.

19. Ibid., p. 75.

20. Ibid., p. 78.

21. Ibid., p. 130.

22. E. Medrich, 'Constant Television: a Background to Everyday Life', *Journal of Communication*, vol. 26, no. 3, 1979, p. 172; cited in Morley, *Television, Audiences and Cultural Studies*, p. 166.

23. Roger Silverstone, 'Television: Text or Discourse?', *Science as Culture*, no. 6, 1989, p. 77; cited in Morley, *Television, Audiences and Cutural Studies*, p. 197. See also Silverstone, *Television and Everyday Life*, London 1994.

24. Joke Hermes, 'Media, Meaning and Everyday Life', *Cultural Studies*, vol. 7, no. 3, October 1993, p. 498.

25. On the commercial importance of durable characters to television series in the United States, see Todd Gitlin, *Inside Prime Time*, revised edition, London 1994, pp. 64f.

26. On this point see Wolfgang Fritz Haug, *Commodity Aesthetics, Ideology and Culture*, New York 1987, p. 123.

27. See Todd Gitlin, 'Television's Screens: Hegemony in Transition', in Lazere, ed., *American Media and Mass Culture*, p. 245.

28. Gitlin, *Inside Prime Time*, pp. 161–2.

29. David Harvey, *The Condition of Postmodernity. An Enquiry into the Origins of Cultural Change*, Oxford 1990, p. 61.

30. Aronowitz, *Dead Artists*, p. 54.

31. Fiske, *TV Culture*, p. 229.

32. Adorno and Horkheimer, *Dialectic of Enlightenment*, p. 163.

33. See Fiske, *TV Culture*, p. 105.

34. Raymond Williams, *The Politics of Modernism. Against the New Conformists*, ed. Tony Pinkney, London 1989, p. 130.

35. Adorno, 'Theorie der Halbbildung', in *Gesammelte Schriften*, vol. 8, p. 115; cited in Peter Dews, *The Logics of Disintegration. Post-Structuralist Thought and the Claims of Critical Theory*, London 1987, p. 142.

36. Federico Fellini, *Le Monde*, January 1986; cited in Jacques Ellul, *The Technological Bluff*, trans. Geoffrey W. Bromley, Grand Rapids, Michigan 1990, p. 339.

37. See Gitlin, *Inside Prime Time*, p. 138.

38. Ibid., p. 187.

39. K. Robins and F. Webster, 'Broadcasting Politics', *Screen*, vol. 27, nos. 3–4, 1986, p. 34; cited in Morley, *Television, Audiences and Cultural Studies*, p. 215.

40. Adorno and Horkheimer, *Dialectic of Enlightenment*, p. 140.

41. Ava Collins, 'Intellectuals, Power and Quality Television', *Cultural Studies*, vol. 7, no. 1, January 1993, pp. 41–2.

42. Morley, *Family Television*, p. 76.

43. Christopher Lasch has seen such self-reference as another technique for bringing about the extreme self-consciousness which characterizes his 'culture of narcissism'. See *The Culture of Narcissism. American Life in an Age of Diminishing Expectations*, New York 1978, p. 96.

44. This is pointed out by Raymond Williams in *Television. Technology and Cultural Form*, New York 1974, p. 92.

45. See Jim Collins, 'Watching Ourselves Watching Television, or Who's your Agent?', *Cultural Studies*, vol. 3, no. 3, October 1989, p. 270.

46. Mark Poster, *The Mode of Information. Poststructuralism and Social Context*, Cambridge 1990, p. 51.

47. Ibid., pp. 62–3. Fiske makes a very similar argument about the pop-video-type sequences in *Miami Vice*: 'the camera pleasures the viewer into the role of consumer, but what is consumed is their [the objects shown] lack of meaning, their postmodern rejection of use and of ideology'. Fiske, *TV Culture*, p. 261.

48. Poster, *The Mode of Information*, p. 68.

49. Haug, *Commodity Aesthetics*, pp. 114–15.

50. See Marx, *Capital*, vol. I, p. 39; cited in Andrew Arato and Eike Gebhardt, eds., *The Essential Frankfurt School Reader*, New York 1982, p. 195.

51. Gitlin, *Inside Prime Time*, p. 333.

52. Barbara Kruger, *Remote Control. Power, Cultures, and the World of Appearances*, Cambridge, Mass. 1993, p. 78.

53. Respondent cited in Morley, *Family Television*, p. 68.

54. Kruger, *Remote Control*, p. 78.

55. Williams, *Television*, p. 77.

56. See ibid., pp. 90–91, 99.

57. Gitlin, *Inside Prime Time*, p. 56.

58. Ibid., p. 61.

59. Jane Feuer, 'The Two Weather Channels', *Cultural Studies*, vol. 1, no. 3, October 1987, p. 383.

60. This is a constant theme of the interviews conducted by Morley in *Family Television*.

61. Ellen Seiter, 'Making Distinctions in TV Audience Research: Case Study of a Troubling Interview', *Cultural Studies*, vol. 4, no. 1, January 1990, p. 63.

10

CAPITAL TO CAPITAL

In a very famous, even notorious, passage, Benjamin wrote:

> The products of art and science owe their existence not merely to the
> effort of the great geniuses that created them, but also to the unnamed
> drudgery of their contemporaries. There is no document of culture
> which is not at the same time a document of barbarism. No cultural his-
> tory has yet done justice to this fundamental state of affairs, and it can
> hardly hope to do so.[1]

Mass culture has never been more widely distributed nor the wealth of
the world so great. As both continue to grow, the gulf between rich and
poor widens and more and more people's most basic needs go unmet.
Unlike many other economic indicators, the growth of this barbarism,
in which half of the world sinks deeper into misery while the other half
distracts itself with fripperies, shows no signs of abating. Benjamin's
point that *cultural* history cannot do justice to this situation is surely correct but the marks of a continued and intensifying barbarism on the
culture can be traced. To dwell on culture alone would be to do an
injustice to those forced to drudgery, and equally it is not enough
simply to juxtapose cultural phenomena with an account of the world's
political and economic setup. It may be, however, that the analysis of
culture can foster an awareness of barbarism. There have of course
been some attempts to achieve this in 'cutting-edge' high-art produc-

tions: unfortunately these tend to appeal only to tiny elite audiences who are already convinced of the art work's point of view. Also relevant, perhaps, are accounts which try to blend the political and the affective, the cultural and the subjective. Just before the First World War, Wyndham Lewis marvelled at a succession of mild British characters – domesticated policemen, aesthetes and socialist playwrights – produced, he wrote, half-jokingly, by a vast global machinery: 'A 1000 mile long, 2 kilometre deep body of water even, is pushed against us from the Floridas, to make us mild. Officious mountains keep out drastic winds.'[2] In the same way, the entire grand apparatus of the culture industry bears down weightily on the point of individual consciousness, if only to make it less individual, and the generalized effect of this consoling, tepid Gulf Stream of culture is exactly to make us mild. Given the enormous material effort which goes into manufacturing our minds, subjective accounts are always, even despite themselves, shot through with objectivity. What follows, then, is a fragment of my own experience, of a certain brief breaking of mass culture's enchantment, recounted by someone who – like almost everybody in the First World – cannot escape complicity in its continued operation.

Once I took a long train journey which began one night and only ended long after dark the next day, taking me from Bucharest to Munich. It was swift in the sense that there was almost no break in the trip, just an hour or so in Budapest, and slow in another, for it enclosed me in a long, enforced peace in which thoughts of Romania and other places along the way could settle in my mind.

What I experienced in this travelling from East to West was, I suppose, a certain slight shift in perception in which the familiar sights and circumstances of a wealthy, Western regional capital were tainted by the fresh memories I trailed with me. The various railway compartments, increasingly sanitized, were capsules in which this transformation was made. I began the journey in a full, dark carriage, with Romanians and a couple of chatty Italian students. The train rocked us slowly, and people stirred, sighed and tried to sleep. I dozed fitfully, breathing in the stuffy air, often waking when the train lurched to a halt in the blackness, where fragments of some shabby urban scene would be cut from the night by a solitary lamp. Guards and passport officials also regularly disturbed our attempts at rest. Half asleep and lulled by the movement of the train, I had the sensation of traversing a vast country stretching out from either side of the carriage into the blackness and filled with peasants, horse-drawn wagons and a filthy, ramshackle industry of which in my travels I had only had a glimpse. The journey ended with my standing alone in a long, air-conditioned corridor on a very fast train, escaping the solitude of my pristine carriage, watching the complex arrangement of lights that was Munich approach. I had been standing there a long time, impatient to arrive at the city I had long wanted to visit since looking at textbook illustrations of its collection of ancient sculpture.

On the train I thought of the railway station at Bucharest; it was a crowded, chaotic place, like much of the capital, coated with a grime which seemed to adhere to surfaces and become part of them. The grand entrance was flanked by bootblacks and unofficial money-changers. Sometimes around the station you could see unshod children sleeping on the cracked pavements, surrounded by rubbish. Inside, legless beggars dragged themselves about on pallets and people slept in old cabinets which had once been used to display some fancy goods. The station was a huge, shadowy, begrimed place, and to Western Europeans it might have felt threatening. Yet it was only a microcosm of the capital where the collapse of economic and social structures had left so many merely eking out an inadequate living.

You had to show your train ticket to gain entry to the waiting-room. It was a large, deep room, very gloomy, lit only by a few fluorescent lights and a grubby strip of window high up at the far end. At first I could see very little but was aware of the presence of a great many people gathered together in the darkness, and could hear among them little rustlings, stirrings and sighs. As my eyes adjusted to the dark, details of worn clothing and weary faces gradually emerged: a mass of people sat patiently on wooden benches, arranged back to back. Most looked haggard and weary. There was little conversation, though a silent game of cards proceeded in one corner.

After a time a strange couple entered: a robust woman, bolstered by a tight blue uniform, followed by a short, slight, stooped man, apparently very old, carrying a broom handle. The woman approached one seated, waiting man, who to me looked no different from anyone else there, and began noisily berating him. People close to the scene looked on incuriously. Evidently he was one of the many homeless of

Bucharest who had somehow managed to slip in without a ticket and was enjoying the luxury of a hard bench. The station officials must know their faces by now. The man, who looked weak, did not want to go, but the woman kept shouting at him. This went on for some time, the official shouting more and more loudly, to build herself up for some physical confrontation, the man sitting there, head bowed, without speaking, as if willing her out of existence. Then, bending forward cautiously, the woman gave the seated man a tentative shove as one might poke at something distasteful with a stick. He leant over a little. There was more shouting; then eventually she took the broom handle from the frail, expressionless man behind her and rapped it sharply on the bench. The resulting loud crack broke in upon the muffled texture of the room's little noises. This threat was enough and the indigent slowly rose and tramped out quietly between the two of them.

As a spectacle, this was a minor scene of picturesque Dickensian drama, an animated Daumier print of malformed types in crepuscular conditions, and I was ashamed not to be able to see it otherwise. The utter indifference of the other travellers to this no doubt regular occurrence was also disturbing. What was most striking of course was that in the general collapse of prosperity (such as it was), which had left this listless crowd beached in the waiting room, the minuscule distinctions that remained were being insisted upon with such officiousness and severity.

So then to Munich, that immensely wealthy city, with its charming, anodyne centre where shops, pavements and buildings seem manicured – sharpened and scrubbed to a dull perfection. The streets were unspoilt even by a single dropped sweet-wrapper. Bored tourists hung about the historic squares in the sun. But this is also a city where the finest cultural riches, antique sculpture and Western painting, are put on immaculate display in the grand buildings of the German Enlightenment.

Ludwig I, the enlightened monarch of Bavaria who reigned from 1825 to 1848 (he was not a direct victim of the year of revolutions but was forced to abdicate over a sexual scandal), was responsible for collecting and commissioning many of these treasures, building on old aristocratic and royal collections and the confiscation of church property during secularization. The people had been granted certain parliamentary powers and the thinking was that, if they were to exercise these with wisdom, they required an education not only in ethics but aesthetics. So the collections were housed in fine new buildings designed to be open to the public. The Glypothek, built between 1816 and 1830 to house Ludwig's collection of classical statuary, was one of the first public museums. Similarly the Alte Pinakothek, finished in 1836, housed the Wittelsbach collection which Ludwig had given to his subjects. Beauty was considered a source of social harmony and the people were to be made conscious of the links between the true, the beautiful and the good.[3] In these expressions of German classicism, allegory was denigrated in favour of an organic symbolism, the product of artistic genius which went far beyond the merely intellectual assembly of discrete signs.[4] Ludwig's favoured architect, Leo von Klenze, was an archaeologist and writer as well as a builder who hoped to further the ideals of the Greeks by developing their architectural forms.[5] The buildings which he made to house the art collections are expressions of Enlightenment ideals, looking to Greek civilization and the Italian Renaissance for their lineage; ideals of freedom and humanism, and the discovery of truth expressed through a particular aesthetic sensibility. They were of course at the same time an exercise of power, part of Ludwig's plan to make Munich a centre for German and indeed European culture.

The design of both the Glypothek and the Alte Pinakothek reflected the style of their contents.[6] The long galleries of the Pinakothek contain one of the best collections of European painting anywhere. In the now bare halls of the Glypothek (its mural decoration by Peter von Cornelius was destroyed in the last war), beautiful Greek and Roman statuary stands calmly, sometimes damaged and fragmentary yet perfect under the gentle illumination of the sky. Between these two buildings I spent most of the day, meeting old friends (pictures and sculpture long known from reproductions) for the first time, as it were, and making many entirely new ones.

In the Alte Pinakothek there is a curious painting of 1567 by Pieter Brueghel the Elder called *Land of Cockaigne*. It shows a land of plenty where food and drink are always abundant and may be obtained without effort. Pigs and geese run around ready-roasted, pancakes and tarts grow from the roofs, and fences are made from sausages. Here a soldier, a peasant and a clerk lie upon the ground in a stupor following some bout of extreme gluttony. The painting is based on a Dutch

poem of 1546 which tells us that in this fabled land cooked and prepared food would fly into the open mouths of the inhabitants, who
had, however, been obliged to eat their way through three miles of por-
ridge to get there.[7] This animated, readily available food does not
simply presage pre-packaged convenience foods, but may also stand as
a prophecy of the animated, fetishized commodity itself. Brueghel,
living in Antwerp, at the time a powerful commercial and financial
centre set in wealthy Flanders, had the opportunity to glimpse this.

If a legend, which goes back at least to Roman times, has its origin
in the dreams of hungry European peasants, it finds a perverse fulfilment in their descendants' lifestyles in the West, as I soon found on
emerging from the galleries into the evening sunlight, and wandering
about the centre of the city, looking for something I could afford to
eat. The icy perfection of Munich's immaculate display of commodities cast its light back over the experience of the riches of the
galleries. The well-ordered piles of diverse foods in shop windows
and market stalls could not but remind me of the sparse goods of
urban Romania. There goods and the circumstances of their display
seemed to conspire against the creation of the uniform glacis of
Western shop etiquette. Eastern Europeans often try to be good capitalists but still generally fail to get it quite right: it is a little sad that
they try so hard and entirely positive that they do not succeed. The
failures are often to do with curious spaces or gaps in their shop displays or with mismatches of objects which appear in somewhat surreal
combinations, drawing attention to their intrinsic qualities rather
than their status as commodities. Contingency, we are reminded,
always lurks just beyond the field of vision, ready to slip in through any
gap in the phantasmagoria.

The centre of Munich, stuffed with an orderly consumption, the
noise and filth of production being tucked safely out of mind in
another zone or another country, could only summon up by contrast
the extraordinary juxtaposition of disparate environments in
Romania; there an ancient, chaotic but leviathan industry lay down
next to little rural shacks with scrappy backyards in which people
tended chickens or geese; or in streets of finely built houses one
would find huge, stinking piles of rubbish assembled, which had been
festering for months and were picked over by gulls and sick cats; or in
Hunedoara where an acrid, sticky air stung the throat and pollution

from a smelting plant had coated everything – trees, houses, a nearby castle, the plant itself – with a veneer of dull brown.

In the immaculate rooms of the old museums and with the exercise of a tastefully neutral modernity in the attached cafés and other facilities it was as though every surface had been buffed to eliminate all incident. The shabby and contingent feel of rooms in the East seemed more human than these highly polished surfaces. Those old spaces, untouched for so long, sometimes spoke clearly of their recent alteration. The buffet at the railway station in Ceské Budĕbjovice, a town in the Czech Republic, is as high as a church, with bare walls rising up dourly to a vast curved ceiling capped with a stained skylight. Far below, at head height, wall lamps illuminate framed advertisements. Their measured disposition and sober frames suggest that they once carried edifying material, exhorting travellers to socialist ideals. Now they carry adverts for Camel cigarettes or holiday firms, the new official icons. Or in the little Slovakian town of Zilina the old town square, surrounded with a pretty arcade, with its municipal speakers at each corner, now resounds to loud and incessant pop music which, if you stand in the right place, produces weird quadraphonic effects. This music, which is heard outside every bar and shop – and is of the most commercial kind – has uniformly and completely replaced the old music, but is far more inescapable. Something one stumbles upon again and again is the old, authoritarian frames of the command economy culture employed without modification or discomfort in the service of consumer culture. Such experiences were an education in the official, determining nature of capitalist propaganda, which is of course produced not merely by the state but by large corporate bodies more powerful than many states. The ideology stresses choice, freedom, spontaneity and liveliness, which are all positive qualities except when they are forced on us.

The early bourgeois idealism of Ludwig's Munich, now broken, was expressed in the immaculate halls of the Glypothek and their ancient contents. It contrasts painfully with the false, marketed aestheticism of commodity culture, in which pretensions to such ideals have long since been abandoned, but where the barbarism they used to justify has been immeasurably extended. A culture of distraction now swamps a feeling for justice and aesthetic sense together.

In my evening meandering through the city centre, it was as though some wall in my mind had fallen. I felt restless, light-headed and emotional. The façades of buildings and the slick shop frontages appeared as veils over some other, shadowy but already more substantial world, veils that were about to fall away. It could have been the result of hunger or exhaustion from my travels and the day's intensive museum going, of course, or even a sense of relief at returning to a familiar environment where, for instance, credit cards were of some use. Rather, I think, it was the sudden jump from one world to another; from the filth, disorder and poverty of Bucharest to the excessive consumerism and inhuman perfection of Munich's centre. This contrast made me feel, rather than just know, that both are part of the same global system, that the icy sheen of one feeds off the devastation of the other, and that personal implication in this system, through earning and spending, was inescapable. Then there was the shock of seeing so much exceptional art, a display of the most extraordinary human potential, and in the classical statuary and the architecture which sympathetically surrounded it, some glimpse of abandoned ideals and hopes. Most affecting, perhaps, was the further realization that these extraordinary works, at the time of their creation resting on drudgery, and now employed so regularly for commercial purposes, are also implicated in this system. Present in Munich in this concentration because of the past exercise of power, kept there and publicised to maintain its political and cultural prestige, they form a part of its apparently impregnable armour of wealth and stolid probity.

Of course, the problem is that such affective realizations are so transient. It is difficult to hold them steadily before the mind which is the constant target of the culture of distraction. So let us return to this culture and to Gargantua. He is profligate not only in his consumption but in his excretion:

'Once I wiped myself on a lady's velvet mask, and I found it good. For the softness of the silk was most voluptuous to my fundament. Another time on one of their hoods, and I found it just as good. Another time on a lady's neckerchief; another time on some ear-flaps of crimson satin. [. . .]

'Then, as I was sitting behind a bush, I found a March-born cat; I wiped myself on him, but his claws exulcerated my whole perineum. [. . .] Then I wiped myself with sage, fennel, anise, marjoram, roses, gourd leaves, cabbage, beets, vineshoots, marshmallow, mullein – which is red as your bum – lettuces, and spinach leaves. All this did very great good to my legs. Then with dog's mercury, persicaria, nettles and comfrey. But that gave me the bloody flux of Lombardy, from which I was cured by wiping myself with my codpiece.

'Then I wiped myself on the sheets, the coverlet, the curtains, with a cushion, with the hangings, with a green cloth, with a table-cloth, with a napkin, with a handkerchief, with an overall. And I found more pleasure in all those than mangy dogs do when they are combed. [. . .]

'After that', said Gargantua, 'I wiped myself with a kerchief, with a pillow, with a slipper, with a game-bag, with a basket – but what an unpleasant arse-wipe that was! – then with a hat. And note that some hats are smooth, some shaggy, some velvety, some of taffeta, and some of satin. The best of all are the shaggy ones, for they make a very good abstersion of faecal matter. Then I wiped myself with a hen, a cock, and a chicken, with a calf's skin, a hare, a pigeon, and a cormorant, with a lawyer's bag, with a penitent's hood, with a coif, with an otter. But to conclude, I say and maintain that there is no arse-wipe like a well-downed goose [. . .].'[8]

Not manufactured goods, nor beasts, nor plants escape Gargantua's incontinent outpourings. Although the giant may sometimes experience some discomfort, little escapes the ubiquitous smearing of commodification. Capitalism abhors a vacuum, both in the environment and in subjective experience which must both be filled with marketing trivia.

We have seen that many intellectuals and academics have argued that the dominance of mass culture should not be troubling because, in its varied reception, it is reclaimed for the radical and the popular. At the bottom of much of this writing is the assumption that people resist capitalist indoctrination, no matter how constant and insidious its propagation. On the face of it, particularly in the First World, this is not a very plausible assumption – indeed, if this were the case, given the current economic and political travails of the capitalist system we might expect to see more overt and radical opposition. Instead it is the Right, and a populist Right at that, which is in many places ascendant. Furthermore, many of those who are troubled about the current situation often feel powerless to do anything about it and this is surely a result of the most effective cultural and political hegemony. In this situation, to say, for example of television that it 'promotes and provokes a network of resistances to its own power whose attempt to homogenize and hegemonize breaks down on the instability and multiplicity of its meanings and pleasures',[9] is to make a convoluted expression out of plain nonsense.

We must ask ourselves how, at least in some restricted intellectual circles, such foolishness has come close to being accepted as orthodoxy. When capital was still an infant, Shakespeare wrote of gold's magical properties:

> Thus much will make black white, foul fair,
> Wrong right, base noble, old young, coward valiant
> [. . .]
> Thou *visible God!*
> That solder'st close impossibilities,
> And makest them kiss! That speak'st with every tongue,
> To every purpose![10]

From plastic surgery and the Gulf War to the sycophantic biographies of billionaires, how many resonances this passage has today. When Marx cited it in the *Economic and Philosophical Manuscripts*, he noted how money effaces all faults and with them all individuality.[11] Powerful interests lie behind the marketing of cultural products and that many writers, from academics to hacks, are in thrall to them should not be a surprise. Theorizations of consumerism as radical or empowering have significant material consequences for their supporters. Among the most direct is that 'they have acted as a form of permission entitling members of today's left intelligentsia to enjoy consuming images and commodities [. . .] without having to feel anxious about whether these activities are good or correct'.[12]

Many intellectuals serve as courtiers to the powerful: in 1922 Henry Ford, having claimed that only a very few people were capable of genuinely creative work and that the vast majority were happiest on the production line, appealed to the artistic elite to join him in industry:

> if a man wants a field for vital creative work, let him come where he is
> dealing with higher laws than those of sound, or line, or colour; let him

come where he may deal with the laws of personality. We want artists in industrial relationship. We want masters in industrial method – both from the standpoint of the producer and the product. We want those who can mould the political, social, industrial and moral mass into a sound and shapely whole.[13]

This creative skill is to be applied as much to the product as to industrial relations, and its main task is to influence the consciousness of those among the dull masses who are privileged enough to be able to buy Ford's products. Furthermore, to make mass culture effective, to ensure its dominance over society as a whole, an intellectual class is needed to ratify it; they must propagandize it, make it palatable, and divert attention from the less savoury doings of the economic elite. The role of intellectuals taken broadly, of 'the chattering classes' who inhabit the linked worlds of television, journalism and the academy, is crucial to the smooth running of the Gargantuan system.

In any case, the much-vaunted indeterminacy of response in the consumption of mass culture is irrelevant as far as the producers are concerned: the only thing that counts is whether the 'product' is purchased or not. Arnold Becker, the vice-president of CBS television research, put the matter clearly: 'I'm not interested in culture. I'm not interested in pro-social values. I have only one interest. That's whether people watch the program. That's my definition of good, that's my definition of bad.'[14] This binary on/off switch is always the bottom line. Herbert Schiller argues that active reader theories have aided the 'Western effort to stall and deflect the near-global movement for change in the prevailing international information cultural order [. . .]'.[15] He continues that 'whatever the unique experiential history of each of the many subgroups in the nation, they are all subject to the rule of market forces and the domination of capital over those market forces. This is the grand common denominator that insures basic inequality in the social order [. . .]'. There is good evidence, he continues, that manipulation of the media works; where has been the outcry about the fabrication, now so plainly revealed, of the Communist threat over the last fifty years?[16] Schiller concludes: 'It is not a matter of people being dupes, informational or cultural. It is just that human beings are not equipped to deal with a pervasive disinformational system – administered from the command posts of the social order – that assaults the senses through all cultural forms and channels.'[17]

There is a curious episode in *Gargantua* where a monk, Friar John, in reward for his feats in war is made abbott of a new establishment, the Abbey of Thélemè. It is an odd utopia, run effectively by Gargantua himself, where monastic poverty is replaced by riches, celibacy by chastity, and timetabled regulation by the rule of free will.[18] Yet the exercise of free will by the uniformly beautiful and well-born inhabitants leads not to anarchy but conformity. After a time, all the Thelemites willingly dress in the same clothes, simultaneously enjoy the same diversions and eat the same food. Thélemè becomes a fortified refuge of beauty and conformity whose walls protect it against the world of evil, disorder and deformity outside.

Similarly, an icy perfection is being prepared for us – its precursors can be seen clearly enough in the gleaming, uniform surfaces of the richer shopping centres, in the scrubbed historical centres of wealthy ancient cities, which have effaced even the signs of age from their artefacts, and in the glossy artificial environments of television, the decor of game shows, chat shows and advertisements. Already millions of non-conformists wear the same uniform, marketed as rebellious by powerful corporations. The attempt to control contingency is made utterly transparent in the attempted flight to perfect virtual worlds and the political dimension to these dreams of totality is relevant to the culture as a whole. Adorno wrote of how the bourgeois ratio, having destroyed the feudal order, was then faced with the danger of chaos. Since it was not a complete emancipation, bourgeois consciousness feared being exceeded by something more radical: its only defence was the 'theoretical expansion of its autonomy into a system similar to its own coercive mechanisms'.[19] So from inside itself the bourgeois ratio produced the order which it had negated outside itself. Yet as each order it thus produced then ceased to be an order, the need became insatiable. To prevail as a system, the ratio sought to eliminate all qualitative distinctions it came across.

The danger of contingency and of reality's obdurate existence is indicated by attempts to overcome them. What, after all, would be the point of simulating hyperreality? The invention of virtual reality is a sure proof of actuality. In any case, its effects are hardly new: Henri Lefebvre wrote on films, the press, theatre and leisure activities,

> We are now entering the vast domain of the *illusory reverse image*. What we find is a false world: firstly because it is not a world, and because it presents itself as true, and because it mimics real life closely in order to replace the real by its opposite, by replacing real unhappiness by fictions of happiness, for example – by offering a fiction in response to the real need for happiness [. . .].[20]

Cyberspace is the ultimate point in the development of a long-established system of ideology, just the image of a camera obscura expanded to three dimensions. The ever-growing presence of such a consistent, stifling perfection in parts of the First World is founded on an ever greater tide of filth, degradation, disorder and disease everywhere else. This secret is reflected openly enough in what we take as entertainment, where representatives of order, decency and money (generally cops) are thrown against the dark inhabitants of the ghetto.

In the *Economic and Philosophical Manuscripts*, Marx wrote of how both worker and capitalist become shadows of themselves, the worker a mechanized slave who is able to satisfy only the barest physical needs, the capitalist forever deferring desire for the sake of amassing capital itself. As Terry Eagleton describes it, 'Both capitalist and capital are images of the living dead, the one animate yet anaesthetized, the other inanimate yet active.'[21] This situation is less familiar in the First World now, but Eagleton also notes that 'The antithesis of the blindly biologistic wage-slave is the exotic idler, the self-pleasuring parasite for whom "the realisation of man's essential powers is simply the realisation of his own disorderly existence, his whims and his capricious and bizarre notions".'[22] The consumer culture has blurred the distinction between vampires and victims in the First World, but on a global level the division is all too clear, as is the inescapable implication in it of the readers of this text. Postmodern theory, often whimsical, capricious and bizarre, has frequently served as the ideological justification for consumer vampirism. The modern cult of the vampire, which has recently undergone a revival, is not merely a pale reflection of the concern about AIDS but a fitting metaphor for the relation between rich and poor, the former extending their lives and good looks ever further in search of eternal youth, the latter having theirs ever more abbreviated and impoverished, not just in terms of money but also environment and education. The victims of this new vampirism even give their lives or their health by 'donating' organs to the rich yet, after their final demise, they stay firmly beneath ground.

The old question runs: how do people like ourselves, long damaged by the operation of a falsifying culture, begin to form a critique and change the very system which is responsible for our condition? Art has sometimes been held out as the answer, forming a preview of another reality which might provide the grounds for vision and opposition:

> The only possible ingress into art is the idea that something on the other side of reality's veil – a veil woven by the interaction of institutions and false needs – objectively demands art. It demands a kind of art that can speak for what is hidden by the veil. Unlike discursive knowledge, art does not rationally understand reality, including its irrational qualities which stem from reality's law of motion. However, rational cognition has one critical limit which is its inability to cope with suffering.[23]

Art alone can cope with suffering, then: 'art may be the only remaining medium of truth in an age of incomprehensible terror and suffering'.[24] Art may indeed do these things, but under the current system the results tend to be overly subjective, extremely transient and confined to a very few people. At best high art may become an important part of a wider culture of radical opposition. We must do better than this very nearly unspeakable positive.

Opposition can be forced on us, when the contradictions of the system become so intense that they must lead to action. Various aspects of the current situation may lead to such a forced change of consciousness. Most important of these is the prolonged economic crisis which has begun to affect even the comfortable classes. The costs to the individual of the apparatus to build one's own personal cocoon of goods, most of all houses and cars, becomes more burdensome and even unsustainable. The benefits of doing so come to seem ever poorer; the hedonism of television's contents, for instance, so blatantly contradicting the passivity and emptiness of its continued viewing. In addition, the lack of a credible external threat in military or ideological terms throws previous political certainties into the spotlight of critique, and has encouraged extreme cynicism towards mainstream politics. Lastly, frightening changes in the environment, especially the ozone holes over the Antarctic and Arctic (and these are prominent in the public mind only because the effect can be measured without dispute), bring home the cost of uncontained consumerism. Although the culture is geared towards distraction in both work and leisure – it is the very essence of television, and think of the thousands of hours expended at work to be able to buy and run a car – these factors lead to a detailed questioning in the mainstream of previously accepted practices, from road-building, to democracy in the workplace and the size of corporate profits. Most importantly, ubiquitous and powerful though the system of culture may be, it has not made us mild. Frustrated and undirected opposition is forever present and the result is a great deal of misery. I will never forget sitting in the living-room of a children's home, where I was working as a volunteer, while opposite me a teenage boy was calmly, rhythmically cutting at his forearm with a razor blade. While such acts of self-mutilation are widespread and varied, and certainly not the preserve of the disenfranchised, this was in a Welsh mining valley at the height of Thatcher's first recession; how could you tell such adolescents that everything was right with them and the world, when the plain evidence of their eyes and their experiences told them otherwise every moment of the day? There are plainly both immense dangers and possibilities inherent in this situation and the greatest possibility is that it may lead to a break in the monolithic ice of commercial culture.

Just after the First World War, Lukács made an acute analysis of a capitalism he believed to be in decline, trying to account for the trends which seemed to herald an intensification of its power. First, he cited a letter from Lasalle to Marx: 'Hegel used to say in his old age that directly before the emergence of something qualitatively new, the old state of affairs gathers itself up into its original, purely general, essence, into its simple totality, transcending and absorbing back into itself all those marked differences and peculiarities which it evinced when it was still viable.' This is surely a description which has great resonance today. Next, though, he noted that Bukharin was correct to observe that as capitalism dissolves the fetishistic categories collapse and it becomes necessary to have recourse to the natural forms underlying them. The contradiction between these views, argued Lukács, is only apparent. 'For the contradiction has two aspects: on the one hand, there is the increasing undermining of the forms of reification – one might describe it as the cracking of the crust because of the inner emptiness – their growing inability to do justice to the phenomena, even as objects of reflection and calculation. On the other hand, we find the quantitative increase of the forms of reification, their empty extension to cover the whole surface of manifest phenomena. And the fact that these two aspects together are in conflict provides the key signature to the decline of bourgeois society.'[25] Now of course it can be claimed that history proved Lukács wrong in this analysis, but this is to forget just how close the system came to its demise.

Throughout this book judgements of quality have been made; they must be justified in the face of the postmodern claim that different discourses are incommensurable; that advertising, for instance, is a discourse to itself with its own mores and values which cannot be compared with literature. Yet surely such arenas of convention and conversation are formed as wheels within wheels; within any category there are sub-categories which communicate and are judged against each other; similarly all categories have outward effects and some are pursued solely for their effectiveness on an outer world. No discourse is an island. Secondly, the argument is beginning to move on from mere relativism among people to questions of what will supersede them. If, as a biologist once reminded me, a tiger is merely a point on an evolutionary line, then so are we humans. Let us assume that cyberspace does achieve a total flattening out of data and discourses where all that is human is as valuable or as worthless as any other data fragment; that it may be exchanged, destroyed or simply replaced. Are relativist critics really willing to accept this?

There are certain simple and refractory truths which determine the forms of First World culture. Over fifty years ago, Max Horkheimer spelt them out:

> humanity has become so rich and has at its disposal such great natural and human auxiliary powers, that it could exist united by worthy objectives. The need to veil this state of affairs, which is transparent in every respect, gives rise to a sphere of hypocrisy which extends not only to international relations, but which penetrates into even the most private relations; it results in a diminution of cultural endeavours (including

science) and a brutalization of personal and public life, such that spiritual and material misery are confounded.[26]

In the years since this was written, the gap between the possible and the actual has become ever wider as the growth in the world's wealth matched the misery of most of its inhabitants.

This grotesque situation can provide the clue to resolving the opposition which Jean Baudrillard has set up about views of the mass media: either they are the strategy which power uses to mystify the masses and impose their own truth, or they are 'the strategic territory of the ruse of the masses, who exercise in them their concrete power of the refusal of the truth, of the denial of reality', who resist indoctrination, in other words, by their very indifference to the truth.[27] Of course they are both: the elite are benefited by the masses' wilful forgetting of the truth, and this truth is deliberately repudiated because it is too painful to look on steadily. Forgetting through distraction is the major role of the culture industry. It is a distraction not merely from matters we might find distasteful but also from the development of a latent and widespread opposition. Some of those who watch most television also play the most video games and, by distracting the young, the latter, argues Gary Sehow rather quaintly, might be doing us a favour, 'by absorbing time that would otherwise be spent in plotting and executing roguish activities'.[28] Better that they do this, or commit minor acts of vandalism in town centres on Saturday night, than commit themselves to some more dangerous roguery.

The task of dispelling this forgetfulness is urgent. While the victims of totalitarianism are rightly counted and recounted, repeatedly relayed to the public and mourned over, capital's many ghosts lie silent. More than twenty years ago Eduardo Galeano graphically described the incessant murder by manufactured poverty of people in Latin America: 'every year, without making a sound, three Hiroshima bombs explode over communities that have become accustomed to suffering with clenched teeth'.[29] Since then, all over the world, the bombs have continued to explode as regularly and as silently as ever but with ever increasing force. These victims remain uncounted and unaccounted for and each moment, as the First World distracts itself, their numbers mount.

Despite the best efforts of those who would construct a perfectly reasonable and resilient world, the very connectedness of the global economic system makes it fragile and there are oppositional groups who are well aware of the worldwide effects small local actions may produce. If the fluttering of a butterfly's wings can cause a hurricane on the other side of the world, then even the poorest and the weakest may make their mark. There may come a time when the forms of commercial culture will seem as alien as the inscriptions on ancient tombs, when brand names (even the Coca-Cola logo), advertising and the entire apparatus of hypertrophic commerce will be a matter merely for a curious if mystified archaeology, looking on us rather as we look on the ancient Egyptian cult of the dead.

This book has pursued a number of themes, among them various forms of contingency which break with the official culture of capital. Presently, these forms are marginal and relatively friendly; while they are often overlooked, and do not force themselves into our world, they repay attention. Yet it is only fair to end with a threat: the situation as it stands and develops is hardly sustainable. If nothing is done, other forms of contingency will shatter the intricate structures which sustain economy and culture. They may be natural or social, or most likely both. The Gargantuan culture of distraction is conjured up by powerful commercial institutions. If truly material giants are aroused, they will force their way into our minds and our world, crushing this fragile and impoverished culture like a bug. The majority of the world's population will not stand our forgetfulness and our condescension forever.

NOTES

1. Walter Benjamin, 'Edward Fuchs: Collector and Historian', in Andrew Arato and Eike Gebhardt, eds, *The Essential Frankfurt School Reader*, New York 1982, p. 233.

2. Wyndham Lewis, *Blast*, no. 1, 1914, p. 11.

3. See Christopher Heilmann, 'Ludwig I's Munich as a Centre of Artistic Renewal', in Keith Hartley, ed., *The Romantic Spirit in German Art 1790–1990*, London 1994.

4. Hans-Georg Gadamer, *Truth and Method*, London 1975, p. 71.

5. See David Watkin and Tilman Mellinghoff, *German Architecture and the Classical Ideal, 1740–1840*, London 1987, pp. 141–3.

6. See ibid., pp. 144f.

7. See Walter S. Gibson, *Brueghel*, London 1977, p. 178.

8. François Rabelais, *The Histories of Gargantua and Pantagruel*, trans. J.M. Cohen, London 1955, pp. 66–7, 69.

9. John Fiske, *TV Culture*, London 1987, p. 324.

10. William Shakespeare, *Timon of Athens*, Act IV, Scene 3.

11. Karl Marx, *Economic and Philosophical Manuscripts of 1844*, Moscow 1977, p. 130.

12. Mica Nava, 'Consumerism and its Contradictions', *Cultural Studies*, vol. 1, no. 2, May 1987, p. 209.

13. Henry Ford, *My Life and Work*, Garden City, NY 1922, p. 104.

14. Cited in Todd Gitlin, *Inside Prime Time*, revised edition, London 1994, p. 31.

15. Herbert I. Schiller, *Culture Inc. The Corporate Takeover of Public Expression*, Oxford 1989, p. 151.

16. Ibid., pp. 153, 155.

17. Ibid., p. 156.

18. Rabelais, *Gargantua*, pp. 149f. See also M.A. Screech, *Rabelais*, London 1979, pp. 187f.

19. Adorno, *Negative Dialectics*, trans. E.B. Ashton, London 1973, p. 21.

20. Henri Lefebvre, *Critique of Everyday Life*, London 1991, vol. I, p. 35.

21. Terry Eagleton, *The Ideology of the Aesthetic*, Oxford 1990, p. 200.

22. Ibid., p. 200; citing Marx, *Economic and Philosophical Manuscripts of 1844*, p. 119.

23. T.W. Adorno, *Aesthetic Theory*, trans. C. Lenhardt, London 1984, p. 27.

24. Ibid.

25. Georg Lukács, *History and Class Consciousness. Studies in Marxist Dialectics*, trans. Rodney Livingstone, London 1971, p. 208; citing Lasalle, letter of 12 December 1851, ed. G. Mayer, p. 41; and Bukharin, *Ökonomie der Transformationsperiode*, pp. 50–51.

26. Max Horkheimer, 'Materialism and Morality', 1933; cited in Douglas Kellner, *Critical Theory, Marxism and Modernity*, Cambridge 1989, p. 33.

27. Jean Baudrillard, *The Masses*, p. 217; cited in Christopher Norris, *What's Wrong with Postmodernism. Critical Theory and the Ends of Philosophy*, Hemel Hempstead 1990, p. 181.

28. Gary Sehow, 'The Fall and Rise of Video Games', *Journal of Popular Culture*, vol. 21, no. 1, Summer 1987, pp. 55, 56.

29. Eduardo Galeano, *Open Veins of Latin America. Five Centuries of the Pillage of a Continent*, trans. Cedric Belfrage, New York 1973, p. 15.

BIBLIOGRAPHY

Adorno, T. W., *Aesthetic Theory*, trans. C. Lenhardt, ed. Gretel Adorno & Rolf Tiedemann, London 1984.

—— *The Culture Industry, Selected Essays on Mass Culture*, ed. J.M. Bernstein, London 1991.

—— *Minima Moralia. Reflections from Damaged Life*, trans. E.F.N. Jephcott, London 1974.

—— *Negative Dialectics*, trans. E.B. Ashton, London 1973.

—— *Notes to Literature*, ed. Rolf Tiedemann, trans. Shierry Weber Nicholsen, vol. II, New York 1992.

—— *Prisms*, trans. Samuel and Shierry Weber, Cambridge, Mass. 1981.

Adorno, Theodor/Walter Benjamin/Ernst Bloch/Bertolt Brecht/Georg Lukács, *Aesthetics and Politics*, afterword by Fredric Jameson, London 1980.

Adorno, Theodor/Max Horkheimer, *Dialectic of Enlightenment*, trans. John Cumming, London, 1973.

Agamben, Giorgio, *Infancy and History. Essays on the Destruction of Experience*, trans. Liz Heron, London 1993.

Algora, Montxo, *Art Futura 93*, Barcelona 1993.

Althusser, Louis, *Essays on Ideology*, London 1984.

Althusser, Louis/Etienne Balibar, *Reading Capital*, trans. Ben Brewster, London 1979.

Anon., 'The Environmental Street', *The Architectural Review*, vol. 135, no. 807, 1964, pp. 319–20.

—— 'Traffic Signs', *The Architectural Review*, vol. 134, no. 798, 1963, pp. 83–5.

Arato, Andrew/Eike Gebhardt, eds, *The Essential Frankfurt School Reader*, New York 1982.

Aronowitz, Stanley, *Dead Artists, Live Theories and Other Cultural Problems*, New York 1994.

Ascott, Roy, 'Connectivity: Art and Interactive Communications', *Leonardo*, vol. 24, no. 2, 1991, pp. 115–16.

Bagdikian, Ben H., *The Media Monopoly*, 4th edition, Boston 1992.

Ballard, J.G., *Crash*, London 1990.

Barthes, Roland, *A Barthes Reader*, ed. Susan Sontag, London 1982.

—— *Camera Lucida. Reflections on Photography*, trans. Richard Howard, London 1984.

—— *Selected Writings*, Cambridge 1988.

Benedikt, Michael, ed., *Cyberspace. First Steps*, Cambridge, Mass. 1991.

Benhabib, Seyla/Wolfgang Bonß/John McCole, eds, *On Horkheimer. New Perspectives*, Cambridge, Mass. 1993.

Benjamin, Walter, *Charles Baudelaire. A Lyric Poet in the Era of High Capitalism*, London 1973.

—— *Illuminations*, ed. Hannah Arendt, London 1973.

—— *One Way Street and Other Writings*, trans. Edmund Jephcott and Kingsley Shorter, London 1979.

—— *The Origin of German Tragic Drama*, trans. John Osborne, London 1977.

—— *Reflections. Essays, Aphorisms, Autobiographical Writings*, ed. Peter Demetz, New York 1978.

Berman, Russell A., *Modern Culture and Critical Theory. Art, Politics and the Legacy of the Frankfurt School*, Madison 1989.

Blachnicki, Henryk/Kenneth Browne, 'Over and Under. A Survey of Pedestrian/Vehicle Separation', *The Architectural Review*, vol. 129, no. 771, 1961, pp. 321–36.

Bocock, Robert/Kenneth Thompson, *Religion and Ideology*, Manchester 1985.

Borhek, J.T., 'Rods, Choppers, and Restorations: The Modification and Re-creation of Production Motor Vehicles in America', *Journal of Popular Culture*, vol. 22, no. 4, 1989, pp. 97–101.

Bourdieu, Pierre, *Photography. A Middle-brow Art*, with Robert Castel, Jean-Claude Chamboredon, Luc Boltanski, Dominique Schnapper, trans. Shaun Whiteside, Cambridge 1990.

—— *Distinction. A Social Critique of the Judgement of Taste*, trans. Richard Nice, London 1984.

Bowlby, Rachel, *Shopping with Freud*, London 1993.

Brawne, Michael, 'Parking Terminals', *The Architectural Review*, vol. 128, no. 762, 1960, pp. 125–34.

Bronner, Stephen Eric, *Of Critical Theory and Its Theorists*, Oxford 1994.

Buck-Morss, Susan, *The Dialectics of Seeing. Walter Benjamin and the Arcades Project*, Cambridge, Mass. 1989.

Bukatman, Scott, *Terminal Identity. The Virtual Subject in Postmodern Science Fiction*, Durham, NC 1993.

Burnham, Jack, *Beyond Modern Sculpture. The Effects of Science and Technology on the Sculpture of This Century*, New York 1968.

Bürger, Peter, *Theory of the Avant-Garde*, trans. Michael Shaw, Manchester 1984.

Caillois, Roger, *Cases d'un échiquier*, Paris 1970.

Castleman, Craig, *Getting Up. Subway Graffiti in New York*, Cambridge, Mass. 1982.

Chalfant, Henry/James Prigoff, *Spraycan Art*, London 1987.

Chomsky, Noam, *Year 501. The Conquest Continues*, London, 1993.

Coffield, Frank, *Vandalism and Graffiti. The State of the Art*, London 1991.

Cohen, Margaret, *Profane Illumination. Walter Benjamin and the Paris of Surrealist Revolution*, Berkeley 1993.

Collins, Ava, 'Intellectuals, Power and Quality Television', *Cultural Studies*, vol. 7, no. 1, 1993, pp. 28–45.

Collins, Jim, 'Watching Ourselves Watching Television, or Who's Your Agent?', *Cultural Studies*, vol. 3, no. 3, 1989, pp. 261–81.

Cooper, Martha/Henry Chalfant, *Subway Art*, London 1984.

Cooper, Martha/Joseph Sciorra, *R.I.P. New York Spraycan Memorials*, London 1994.

Crary, Jonathan, 'Critical Reflections', *Artforum*, Feb. 1994, pp. 58–9, 103.

Crary, Jonathan/Sandford Kwinter, *Zone 6*, New York 1992.

Davidson, Martin P., *The Consumerist Manifesto. Advertising in Postmodern Times*, London 1992.

Derrida, Jacques, *The Truth in Painting*, trans. Geoff Bennington and Ian McLeod, Chicago 1987.

DeWitt, Tom, 'Dataism', *Leonardo. Supplemental Issue. Computer Art in Context: SIGGRAPH '89 Art Show Catalog*, 1989, pp. 57–61.

Dews, Peter, *The Logics of Disintegration. Post-Structuralist Thought and the Claims of Critical Theory*, London 1987.

Dienst, Richard, *Still Life in Real Time. Theory After Television*, Durham, NC 1994.

Druckrey, Timothy, ed., *Iterations: The New Image*, New York and Cambridge, Mass. 1993.

Eagleton, Terry, *The Ideology of the Aesthetic*, Oxford 1990.

—— *Walter Benjamin or Towards a Revolutionary Criticism*, London 1981.

Edinburgh, Scottish National Gallery of Modern Art, *The Romantic Spirit in German Art 1790–1990*, London 1994.

Ellul, Jacques, *The Technological Bluff*, trans. Geoffrey W. Bromley, Grand Rapids, MI 1990.

Featherstone, Mike, *Consumer Culture and Postmodernism*, London 1991.

Fekete, John, ed., *Life After Postmodernism. Essays on Value and Culture*, London 1988.

Feuer, Jane, 'The Two Weather Channels', *Cultural Studies*, vol. 1, no. 3, 1987, pp. 383–5.

Fiske, John, *Power Plays. Power Works*, London 1993.
—— *Reading the Popular*, London 1989.
—— *TV Culture*, London 1987.
Fletcher, Angus, *Allegory, The Theory of a Symbolic Mode*, Ithaca, NY 1964.
Flink, James J., *The Automobile Age*, Cambridge, Mass. 1988.
—— *The Car Culture*, Cambridge, Mass. 1975.
Ford, Henry, *My Life and Work*, with Samuel Crowther, Garden City, NY 1922.
Franke, Herbert W., 'Mathematics as an Artistic-Generative Principle', *Leonardo. Supplemental Issue. Computer Art in Context: SIGGRAPH '89 Art Show Catalog*, 1989, pp. 25–6.
Gadamer, Hans-Georg, *Truth and Method*, London 1975.
Gailey, Christine Ward, 'Mediated Messages. Gender, Class and Cosmos in Home Video Games', *Journal of Popular Culture*, vol. 27, no. 1, 1993, pp. 81–97.
Galeano, Eduardo, *Open Veins of Latin America. Five Centuries of the Pillage of a Continent*, trans. Cedric Belfrage, New York 1973.
Gardner, Carl/Julie Sheppard, *Consuming Passion. The Rise of Retail Culture*, London 1989.
Gibson, Walter S., *Brueghel*, London 1977.
Gibson, William, *Burning Chrome*, London 1993.
—— *Count Zero*, London 1986.
—— *Mona Lisa Overdrive*, London 1989.
—— *Neuromancer*, London 1984.
Gitlin, Todd, *Inside Prime Time*, revised edition, London 1994.
Glazer, Miriyam, '"What is Within Now Seen Without": Romanticism, Neuromanticism and the Death of the Imagination in William Gibson's Fictive World', *Journal of Popular Culture*, vol. 23, no. 3, 1989, pp. 155–64.
Gripsrud, Jostein, '"High Culture" Revisited', *Cultural Studies*, vol. 3, no. 2, 1989, pp. 194–207.
Gurevitch, Michael/Tony Bennett/James Curran/Janet Woollacott, *Culture, Society and the Media*, London 1982.
Harvey, David, *The Condition of Postmodernity, An Enquiry Into the Origins of Cultural Change*, Oxford 1990.
Haug, Wolfgang Fritz, *Commodity Aesthetics, Ideology and Culture*, New York 1987.
Hayward, Philip, ed., *Culture, Technology and Creativity in the Late Twentieth Century*, London n.d.
Hermes, Joke, 'Media, Meaning and Everyday Life', *Cultural Studies*, vol. 7, no. 3, 1993, pp. 493–506.
Hickman, Larry A., ed., *Technology as a Human Affair*, New York 1990.
Hook, Donald D., 'American and German Driving Habits', *Journal of Popular Culture*, vol. 19, no. 1, 1985, pp. 91–8.
Huxley, Aldous, *Brave New World*, Harmondsworth 1955.

Jameson, Fredric, *Late Marxism, Adorno, or, the Persistence of the Dialectic,* London 1990.

—— *Marxism and Form. Twentieth Century Dialectical Theories of Literature,* Princeton 1971.

—— *The Political Unconscious. Narrative as a Socially Symbolic Act,* London 1981.

—— *Postmodernism or, the Cultural Logic of Late Capitalism,* London 1991.

Jay, Martin, *The Dialectical Imagination. A History of the Frankfurt School and the Institute of Social Research, 1923–1950,* Boston 1973.

—— *Downcast Eyes. The Denigration of Vision in Twentieth-Century French Thought,* Berkeley 1993.

Jones, Beverley, 'Computer Imagery: Imitation and Representation of Realities', *Leonardo. Supplemental Issue. Computer Art in Context: SIGGRAPH '89 Art Show Catalog,* 1989, pp. 31–8.

Kaplan, Sidney J., 'The Image of Amusement Arcades and Differences in Male and Female Video Game Playing', *Journal of Popular Culture,* vol. 17, no. 1, 1983, pp. 93–8.

Kellner, Douglas, *Critical Theory, Marxism and Modernity,* Cambridge 1989.

Kochman, Thomas, ed., *Rappin' and Stylin' Out. Communication in Urban Black America,* Urbana 1972.

Kroker, Arthur/Michael A. Weinstein, *Data Trash. The Theory of the Virtual Class,* Montreal 1994.

Kruger, Barbara, *Remote Control. Power, Cultures, and the World of Appearances,* Cambridge, Mass. 1993.

Kurzweil, Raymond, *The Age of Intelligent Machines,* Cambridge, Mass. 1990.

Kuspit, Donald, *The New Subjectivism, Art in the 1980s,* New York 1993.

Lasch, Christopher, *The Culture of Narcissism. American Life in an Age of Diminishing Expectations,* New York 1978.

Lazere, Donald, ed., *American Media and Mass Culture. New Perspectives,* Berkeley 1987.

Le Corbusier, *The City of Tomorrow and Its Planning,* trans. Frederick Etchells, London 1971.

Lefebvre, Henri, *Critique of Everyday Life,* London 1990.

Levy, Stephen, *Artificial Life. The Quest for a New Creation,* London 1992.

Lewis, Jon, 'Punks in L.A.: It's Kiss or Kill', *Journal of Popular Culture,* vol. 22, no. 2, 1988, pp. 87–97.

London, Barbican Art Gallery, *Who's Looking at the Family?,* London 1994.

London, Hayward Gallery, *L'Amour Fou. Photography and Surrealism,* London 1986.

Lukács, Georg, *History and Class Consciousness. Studies in Marxist Dialectics,* trans. Rodney Livingstone, London 1971.

Lunt, Peter K./Sonia M. Livingstone, *Mass Consumption and Personal Identity. Everyday Economic Experience,* Buckingham 1992.

McCaffery, Larry, ed., *Storming the Reality Studio. A Casebook of Cyberpunk and Postmodern Fiction*, Durham, NC 1991.

McCole, John, *Walter Benjamin and the Antimonies of Tradition*, Ithaca 1993.

McLuhan, Marshall, *Understanding Media. The Extensions of Man*, London 1964.

Madrid, Centro de Arte Reina Sofia, *Art Futura 94*, Madrid 1994.

Marx, Karl, *Capital. A Critique of Political Economy, Volume I*, trans. Ben Fowkes, Harmondsworth 1976.

—— *Economic and Philosophical Manuscripts of 1844*, Moscow 1977.

—— *Grundrisse. Foundations of the Critique of Political Economy (Rough Draft)*, trans. Martin Nicolaus, Harmondsworth 1973.

Marx, Karl/Frederick Engels, *Collected Works. Vol. 5. Marx and Engels, 1845–47*, London 1976.

Michaux, Henri, *Ecuador. Journal d'un voyage*, Paris 1929.

Miller, Daniel, *Material Culture and Mass Consumption*, Oxford 1987.

Mitchell, William J., *The Reconfigured Eye. Visual Truth in the Post-Photographic Era*, Cambridge, Mass. 1992.

Morley, David, *Family Television. Cultural Power and Domestic Leisure*, London 1986.

—— *Television Audiences and Cultural Studies*, London 1992.

Morris, Meaghan, 'Banality in Cultural Studies', *Block*, no. 14, Autumn 1988, pp. 15–26.

Nader, Ralph, *Unsafe at Any Speed. The Designed-in Danger of the American Automobile*, New York 1965.

Nairn, Ian, 'The Mindless Masters', *The Architectural Review*, vol. 127, no. 758, 1960, pp. 229–31.

Nava, Mica, 'Consumerism and Its Contradictions', *Cultural Studies*, vol. 1, no. 2, 1987, pp. 204–10.

New York, Museum of Modern Art, *Pleasures and Terrors of Domestic Comfort*, New York 1991.

Norris, Christopher, *Uncritical Theory. Postmodernism, Intellectuals and the Gulf War*, London 1992.

—— *What's Wrong with Postmodernism. Critical Theory and the Ends of Philosophy*, Hemel Hempstead 1990.

Owens, Craig, *Beyond Recognition. Representation, Power, and Culture*, eds Scott Bryson/Barbara Kruger/Lynne Tillman/Jane Weinstock, Berkeley 1992.

Packard, Vance, *The Hidden Persuaders*, London 1981.

—— *The Status Seekers. An Exploration of Class Behaviour in America*, Harmondsworth 1961.

Paris, Centre National des Arts Plastiques/Prato, Museo d'Arte Contemporanea Luigi Pecci, *Un'altra obiettività/Another Objectivity*, Milan 1989.

Parr, Martin, *The Cost of Living*, Manchester 1989.

Parr, Martin/Nicholas Barker, *From A to B. Tales of Modern Motoring*, London 1994.

Penley, Constance/Andrew Ross, eds, *Technoculture*, Minneapolis 1991.

Poster, Mark, *The Mode of Information. Poststructuralism and Social Context*, Cambridge 1990.

Pynchon, Thomas, *V. A Novel*, Philadelphia 1961.

Rabelais, François, *The Histories of Gargantua and Pantagruel*, trans. J.M. Cohen, London 1955.

Rheingold, Howard, *The Virtual Community. Finding Connection in a Computerized World*, London 1994.

Ritchin, Fred, *In Our Own Image. The Coming Revolution in Photography*, New York 1990.

Robinson, David, *Soho Walls. Beyond Graffiti*, New York 1990.

Ross, Andrew, *Strange Weather, Culture, Science and Technology in the Age of Limits*, London 1991.

Ross, Kristin, *Fast Cars, Clean Bodies. Decolonization and the Reordering of French Culture*, Cambridge, Mass. 1995.

Roszak, Theodore, *The Cult of Information. A Neo-Luddite Treatise on High-Tech, Artificial Intelligence and the True Art of Thinking*, Berkeley 1994.

Schiller, Herbert I., *Culture Inc., The Corporate Takeover of Public Expression*, Oxford 1989.

Screech, M.A., *Rabelais*, London 1979.

Sehow, Gary, 'The Fall and Rise of Video Games', *Journal of Popular Culture*, vol. 21, no. 1, 1987, pp. 53–60.

Seiter, Ellen, 'Making Distinctions in TV Audience Research: Case Study of a Troubling Interview', *Cultural Studies*, vol. 4, no. 1, 1990, pp. 61–84.

Sheff, David, *Game Over. Nintendo's Battle to Dominate an Industry*, London 1993.

Shields, Rob, ed., *Lifestyle Shopping. The Subject of Consumption*, London 1992.

Silverstone, Roger, *Television and Everyday Life*, London 1994.

Smith, Gary, ed., *Benjamin, Philosophy, Aesthetics, History*, Chicago 1983.

— ed., *On Walter Benjamin. Critical Essays and Recollections*, Cambridge, Mass. 1988.

Socialist Review Collectives, ed., *Unfinished Business. Twenty Years of the Socialist Review*, London 1991.

Spurrier, Raymond, 'Road-Style on the Motorway', *The Architectural Review*, vol. 128, no. 798, 1960, pp. 406–11.

— 'The Urban Choice. The Architectural Implications of the Buchanan Report', *The Architectural Review*, vol. 135, no. 807, 1964, pp. 355–7.

Sterling, Bruce, ed., *Mirrorshades. The Cyberpunk Anthology*, London 1994.

Stoll, Clifford, *Silicon Snake Oil. Second Thoughts on the Information Highway*, London 1995.

Tagg, John, *The Burden of Representation. Essays on Photographies and Histories*, Basingstoke 1988.

Taylor, Mark C./Esa Saarinen, *Imagologies. Media Philosophy*, London 1994.

Thompson, D'Arcy Wentworth, *On Growth and Form*, second edition, Cambridge 1942.

Thompson, Michael, *Rubbish Theory. The Creation and Destruction of Value*, Oxford 1979.

Todd, Stephen/William Latham, *Evolutionary Art and Computers*, London 1992.

Updike, John, *Rabbit Redux*, London 1972.

Virilio, Paul, *War and Cinema. The Logistics of Perception*, trans. Patrick Camiller, London 1989.

Wachs, Martin/Margaret Crawford, eds, *The Car and the City. The Automobile, the Built Environment and Daily Urban Life*, Ann Arbor 1992.

Watkin, David/Tilman Mellinghoff, *German Architecture and the Classical Ideal, 1740–1840*, London 1987.

Williams, Raymond, *Keywords. A Vocabulary of Culture and Society*, revised edition, London 1983.

—— *The Politics of Modernism. Against the New Conformists*, ed. Tony Pinkney, London 1989.

—— *Problems in Materialism and Culture. Selected Essays*, London 1980.

—— *Television. Technology and Cultural Form*, New York 1974.

—— *Towards 2000*, Harmondsworth 1985.

Willis, Susan, *A Primer for Daily Life*, London 1991.

Wolfe, Tom, *The Kandy-Kolored Tangerine-Flake Streamline Baby*, London 1981.

Wolin, Richard, 'Utopia, Mimesis, and Reconciliation: A Redemptive Critique of Adorno's *Aesthetic Theory*', *Representations*, no. 32, Fall 1990, pp. 33–49.

—— *Walter Benjamin. An Aesthetic of Redemption*, Berkeley 1994.

Wollen, Peter, *Raiding the Icebox. Reflections on Twentieth-Century Culture*, London 1993.

Wombell, Paul, ed., *Photovideo. Photography in the Age of the Computer*, London 1991.

Woolley, Benjamin, *Virtual Worlds. A Journey in Hype and Hyperreality*, London 1993.

Yelanjian, Mary, 'Rhythms of Consumption', *Cultural Studies*, vol. 5, no. 1, 1991, pp. 91–7.

Zuidervaart, Lambert, *Adorno's Aesthetic Theory. The Redemption of Illusion*, Cambridge, Mass. 1991.

INDEX